EC Environm

European Law Series

Series Editor:
PROFESSOR JOHN A. USHER

Published Titles

International Relations Law of the European Union
DOMINIC McGOLDRICK

EC Public Procurement Law
CHRISTOPHER BOVIS

EC Insurance Law
ROBERT MERKIN AND ANGUS RODGER

EC Consumer Law and Policy
STEPHEN WEATHERILL

EC Tax Law
DAVID WILLIAMS

General Principles of EC Law
JOHN A USHER

EC Environmental Law
JOANNE SCOTT

EU Law and Human Rights
LAMMY BETTEN and NICHOLAS GRIEF

EC Institutions and Legislation
JOHN A. USHER

European Social Law and Policy
TAMARA HERVEY

EC Environmental Law

JOANNE SCOTT
Senior Lecturer in European Community Law,
Queen Mary and Westfield College,
University of London

LONGMAN
London and New York

Addison Wesley Longman Limited
Edinburgh Gate
Harlow, Essex
CM20 2JE
England

and Associated Companies throughout the world

*Published in the United States of America
by Addison Wesley Longman Inc., New York*

First published 1998

ISBN 0 582 29190-9 Paper

British Library Cataloguing-in-Publication Data

A catalogue record for this book is
available from the British Library

Library of Congress Cataloging-in-Publication Data

A catalog entry for this title is available from the
Library of Congress

Set by 7 in 10/12pt Sabon
Produced through Longman Malaysia, ACM

Contents

Acknowledgements   vi

General Editor's Preface   vii

Table of Cases   viii

Table of Legislation   xl

Abbreviations   xiii

Introduction   1

1   The European Community as an environmental actor   3

2   Instruments for environmental protection: 'command and
    control'   24

3   Economic instruments for environmental protection   44

4   Trade and environment: an internal market perspective   64

5   Trade and environment: an external relations
    perspective   86

6   Nature conservation and environmental impact
    assessment   106

7   Regional policy and environment   128

8   Enforcing EC environmental law   148

Further reading   169

Appendix: Treaty of Amsterdam (extracts)   171

Bibliography   177

Index   184

Acknowledgements

Many people have helped me in the course of writing this book. Wade Mansell, though no longer a colleague, continued to read and comment upon drafts of my work. And this though he no longer has anything to gain, as Director of Research at the University of Kent. Paul Beaumont and Rajan Subberwal also offered constructive comments on parts of the book. Rajan also learnt more about looking for European law cases than he really ever wanted to know. Many thanks to all three. Marise Cremona and Nick Bernard were disturbed, by e-mail, on more than one occasion with yet another question from Joanne. Both, I think, fled to France during the summer for some peace and quiet, the former lending me her house in Oxford. Thanks to both of them. Bob Burns, the law librarian at QMW demonstrated inhuman patience and finally, not for want of trying earlier, persuaded me of the value of CELEX. This may turn out to be the most important thing I learnt in writing this book. Thanks also to the extended NLDEU network, and to my environmental law colleagues in London. As ever it is the quality of the company – and of the G&Ts at the Russell Hotel – that makes studying European law such a pleasure. Ann Adams, and Malcolm Buchanan of South-East Library Board Headquarters in Ballynahinch, helped me with the introduction by providing information on The Plough and the Stars. Thanks! I am grateful also to John Usher for asking me to contribute to this series and for his help on the way through.

Finally, thanks to my colleagues at Queen Mary and Westfield College. The Law Faculty there has proved a most congenial environment in which to work.

General Editor's Preface

The Longman European Law Series is the first comprehensive series of topic-based books on EC Law aimed specifically at a student readership, though it is hoped that they will also be found useful by academic colleagues and interested practitioners. It has become more and more difficult for a single course or a single book to deal comprehensively with all the major topics of Community law, and the intention of this series is to enable students and teachers to 'mix and match' topics which they find to be of interest; it may also be hoped that the publication of this series will encourage the study of areas of Community law which have historically been neglected in degree courses. However, while the series may have a student readership in mind, the authors have been encouraged to take an academic and critical approach, placing each topic in its overall Community context, and also in its socio-economic and political context where relevant.

EC environmental law involves the development of Community competence through the use of general Treaty provisions, followed by successive Treaty amendments introducing express powers in the area, and elevating the topic to its present pervasive status. It has become one of the major areas of Community activity, as will clearly be seen from Joanne Scott's book, which in particular brings to life the relationship between environmental protection and the Community's older-established trading objectives.

J.A. Usher

Table of Cases

European Community

Case 30/59 *Steenkolenmijnen* v *High Authority* [1961] ECR 1 **51**

Case 25/62 *Plaumann* v *Commission* [1963] ECR 95 **138**

Cases 21-4/72 *International Fruit Company* [1972] ECR 1219 **94**

Case 8/74 *Procureur du Roi* v *Dassonville* [1974] ECR 837 **66**

Case 104/75 *De Peijper* [1976] ECR 613 **72**

Case 41/76 *Donckerwolcke* v *Procureur de la République* [1976] ECR 1921 **88**

Case 106/77 *Ammistrazione dello Stato* v *Simmenthal SpA* [1978] ECR 629 **163**

Case 120/78 *Rewe-Zentrale AG* v *Bundesmonopolverwaltung für Branntwein* [1979] ECR 649 **67**

Case 15/79 *Groenveld* v *Produktschap voor Bee en Vlees* [1979] ECR 3409 **66**

Case 92/79 *Commission* v *Italy* [1980] ECR 1115 **5**

Case 788/79 *Gilli & Andres* [1980] ECR 2071 **175**

Case 40/82 *Commission* v *United Kingdom* [1982] ECR 2793 **75**

Case 42/82 *Commission* v *France* [1983] ECR 1013 **68**

Case 174/82 *Officier van Justitie* v *Sandoz BV* [1983] ECR 2245 **71**

Case 227/82 *Van Bennekom* [1983] ECR 3883 **71**

Case 16/83 *Prantl* [1984] ECR 1299 **75**

Case 14/83 *Von Colson & Kamann* v *Land Nordrhein Westfalen* [1984] ECR 1891 **157**

Case 97/83 *Criminal Proceedings against Melkunie BV* [1984] ECR 2367 **72**

Case 207/83 *Commission* v *United Kingdom* [1985] ECR 1202 **74**

Case 240/83 *Procureur de la République* v *Association de Défense des Bruleurs dhuiles* [1983] ECR 531 **6, 79**

Case 169/84 *Cofaz* v *Commission* [1986] ECR 391 **140**

Case 178/84 *Commission* v *Germany* [1987] ECR 1227 **71, 75**

Case 67-8 & 70/85 *Van der Kooy* v *Commission* [1988] ECR 219 **140**

Case 412/85 *Commission* v *Germany* [1987] ECR 3503 **117**

Case 45/86 *Commission* v *Council* [1987] ECR 1493 **88, 89**

Case 80/86 *Criminal Proceedings Against Kolpinghuis Nijmegen* [1987] ECR 3969 **157**

Case 302/86 *Commission* v *Denmark* [1988] ECR 4607 **66–9, 70**

TABLE OF CASES

Case 187/87 *Saarland and Others* v *Ministry of Industry & Others* [1988] ECR 5013 **112**

Case 380/87 *Enichem Base & Others* v *Commune Di Cinisello Balsamo* [1989] ECR 2491 **43**

Opinion 1/78 [1979] ECR 2871 **89**

Case C-21/88 *Du Pont de Nemours Italiana SpA* v *Unita Sanitaria Locale No 2* [1990] ECR I-889 **78**

Case C-62/88 *Greece* v *Council* [1990] ECR I-1527 **88–9**

Case C-131/88 *Commission* v *Germany* [1991] ECR I-825 **160**

Cases 143/88 and 92/89 *Zuckerfabrik Süderdithmarschen AG* v *Haputzollamt Itzehow and Paderborn* [1991] ECR I-415 **162**

Case C-361/88 *Commission* v *Germany* [1991] ECR I-2567 **160**

Case C-42/89 *Commission* v *Belgium* [1993] ECR I-2821 **152**

Case C-57/89 *Commission* v *Germany* [1991] ECR I-883 **109–10, 112**

Case C-58/89 *Commission* v *Germany* [1991] ECR I-4983 **160**

Case C-59/89R *Commission* v *Germany* [1989] ECR 2607 **162–3**

Case C-106/89 *Marleasing* v *La Comercial Internacionale de Alimentacion SA* [1990] ECR I-4135 **157**

Case C-169/89 *Criminal Proceedings against Gourmetterie van den Burg* [1990] ECR I-2143 **80–3**

Case C-213/89 *R* v *Secretary of State for Transport, ex p Factortame (No.2)* [1991] ECR I-2433 **163**

Case C-300/89 *Commission* v *Council* [1991] ECR 2867 **8–9**

Case C-246/89R *Commission* v *United Kingdom* [1989] ECR 3125 **163**

Case C-337/89 *Commission* v *United Kingdom and Ireland* [1992] ECR I-6103 **161**

Case C-2/90 *Commission* v *Belgium* [1992] ECR I-4431 **77–9**

Cases C-6/90 & 9/90 *Francovich and Bonifaci* v *Italian State* [1991] ECR I-5357 **124, 158**

Case C-56/90 *Commission* v *United Kingdom* [1993] ECR I-4109 **152**

Case C-355/90 *Commission* v *Spain* [1993] ECR I-4221 **109, 110**

Case C-155/91 *Commission* v *Council* [1993] ECR I-939 **9**

Case C-198/91 *Cook* v *Commission* [1993] ECR I-2487 **140**

Cases C-267-68/91 *Keck & Mithouard* [1993] ECR I-6097 **66, 75–7**

Case T-37/92 *BEUC & NCC* v *Commission* [1994] ECR II-285 **140**

Case C-91/92 *Faccini Dori* v *Recreb* [1994] ECR I-3325 **157**

Case C-315/92 *Verband Sozialer Wettbewerb* v *Clinique* [1994] ECR I-317 **76**

Case C-396/92 *Bundnaturschutz in Bayern and Others* v *Freistaat Bayern* [1994] ECR I-3717 **120**

Case C-431/92 *Commission* v *Germany* [1995] ECR I-2189 **120, 122**

Case C-17/93 *Openbaar Ministerie* v *Van der Veldt* [1994] ECR I-3537 **76**

Case C-41/93 *France* v *Commission* [1994] ECR I-829 **41**

Cases C-46 & 48/93 *Brasserie de Pecheur* v *Germany* and *R* v *Secretary of State for Transport* ex p *Factortame Ltd and Others* [1996] ECR I-1029 **159, 161**

Cases 69 & 258/93 *Punto Casa Spa* v *Sindaco del Commune di Capena* [1994] ECR I-2355 **76**

Case C-131/93 *Commission* v *Germany* [1994] ECR I-3303 **69**

Case C-187/93 *Parliament* v *Council* [1994] ECR I-2857 **9, 90**

Case C-255/93 *Commission* v *France* [1994] ECR I-4949 **166**

Case C-280/93 *Germany* v *Council* [1994] ECR I-4973 **94**

Case C-384/93 *Alpine Investments BV* v *Minister van Financien* [1995] ECR I-1141 **66, 83**

Case C-392/93 *R* v *HM Treasury* ex p *British Telecommunications* [1996] ECR I-1631 **159**

Case C-412/93 *Leclerc-Siplec* v *TF1 Publicité and Another* [1995] ECR I-179 **76**

Case T-461/93 *An Taisce & WWF (UK)* v *Commission* [1994] ECR II-733 **130–4**

Case T-465/93 *Conzorzio Gruppo di Azione Locale Murgia Messapica* v *Commission* [1994] ECR II- 361 **140**

Cases C-465-6/93 *Atlanta Fruchhandelsgesellschaft mbH* v *Bundesamt für Ernahrung und Forstwirschaft* [1995] ECR I-3761 **165**

Case T-585/93 *Stichtung Greenpeace Council and Others* v *Commission* [1995] ECR II-2205 **134–6, 138–41**

Opinion 1/94 [1994] ECR I-5267 **93**

Case C-5/94 *R* v *MAFF, ex p Hedley Lomas (Ireland) Ltd* [1996] ECR I-2553 **84, 159**

Case C-21/94 *Parliament* v *Council* [1996] ECR I-1827 **45**

Case C-70/94 *Werner* v *Germany* [1995] ECR I-3189 **89, 91**

Case C-83/94 *Criminal Proceedings against Liefer* [1995] ECR I-3231 **89, 91**

Case C-129/94 *Criminal Proceedings Against Rafael Ruiz Bernaldez.* [1996] ECR 1-1829 **157**

Case 133/94 *Commission* v *Belgium* [1996] ECR I-2323 **118**

Cases C-140-42/94 *DIP SpA* v *Commune Di Bassano Del Grappa* [1995] ECR I-3257 **76**

Case C-194/94 *C.I.A. Security International SA* v *Signalson SA and Another* [1996] ECR I- 2201 **142**

Case C-325/94P *An Taisce & WWF (UK)* v *Commission* [1996] ECR I-3727 **130–4**

Case C-44/95 *R* v *Secretary of State for the Environment ex p RSPB* [1996] ECR I-3805 **110, 111**

Case C-72/95 *Kraaijeveld BV* v *Gedeputeerde Staten van Zuid- Holland* [1996] ECR I- 5403 **123, 157**

Case C-105/95 *WWF* v *Commission* judgment of 5 March 1997, nyr **133**

Case C-107/95P *Bundesverband der Bilanzbuchhalter* v *Commission* [1997] ECR I-947 **133**

Case C-168/95 *Criminal Proceedings Against Arcaro* [1996] ECR I-4705 **157**

Case T-288/95R *Lehrfreund* v *Council and Commission* [1996] ECR II-111 **96**

Case C-10/96 *Ligue royal Belge pour la protection des oiseaux ASBL and Another* v *Région Wallonne* [1996] ECR I-6775 **117**

Case C-13/96 *Bic Benelux* v *Belgian State* judgment of 20 March 1997, nyr **50**

Case C-114/96 *Criminal Proceedings against Kieffer and Thill* judgment of 25 June 1997, nyr **51**

Case 180/96R *United Kingdom and Northern Ireland* v *Commission* [1996] ECR I-3903 **72–3**

France

The State v *Vituret & Chambon* [1995] 1 CMLR 185 **82**

Ireland

Howard v *Commissioners for Public Works* [1994] IR 101 **130–1**

United Kingdom

Twyford Down Parish Council v *Secretary of State for the Environment* [1990] 1 Env. L.R. 37 **120**

R v *HM Treasury, ex p British Telecommunications* [1994] 1 CMLR 621 **164**

R v *Secretary of State for the Environment & Others ex p Greenpeace & Others* [1994] 4 All ER 352 **120**

R v *Secretary of State for the Environment ex p RSPB* (1995) 7 JEL 255 **164**

R v *Secretary of State for the Environment ex p Kingston-upon-Hull City Council and R* v *Secretary of State for the Environment ex p Bristol City Council and Woodspring District Council* [1996] 8 JEL 336 **155–6**

Table of Legislation

European Community environmental legislation is constantly amended and updated. Some directives have been amended more than 20 times. Amendments are consequently not listed below, apart from the occasional extremely important amendment. Sands & Tarasofsky, *Documents in European Community Environmental Law* (MUP, 1995) is very useful as it provides consolidated versions of much of the relevant legislation. The easiest way to keep up to date with changes is to consult the electronic database 'CELEX' (see further reading).

Regulations

Financial Regulation OJ 1977 L356/1 **135, 136**

Council Regulation EEC/1210/90 OJ 1990 L120/1 **153**

Council Regulation EEC/594/91 OJ 1991 L67/1 **86**

Council Regulation EEC/3254/91 OJ 1991 L308/1 **86, 96, 101, 102**

Council Regulation EEC/880/92 OJ 1992 L99/1 **168**

Council Regulation EEC/1973/92 OJ 1992 L206/1 **53**

Council Regulation EEC/2078/92 OJ 1992 L215/85 **54**

Council Regulation EEC/2455/92 OJ 1992 L251/13 **86**

Council Regulation EEC/259/93 OJ 1993 L30/1 **86**

Council Regulation EEC/1836/93 OJ 1993 L168/1 **168**

Council Regulation EEC/2081/93 OJ 1993 L193/5 **128, 132, 137, 142, 144**

Council Regulation EEC/2082/93 OJ 1993 L193/20 **128, 133, 135, 136, 137, 144, 145**

Council Regulation EC/1164/94 OJ 1994 L130/1 **129**

Commission Regulation EC/1771/94 OJ 1994 L184/3 **96**

Council Regulation EC/3285/94 OJ 1994 L349/53 **91**

Commission Regulation EC/35/97 OJ 1997 L8/2 **86, 97**

Council Regulation EC/338/97 OJ 1997 L61/1 **86**

Commission Regulation 2064/97 OJ 1997 L290/1 **145**

Directives

Council Directive 70/220/EEC OJ 1970 L76/1 **27**

Council Directive 75/440/EEC OJ 1975 L194/26 **160**

Council Directive 76/160/EEC OJ 1976 L31/1 **151, 152**

Council Directive 77/102/EEC OJ 1977 L32/32 **27**

Council Directive 79/409/EEC OJ 1979 L103/1 **6, 17, 80, 81, 82, 106–7, 108–12**

Council Directive 80/68/EEC OJ 1980 L20/43 **130, 160**

Council Directive 80/778 OJ 1980 L229/11 **152**

Council Directive 80/779/EEC OJ 1980 L229/30 **25**

Council Directive 82/884/EEC OJ 1982 L378/15 **25**

Council Directive 82/806/EEC OJ 1982 L339/55 **29**

Council Directive 83/129/EEC OJ 1983 L91/30 **86**

Council Directive 83/189/EEC OJ 1983 L109/8 **42, 50**

Council Directive 84/360/EEC OJ 1984 L188/20 **26, 28, 32, 33**

Council Directive 85/203/EEC OJ 1985 L87/1 **25**

Council Directive 85/210/EEC OJ 1985 L96/25 **29**

Council Directive 85/337/EEC OJ 1985 L91/30 **107, 117–25, 130, 142, 159**

Council Directive 87/416/EEC OJ 1987 L225/33 **29**

Council Directive 88/436/EEC OJ 1988 L214/1 **127**

Council Directive 88/609/EEC OJ 1988 L336/1 **27, 33, 38, 39**

Council Directive 89/369/EEC OJ 1989 L163/32 **27**

Council Directive 89/429/EEC OJ 1989 L203/50 **27**

Council Directive 90/313/EEC OJ 1990 L158/56 **159**

Council Directive 91/271/EEC OJ 1991 L135/40 **155**

Council Directive 91/692/EEC OJ 1991 L337/48 **153**

Council Directive 92/3/Euratom OJ 1992 L35/24 **86**

Council Directive 92/43/EEC OJ 1992 L206/7 **17, 106, 112–17**

Council Directive 92/82/EEC OJ 1992 L316/19 **46**

Council Directive 93/12/EEC OJ 1993 L74/81 **29**

Council Directive 93/89/EEC OJ 1993 L279/32 **45, 46**

European Parliament and Council Directive 94/62/EC OJ 1994 L365/10 **103, 166**

Council Directive 94/67/EEC OJ 1994 L365/35 **33**

Council Directive 96/22/EC OJ 1996 L125/3 **103**

Council Directive 96/61/EC OJ 1996 L257/26 **25, 30, 31, 32**

Council Directive 96/62/EC OJ 1996 L296/55 **25, 31**

Council Directive 97/11/EC OJ 1997 L73/5 **107, 119–25**

Decisions

Commission Decision 93/701/EC OJ 1993 L328/53 **22**

Council Decision 94/800/EC OJ 1994 L336/1 (WTO Agreement) **93**

Commission Decision 96/239/EC OJ 1996 L78/47 **72**

Commission Decision 97/602 OJ 1997 L242/64 **97**

Environmental Action Programmes

First Environmental Action Programme 1973 OJ C112/1 **6**

Second Environmental Action Programme OJ 1977 C139/1 **6**

Third Environmental Action Programme OJ 1983 C46/1 **6**

Fourth Environmental Action Programme OJ 1987 C328/1 **6**

Fifth Environmental Action Programme OJ 1993 C138/1 **6, 24**

Abbreviations

AJIL:	American Journal of International Law
BAT:	Best Available Techniques
BATNEEC:	Best Available Technology Not Entailing Excessive Costs
CAP:	Common Agricultural Policy
COM:	Commission
CMLR:	Common Market Law Reports
CMLRev.:	Common Market Law Review
CUP:	Cambridge University Press
EC:	European Community
ECR:	European Court Reports
ECU:	European Currency Unit
EEC:	European Economic Community
EELR:	European Environmental Law Review
EIA:	Environmental Impact Assessment
ELJ:	European Law Journal
ELQ:	Ecology Law Quarterly
ELR:	European Law Review
EPA:	Environmental Protection Agency (US)
EQS:	Environmental Quality Standards
EU:	European Union
GATT:	General Agreement on Tariffs and Trade
GSP:	Generalized System of Preferences
ICLQ:	International Comparative Law Quarterly
IPPC:	Integrated Pollution Prevention and Control
JEL:	Journal of Environmental Law
JWT:	Journal of World Trade
LIEI:	Legal Issues of European Integration
LIFE:	Community Financial Instrument for the Environment
LJ:	Law Journal
MLR:	Modern Law Review

MUP:	Manchester University Press
MW:	Megawatt
OJ:	Official Journal
OUP:	Oxford University Press
RECIEL:	Review of European Community and International Environmental Law
RSPB:	Royal Society for the Protection of Birds
SAsC:	Special Areas of Conservation
SEA:	Single European Act
SMEs:	Small and Medium Sized Enterprises
SPAs:	Special Protection Areas
SPS:	Agreement on Sanitary and Phytosanitary Measures
TEU:	Treaty on European Union
TBT:	Agreement on Technical Barriers to Trade
UN:	United Nations
UNCED:	United Nations Conference on Environment and Development
WTO:	World Trade Organization
WWF:	World Wide Fund for Nature

Introduction

Environmental law is an overtly attractive subject for study, appealing to those on the side of the angels who are concerned to preserve and protect wildlife, biodiversity and life quality. The emotive appeal is never better illustrated than in the popular hero status accorded to one 'Swampy', who has devoted his young life to tunnelling relentlessly in the path of any new intended road or airport runway development; thus causing massive disruption. Swampy has tunnelled not only relentlessly but also thoughtlessly, both of his own safety and of the wider issues which lead to decisions to construct, or in his view 'destruct'. Would-be environmental lawyers must, unfortunately, eschew such an example. Regrettably, responsible decision making is infinitely more difficult. That is not to say that there is not a place for Swampy. There is a place for such passion, not least in placing environmental issues high on the agenda for political and public debate. Direct action of this kind has a long, and in many cases happy, history. But even if, as lawyers, we are committed to environmental protection and preservation, we have (rightly or wrongly) chosen to express our commitment through reason and argument, albeit if in some cases this may be harnessed in the name of Swampy and his like.

Protection of the environment in European Community law resonates with the title of one of Séan O'Casey's most famous plays, *The Plough and the Stars* (1926). The title, which was intended to draw attention to both the grandeur and the mundanity of the Irish struggle with the British, derives from the flag of the Irish Citizen Army, at the time of the 1916 rising. This shows a representation of an agricultural plough, upon which is superimposed a representation of the constellation *Ursa Major*, sometimes known as The Plough (or the Great Bear). The coulter (the ironcutter at

1

the front of the ploughshare) of the plough is a serrated sword; a symbol of struggle. No doubt O'Casey realized the duality of the image of the plough – both an instrument of cultivation and itself a constellation. Even the symbol of toil was not free from the celestial.

> Be worthy, men, of following such a banner, for this is your flag of the future. Whatever may happen to me; though I should mingle with the dust, or fall to ashes in a flame, the plough will always remain to furrow the earth, the stars will always be there to unveil the beauty of the night, and a new people, living a newer life, will sing like the sons of the morning.
>
> But it was hard going ... [1]

I very much hope that it should be recognized by readers that, while there is the clearest possible distinction between the apparent normative simplicity of environmental issues and the appalling complexity of the law required to realize environmental objectives, the intellectual challenge of this complexity is not without attraction. Environmental law, appropriately, demands an holistic approach. Unless an environmental lawyer can come to terms with some of the problems and implications of the views of economists, politicians, political theorists and scientists, she will remain an artisan whose task is to give effect to the decisions of others. If, unlike Swampy, one is to articulate a coherent argument for environmental protection, a significant amount of toil, ploughing upwards towards the heavens, will be required.

This book is an attempt to introduce some of the important issues arising in EC environmental law. At a time when it may appear that there are more legislative enactments than there are stars, it makes no claim to be comprehensive. It represents, I hope, an accessible starting point for those interested in the study of environmental politics, as well as law. If at times the legal complexity tends to overshadow the intellectual richness of the discipline, I ask readers to recall the starry plough.

[1] O'Casey, S., *Drums under the Windows* (Macmillan, 1946) p. 270.

CHAPTER ONE

The European Community as an environmental actor

All is not well in the South-West of County Cork. The locals in this part of Ireland are restless – no longer prepared to 'tolerate being dictated to' by the 'blow-ins' – the complacent rich preaching an allegedly romantic and misguided species of environmentalism.[1] Co-operation may well be the 'Irish way . . . [b]ut we will not have people coming along telling us how to live our lives. We will not take that from anybody – no matter what nationality they are'.[2] The leader writer in *The Times* can barely conceal her frustration: 'Ireland has not always been the best steward of its own heritage. . . . As Ireland takes its proper place in the front rank of Europe so Europeans may be allowed a role in Ireland's back garden.'[3] The blow-ins represent the 'Europe' to which the leader writer refers. Their standing, like that of the European Community, to intervene in the environmental life of the rugged Beara peninsula, is contested.

This everyday tale of local conflict highlights the themes to be addressed in this chapter. The first relates to the scope of the Community's competence in environmental matters, and the second to the circumstances in which the Community ought to exercise those powers conferred. The concerns of the residents of the Beara peninsula resonate in an age of subsidiarity, one in which the Community has endorsed the principle that decisions be taken as closely as possible to the citizens of the Union. It is incumbent upon the Community to justify its actions; the imperial 'we know

---

1 Magee, A., 'Irish clash with new invaders over their land and heritage'. *The Times*, 26 August 1996.
2 Ibid.
3 'Shades of Green: Foreign intervention can be in Ireland's interests', *The Times*, 26 August 1996.

best what is good for you' attitude of The Times offers no credible foundation for Community intervention.

Community competence and the environment

Since its inception, the Community legal order has been predicated upon the concept of enumerated powers. The Community may act only within the limit of the powers conferred upon it. Since the early 1970s, however, this principle has been substantially eroded, leading one commentator to speak of jurisdictional 'mutation', and to characterize this mutation as the defining feature of the 'second and fundamental phase in the transformation of Europe'.[4] Mutation implies the disintegration of the line delineating the outer parameters of Community competence, culminating in jurisdictional 'expansion', whereby the Community enters a sphere in which power has not been explicitly granted to it. Early experiences in the environmental sphere exemplify this phenomenon in that, until 1987, with the entry into force of the Single European Act (SEA), the Community enjoyed no explicit legislative mandate in respect of environmental policy. Indeed, the term 'environment' was nowhere to be found in the original Treaty. This notwithstanding, the Community, during the period 1967–86, promulgated more than 150 pieces of environmental legislation. The Community's attitude to environmental protection, at this time, has been described not merely as 'reactive' and 'incidental', but also as 'unarticulated'.[5]

The emergence of the Community as an environmental actor during this early period is attributable to a variety of factors; both political and legal. As a matter of law, the origins of Community intervention lie in two Treaty articles, each conferring extensive competence within remarkably loosely defined parameters. Significant, also, has been the permissiveness of the European Court in sanctioning recourse to these provisions.

Article 100 provides for the adoption of directives for the 'approximation' (harmonization) of Member State laws which directly affect the establishment or functioning of the common market.

---

[4] Weiler, J., 'The Transformation of Europe' (1991) 100 Yale LJ 2403, pp. 2431–2453.
[5] Brinkhorst, L., *The Road to Maastricht* (1993) 20 ELQ 7, p. 9.

In the first instance this was deployed to achieve harmonization of product regulation; that is to say of the laws prescribing the essential characteristics of goods to be offered for sale. In the absence of such harmonization, and in the absence of a doctrine of mutual recognition (such as emerged later[6]) disparities in national law would have the effect of perpetuating market fragmentation and inhibiting the free movement of goods. Perhaps more interestingly, and certainly more controversially, Article 100 was also used to promote harmonization of national laws in a bid to promote a level playing field of competition among Member States. Environmental standards, including production process standards, are assumed to impose substantial costs upon industry. Significant disparities between the national regulatory practices of Member States would tend to lead to a distortion of competition, which would negatively affect the functioning of the common market. According to the European Court, '[p]rovisions which are made necessary by considerations relating to the environment and health may be a burden upon undertakings to which they apply and if there is no harmonization of national provisions on the matter, competition may be appreciably distorted'.[7] The Court, therefore, recognized the adequacy of Article 100 in providing a suitable legal basis for environmental measures. To what extent market integration does necessitate Community level environmental intervention is a theme to which we will return, both in the next section and in Chapter 4.

Article 235 provides for the adoption of Community measures where these 'prove necessary to attain, in the course of operation of the common market, one of the objectives of the Community and [where the] ... Treaty has not provided the necessary powers'. One of the Community's original tasks, as stated in Article 2, was to promote throughout the Community a harmonious development of economic activities, and a continuous and balanced expansion. Expansion, the heads of state or government of the Member States declared in the Declaration to the Paris Summit, was not to be viewed as an end in itself, but rather as a means of achieving not only a raising of the standard of living but of enhancing life quality. In keeping with this, particular attention was to be paid to non-material values and wealth and to environmental

6   For a discussion of mutual recognition see Chapter 4.
7   Case 92/79 *Commission* v *Italy* [1980] ECR 1115, para. 8.

protection.[8] To this end the political leaders requested that a strategic action programme be drawn up by the Commission and Council. This first action programme, adopted in 1973, was the first of five to have emerged to date.[9] It reaffirmed that continuous and balanced expansion was not conceivable in the absence of measures to combat pollution and nuisance to improve the quality of life and protection of the environment. In Brinkhorst's previously quoted terms, this political conversion to a doctrine of environmental protection, made possible through an expansive interpretation of Article 2, might be viewed as a *reaction* to the high profile Stockholm (United Nations) Conference on the Human Environment (1972). In the language of one commentator, the period following the Stockholm Declaration 'was marked by a proliferation of international environmental organisations . . . and greater efforts by existing institutions to address environmental issues'.[10] 'EC Environmental law is one of the most tangible outcomes of the Stockholm Conference.'[11] The European Court lent support to these political developments by acknowledging that environmental protection does indeed constitute one of the Community's 'essential objectives'.[12] A small number of measures were adopted solely on the basis of Article 235, the most famous example being the Wild Birds Directive of 1979.[13] More commonly, however, Article 235 was deployed as a supplementary source of legislative authority, to be used alongside Article 100.

The willingness of the Member States to condone Community participation in environmental policy-making, even in the absence of any self-evident, explicit, legal basis, is most readily explicable in terms of the unanimity requirement which underpins both articles under discussion. Jurisdictional mutation, occurring by way of recourse to these, did not – by virtue of the veto – threaten to impinge upon the sovereign prerogatives of the Member States. Their capacity to define and protect their own interests was to re-

---

[8] See Declaration from Paris summit – Bulletin 1972 10.

[9] First Environmental Action Programme, 1973 OJ C112/1; Second Environmental Action Programme, OJ 1977 C139/1; Third Environmental Action Programme, OJ 1983 C46/1; Fourth Environmental Action Programme, OJ 1987 C328/1; Fifth Environmental Action Programme, OJ 1993 C138/1.

[10] Sands, P., *Principles of International Environmental Law* (MUP, 1995), p. 38.

[11] Ibid., p. 545.

[12] Case 240/83 *Procureur de la République* v *Association de défense des Bruleurs d'huiles usagées* [1983] ECR 531, p. 549.

[13] OJ 1979 L103/1. See Chapter 6.

main unimpaired. Not only would regulatory policies of this kind not necessitate the transfer to the Community of substantial financial resources, but Member States remained secure in their ability to block measures which threatened to impose excessive costs upon either the state or national industry.

When, in 1987, the SEA introduced a new Treaty title on 'Environment' (Articles 130r–130t), this served both to underwrite, politically and legally, the Community's earlier initiatives, and to articulate the objectives and principles (Article 130r) which were to guide future action. As with Articles 100 and 235, the new Article 130s, conferring concurrent competence upon the Community, provided that decisions were to be adopted by consensus in Council. In this sense, the SEA represented merely a modest step forward.

In another sense, however, the constitutional implications of the SEA were profound. It generated a fundamental shift in the balance of power underpinning the Community legal order. The new Article 100a, conferring competence upon the Community to adopt measures to achieve its internal market objective, and to harmonize national laws affecting the establishment or functioning of this internal market, provided – albeit with exceptions – for qualified majority voting.[14] It further reinforced the role of the European Parliament, through the introduction of the so-called 'co-operation' procedure.[15]

Inevitably, in the period following the SEA, the question of choice of legal basis assumed a significance hitherto unknown. Vigorous debate ensued as to the extent to which Article 100a might constitute an adequate legal basis for environmental provisions, in view of the existence of Article 130s. The Commission, in particular, with the support of the European Parliament, pushed relentlessly in the direction of Article 100a, perceiving it as facilitating a move beyond lowest common denominator decision-making. This issue spawned a vigorous debate among Community lawyers, framed at times in the emotive language of an emerging threat to the rule of law.[16] The intensity of the debate is indicative of the sig-

---

[14] Article 100a(2) provides for unanimous voting in respect of fiscal provisions, free movement of persons and measures relating to the rights and interests of employed persons.

[15] See Article 189c.

[16] Compare Crosby, S., 'The Single Market and the Rule of Law' (1991) 16 ELR 451 and Chalmers, D., 'Environmental Protection and the single Market: An Unusual Development. Does the EC Treaty Need a Title on the Environment?' (1995) LIEI 65.

nificance of the question in determining the relative balance of power between institutional actors. Inevitably, the issue fell for consideration before the European Court.

The famous *Titanium Dioxide*[17] case took the form of an action for judicial review instituted by the Commission pursuant to Article 173. The Commission sought the annulment of Council Directive 89/428 harmonizing national rules for the reduction and elimination of pollution caused by waste from the titanium dioxide industry. The Commission had proposed that the directive be adopted on the basis of Article 100a, while the Council engineered a change in legal basis, in favour of Article 130s. Both parties to the case presented arguments formulated in terms of a 'centre of gravity' approach. Whereas the Commission argued that the primary purpose of the measure was to improve conditions of competition in the titanium dioxide industry, the Council maintained that its centre of gravity lay in the elimination of pollution and hence in the realm of environmental protection. The European Commission was thus pushing in the direction of majority voting; while the Council was keen to preserve the right of any individual state to veto the proposals. The European Court accepted that the measure pursued a dual objective and that it was 'concerned, *indissociably*, with both the protection of the environment and the elimination of disparities in conditions of competition'.[18] It was scrupulous in avoiding ranking these objectives in order of importance. Nevertheless, the Court refused to countenance a dual legal basis solution. Such a solution would have implied a marrying of procedural norms which are essentially incompatible; co-operation with the European Parliament and unanimity in Council. The Court then proceeded, by way of textual exegesis, to demonstrate the sufficiency of Article 100a for a directive which aimed (*inter alia*) to contribute to the proper functioning of the internal market. The directive, having been based on Article 130s, was annulled.

The judgment of the Court is susceptible to criticism. Its tone is excessively negative. It explains, credibly, why recourse to Article 100a is not precluded in respect of environmental measures but not why, on this occasion, recourse to it was to be preferred. It may be thought that the Court was influenced by procedural considerations, relating in particular to the enhanced role of the Euro-

---

[17] Case C-300/89 *Commission* v *Council*, [1991] ECR 2867.
[18] Ibid., para. 13.

pean Parliament pursuant to Article 100a; 'that participation reflects a fundamental democratic principle that the peoples should take part in the exercise of power through the intermediary of a representative assembly'.[19] Such a conclusion sits uneasily with the Court's rhetorical insistence that 'the choice of legal basis for a measure . . . must be based on objective factors which are amenable to judicial review'.[20]

What is interesting for our purposes here is the constitutional significance of this judgment in terms of the evolution of the Community's status as an environmental actor. Its implications were profound. Any measure in respect of which it might be claimed that it has some bearing upon the establishment or functioning of the internal market, however secondary, might legitimately be adopted on the basis of Article 100a, and consequently by way of qualified majority, following co-operation with the European Parliament.

The judgment of the Court in this case preceded, in time, those inter-governmental negotiations which were ultimately to lead to the conclusion of the Treaty on European Union (TEU). At Maastricht the Member States condoned a move toward qualified majority voting (and co-operation with the European Parliament) in relation to (most) environmental legislation predicated upon Article 130s. Their willingness to do so may be viewed as being not entirely disassociated from the Court's position in *Titanium Dioxide*. Retention of the veto under Article 130s would not have served to increase the power of individual Member States, given the strength of the European Court's preference for Article 100a, in a dual objective scenario. It is interesting to observe that, following the conclusion of the Maastricht negotiations (though prior to the entry into force of the Treaty due to the ratification difficulties experienced in a number of Member States), the Court retreated from *Titanium Dioxide*, endorsing a centre of gravity (principal/ancillary objective) approach such as had been put forward by the parties in that case.[21] In terms of the legal basis debate, *Titanium Dioxide* appears today as a temporary aberration. However, its significance in shaping the evolution of the Treaty framework for environment should not be discounted.

19 Ibid., para. 20.
20 Ibid., para. 10.
21 See, especially, Case C-155/91 *Commission* v *Council* [1993] ECR I-939 and Case C-187/93 *Parliament* v *Council* [1994] ECR I-2857.

Already, however, Maastricht is yesterday's news. As we proceed we must also take care to observe the implications of the more recently concluded, though not yet ratified, Treaty of Amsterdam (1997). This would bring about a further reconciliation of the legislative procedures governing Articles 100a and 130s. In the case of the latter, co-operation with the European Parliament would be replaced by co-decision. Those areas currently requiring unanimity under Article 130s would continue to do so, even in the wake of the entry into force of the Treaty of Amsterdam. With the European Court's retreat from *Titanium Dioxide* the unanimity exceptions retain considerable practical significance.

What, though, would the residents of the Beara peninsula make of this? Might it not confirm their worst fears that the Community had somehow muscled into territory in which it had no business; the result of a dubious alliance between Community and Member States? While today there can be little doubt, in law, as to the Community's status as an environmental actor, this offers little by way of consolation to those who seek solace in self-rule. In the next section it is necessary to consider, not whether the Community enjoys competence, but whether, and in what circumstances, it ought to exercise that competence. This issue will be approached through the lens of subsidiarity, a concept first introduced into Community law specifically in the context of Treaty's environmental title.

Justifying Community environmental action: the Community's subsidiary role in an age of subsidiarity

Appended to the recently concluded Amsterdam Treaty is a protocol which seeks to clarify the application of the principles of subsidiarity and proportionality. It is with the former that this section is concerned. The concept of subsidiarity rests upon considerations of comparative efficiency in the delimitation of the respective powers of the Community and its Member States. The Community (in areas which do not fall within its exclusive competence[22]) is to

---

22 For a measured analysis of the scope of the Community's exclusive competence see Steiner, J., 'Subsidiarity under the Maastricht Treaty' in O'Keefe and Twomey (eds), *Legal Issues of the Maastricht Treaty* (Wiley Chancery, 1994); c.f. Toth, A., in the same volume.

act only where Member State intervention would be insufficient having regard to the objective pursued, and where Community action adds value in contributing to the achievement of that objective. The Amsterdam protocol provides that Community legislation must state the reasons upon which it is based with a view to demonstrating compliance with subsidiarity and proportionality. '[T]he reasons for concluding that a Community objective can be better achieved by the Community must be substantiated by qualitative, or wherever possible, quantitative indicators.'[23]

Before turning to examine – through the lens of subsidiarity – the rationale for, and proper scope of, Community action in the environmental field, it is helpful to consider first why, in an era which celebrates the market as the central organizing principle of economic life, there is perceived to be a need for state intervention to regulate environmental consumption.

Michael Jacobs, exploring the relationship between market forces and the environment, calls forth the image of an 'invisible elbow'.[24] This 'anatomical choice', he explains, is not arbitrary, in that elbows may be used to push people aside deliberately or merely cause damage inadvertently. The 'environmentally unconstrained' interplay of market forces will, he argues, tend to exacerbate environmental harm. This he attributes to a number of factors, not least to the impetus for continuing economic growth inherent in the functioning of the market. '[C]ompetition tends to stimulate [and necessitate] increased production'.[25]

Central to his analysis is the well-known, and much discussed, concept of environmental externalities. Negative externalities comprise those costs associated with any given activity, borne not by the parties engaging in that activity but by third parties, present or future. These take the form of social costs and constitute a manifestation of market failure. This phenomenon of social cost may take a variety of forms. Externalities may be physical in nature, whereby, for example, we are forced to breath the airborne pollutants emitted when others drive cars. They may be economic in that, for example, the value of our property may diminish due to the construction of a factory treating toxic waste at the gate to our

---

[23] Protocol on the application of the subsidiarity and proportionality principles, Treaty of Amsterdam.
[24] *The Green Economy* (Pluto, 1991), Ch. 3.
[25] Ibid., p. 25.

back garden. They may, it is often suggested, be psychological in nature, implying a decline in our psychic, as opposed to physical, well-being.[26] Those of us who drive cars, centrally heat our homes, or ski down mountains (taking lifts up) are all too familiar with this concept, albeit perhaps not by name. Yet, though we, as consumers, generate negative externalities in that we do not pay the full social cost of our activities, our incentive to alter our behaviour is weak. Externalities tend to be remote, both in time and space. Causation patterns tend to be ill-defined and uncertain. Ignorance is bliss.

The phenomenon of social cost has its origins in the construction of the individual in liberal economics. We behave, and are expected to behave, as utility-maximising producers and consumers of goods; to look out for number one. It might be that, collectively, we would all benefit from a change in patterns of behaviour. However, the value of one individual desisting from any given activity is likely to be of marginal benefit to the collectivity, and yet to impose significant costs upon that individual. One's desisting may well merely enable others to 'free ride' on the back of our (in economic terms, irrational) willingness to sacrifice individual benefit in the name of the common good. The nature of environmental goods (benefits) is frequently such as to render it impossible to exclude free-riding. In the case of common resources (for example, fish stocks) – those goods owned by no-one – it is impossible to prevent others from stepping in to consume those goods which we have foresworn. In the case of public goods (for example, the air) – goods characterized by indivisibility – the benefits which ensue by virtue of our self-restraint will be shared by all, at no cost to those others. Hence, even where we acknowledge the need for a change in behaviour, our willingness to co-operate may be contingent upon the existence of a guarantee that others will likewise contribute to the task at hand, and that the costs associated with such endeavours will be shared fairly among all beneficiaries. The 'tragedy of the commons' is that '. . . we are locked into a system of "fouling our own nest", so long as we behave only as independent, rational free enterprisers'.[27]

Such concepts of externalities and free-riding are of assistance in considering the rationale for Community intervention in matters

---

[26] See Turner, Pearce and Bateman, *Environmental Economics: an Elementary Introduction* (Harvester Wheatsheaf, 1994).
[27] Hardin, G., 'The Tragedy of the Commons' (1968) 162 Science 1243.

environmental; in assessing the legitimacy, and proper parameters, of 'Europe's' role in Ireland's 'back garden'. Ireland is a nation, albeit it one whose boundaries are violently contested. A nation – Benedict Anderson famously tells us – is an 'imagined political community – and imagined as both inherently limited (in terms of membership and territory) and sovereign'.[28] Sovereignty (freedom), David Held asserts, may be *de jure* or *de facto*.[29] The former speaks, in positivist terms, to 'the absence over and above the [nation] state of a superior authority'.[30] The latter is concerned with what Held calls the 'autonomy' of nations, which is tied up with a capacity to define policy objectives, and to implement and effectively realize those objectives.

The autonomy of the modern nation-state is diminished by virtue of its inclusion in a network of states, membership of which implies, more or less profound, interdependence. Such interdependence may be analysed in the language of transnational externalities or 'spillovers'. In the presence of such spillover effects, nations may only 'dream of being free'.[31] They operate to undermine the autonomy of the state, and hence to deny the effectiveness (or sufficiency) of Member State action in addressing a given problem, or in achieving a given objective.

Wils,[32] in a short and provocative article, proposes a tripartite taxonomy of transnational externalities, each in his view operating to legitimate Community intervention in accordance with the subsidiarity principle. He points first to those transnational externalities which are physical in form. It is a truism to assert that pollution respects no national boundaries. Activities in any one state may impinge physically upon environmental quality in another state, or in an area beyond the jurisdiction of any state; in the global commons. Transboundary river pollution, acid rain, global warming, and disposal of waste at sea all attest, by way of example, to this phenomenon. In the language of the Amsterdam guidelines, 'the issue under consideration has [physically expressed] transnational aspects which cannot be satisfactorily regulated by action by Member States'.[33] In the face of such physical

---

[28] *Imagined Communities* (Verso, 1983) p. 15.
[29] *Political Theory and the Modern State* (Polity, 1989) p. 228.
[30] Hinsley, F.H., *Sovereignty* (CUP, 1986) p. 226.
[31] Supra, n. 28.
[32] Wils, W.P.J., 'Subsidiarity and EC Environmental Policy: Taking People's Concerns Seriously' (1994) 6 JEL 85.
[33] Supra, n. 23, para. 5.

spillovers, Ireland is no longer mistress of her own backyard. Her capacity for autonomous (effective) action is limited. Wils points next to a second kind of spillover effect; that which is economic in nature:

> Environmental protection measures, both product and process (or emission) standards, affect trade and competitiveness. Many pieces of EC environmental legislation are justified, at least in part, by the concern to eliminate barriers to trade or unfair competition resulting from disparate environmental standards in the Member States.[34]

For Wils, Community action may be considered indispensable, from the perspective of the Community's internal market objective, both where this may be demonstrated to be necessary to avoid restrictions on trade, or to correct distortions of competition. It is the latter proposition which remains so deeply contested. It may well be the case that the unilateral regulatory preferences of a single state give rise to consequences which are felt beyond the territory of that state. In a context of intense market integration, Member States form part of the same economic, as well as ecological, network. Shifting regulatory patterns may alter the competitive balance between states; both in terms of their relative capacity to attract investment, and in terms of (price sensitive) consumer demand for their goods. As such, one state may endure financial losses as a result of decisions taken by their trading partners. These may be viewed as representing transnational externalities of a sort; 'pecuniary' externalities.[35]

Even to the extent that the existence of such externalities may be empirically verifiable, it is by no means certain that, in and of themselves, they justify Community intervention. From an economic perspective, they do not represent an instance of market failure. On the contrary, they constitute evidence of the efficient functioning of a dynamic market, operating in accordance with the principle of regulatory competition. They are an endemic feature of healthy market relations. To quote Bernard, 'a model of regulation based on "competition between [Member State] rules" . . . may be economically just as, if not more, efficient'.[36]

---

[34] Supra, n. 32, p. 89.

[35] See Ogus, A., *Regulation: Legal Form and Economic Theory* (OUP, 1994), pp. 37–8.

[36] Bernard, N., 'The Future of European Economic Law in the light of the Principle of Subsidiarity' (1996) 33 CMLRev. 633, p. 643.

The above analysis is by no means unconvincing; albeit that it flies in the face of the Amsterdam guidelines, which assume the legitimacy of Community-level action in so far as it seeks to correct competitive distortions.[37] However, it does not, in this writer's view, tell the whole story of economic externalities. It is predicated upon a sharp distinction between physical and economic spillovers; the latter conceived as purely financial in nature. Such a distinction may be tenable in theory, but misleading in practice. Both physical and economic externalities may be capable of undermining the autonomy of Member States to regulate the quality of the domestic environment. Whereas the former may render this physically impossible, the latter may render it economically untenable.[38] The result, ultimately, may be the same. Member States, thrust onto a treadmill of regulatory competition, may – *de facto* – be obliged to abandon environmental policy objectives which they previously endorsed; to adopt standards which are less stringent than those which they would independently prefer. Economic externalities may, in the first instance, be financial (pecuniary) in nature but may, in the second, find physical expression. Where, as Held puts it, there is a 'gap between the formal domain of political authority and the actual economic system of production, distribution and exchange', such as 'serves to limit or undermine the actual power or scope of national political authorities',[39] the apparent autonomy of nations may prove illusory. In such circumstances it may be thought that it is not the Community's internal market objective which is threatened, but rather the quality of the Community's environment. The Community is committed to the objective of sustainable development, protecting the environment, and to contributing to the broadly expressed objectives laid down in Article 130r. Locked into a cycle of competitive de-regulation, Member State action may prove insufficient to achieve these objectives. It remains for the Community to demonstrate that this is, in practice, the case in any specific regulatory context.

Before moving on to consider Wils's third, and most controversial, category of externality, it is necessary to allude to the signific-

---

37 Supra, n. 23.
38 For a fuller discussion of this argument see Scott, J., 'The GATT and Community Law: Rethinking the Regulatory Gap' in Shaw and More, *New Legal Dynamics of European Union* (OUP, 1995) and Bernard, supra, n. 36, pp. 642–7.
39 Supra, n. 29, p. 229.

ance of the above in terms of the legal basis debate. It has been suggested that regulatory competition may preclude realization of the Community's environmental, as opposed to internal market, objectives. An efficient internal market is not only capable of accommodating diversity in regulatory response, but may be thought to demand such diversity to function properly (efficiently). It should not therefore be assumed that harmonization measures, adopted in the face of economic spillovers, be predicated upon Article 100a, except where these aim principally at eliminating barriers to trade. Such a conclusion is important, given the uncertainty surrounding the scope of the Community's exclusive competence, particularly in an internal market context, and hence in relation to the scope of application of the subsidiarity principle.[40]

The above discussion has highlighted the insufficiency of Member State action in a context of autonomy sapping transnational externalities, both physical and economic. Wils goes on, however, to argue that this represents an unduly confined conception of subsidiarity which 'fails to explain the compatibility with the principle of subsidiarity of substantial parts of [Community] environmental policy'.[41] This, he suggests, is true above all of 'most' Community law in the area of nature conservation. This approach fails to 'take people's concerns seriously', at least to the extent that these concerns 'transcend physical proximity and economic relevance'.[42] On this basis he argues that 'psychic' (!) spillovers should be written into the subsidiarity equation. According to his thesis, Community level intervention may be justified where the environmental sensibilities of citizens in one Member State are offended by activities in another, resulting in a decline in their psychological well-being. Wils offers illustrations which range from the preservation of wildlife species and natural habitats, to the regulation of bull-fighting in Spain.

Wils's thesis reflects a widespread perception that certain environmental goods situated wholly within the territory of a single state should not be viewed as constituting the exclusive property of that state, to be disposed of at will. Wils seeks to offer an explanation for the 'internationalization' of apparently 'local' environmental goods which is based upon the fact of psychological interdependence or interconnectedness. While Community law,

---

40 See Steiner and Toth, supra, n. 22.
41 Supra, n. 32, p. 87.
42 Ibid.

like international law, has embraced the concepts of 'common heritage of mankind',[43] and 'common concern of mankind',[44] neither has sought, other than at a political level, to delimit their scope of application on the basis of enumerated criteria. Any attempt to do so, Wils would argue, must eschew 'physicism' and 'economism' as the basis for international action.[45]

Wils acknowledges that '[a]t first sight, the concept of psychic spill-overs might appear rather woolly and uncontrollably wide-ranging . . .',[46] but seeks solace in the hard-nosed world of economic rationality. Environmental economics of a fairly orthodox kind has long recognized that externalities may be non-material in form, and that loss of 'psychic' well-being may constitute a valid reason for environmental regulation, including that at an international level.[47] Indeed, Wils concedes that 'not all environmental problems present psychic spill-overs worth mentioning',[48] and appears to endorse economic rationality as a means of assessing their existence and quantifying their scale. Wils emphasizes that environmental economics has, in recent years, been concerned to develop methods for valuing non-material costs and benefits. Whether Wils means it to or not, this takes him deep into the heart of a cost-benefit, efficiency orientated, approach to environmental law and politics. The question of whether the Community ought to regulate bull-fighting in Spain becomes an economic question, to be answered on the basis of a comparison of the relative costs and benefits associated with Community action. The intensity of the psychological damage endured is to be measured (quantified) and, through the application of a cost-benefit analysis, willingness to pay – where there is willingness to pay enough to compensate for the losses associated with a ban on bull-fighting – may result in it

43 See preamble to Council Directive 79/409 (wild birds), supra, n. 13.
44 See preamble to Council Directive 92/43 (habitats) OJ 1992 L206/7.
45 The concept of physical spillovers, in this writer's view, operates to justify more of the Community's legislation in the area of nature conservation than Wils acknowledges. This is self-evidently the case as regards migratory species. Equally, however, it may legitimate Community action in so far as this is concerned with the conservation of wildlife species and habitats whose conservation status is threatened. A single state may adopt drastic measures to improve the conservation status of a particular species or habitat type. Nonetheless, by virtue of the limited scale of intervention, its viability may remain precarious. The autonomy of a single Member State is thus diminished.
46 Supra, n. 32, p. 89.
47 Supra, n. 26, p. 229.
48 Supra, n. 32, p. 90.

being efficient, and hence justifiable, for the Community to intervene. The end, according to which the insufficiency of Member
State action is to be adjudged, is understood in terms of (alloca-
tive) efficiency; not, as was suggested above, in terms of effectiveness or autonomy or, as Wils appears to countenance in relation to
economic spillovers, in terms of fairness (of competition). It is the
enthusiasm with which Wils endorses the methodology of environmental economics, and his alacrity in offering allegiance to efficiency as a policy goal, which is, arguably, the most striking and
problematic facet of his analysis. Yet it should be readily conceded
that such an analysis is instinctively compelling. An efficiency-in-
spired approach to subsidiarity, in the sphere of social regulation,
implies the existence of an objectively correct outcome, one which
is susceptible to substantiation on the basis of quantitative indicators.[49] It promises 'right' answers, not only in respect of the 'level
of governance' issue, but in relation to the setting and stringency
of standards and to the choice of policy instruments. It militates in
the direction of government by expert (technocracy), and for many
in the direction of an independent agency approach to regulation,
such as is characteristic in the United States. Economic analysis has
much to offer environmental law but, in the language of Sagoff,[50]
not all political questions are economic. Wils's thesis necessitates a
brief excursion into the world of economic theory, and specifically
into the highly technical world of cost-benefit analysis.

The 'curious comeback' of cost-benefit analysis

Cost-benefit analysis has been subjected to a barrage of criticism
over recent years.[51] One author, drawing on the writings of John
Barth, compares the related principles of efficiency, welfare
maximization and cost-benefit balancing to the principles of sinis-
trality (if the alternatives are side by side, choose the one on the
left), antecedence (if they are consecutive in time, choose the ear-

---

49 See again para. 4 of the Amsterdam subsidiarity protocol, supra, n. 23.
50 Sagoff, M., *The Economy of the Earth* (CUP, 1990), p. vii.
51 See Mishan, E.J., *Cost Benefit Analysis* (Allen & Unwin, 1988) for an excellent
and entertaining exploration of this topic. See also Jacobs, supra, n. 24, Chs
16–19 and Kelman, S., 'Cost-Benefit Analysis: an Ethical Critique' (1981) 5
Regulation 33. Ogus, supra, n. 35 provides an accessible account and references
to much of the relevant literature.

lier) and alphabetical priority (choose the alternative whose first letter appears earlier in the alphabet).[52] This notwithstanding, cost-benefit analysis appears to be enjoying a 'curious comeback'.[53]

Cost-benefit analysis measures the relative efficiency of any given course of action (or inaction). Efficiency, increasingly, is understood in 'Kaldor-Hicks' terms; '[t]his stipulates as efficient a policy which results in sufficient benefits for those who gain such that *potentially* they can compensate fully all the losers and still remain better off'.[54] It may be efficient for the state (or Community) to step in to regulate an externality generating activity where this would lead to an overall (net) increase in well-being, whereby the gainers gain more than the losers lose.

Sagoff, in his book *The Economy of the Earth*, provides an elegant and insightful critique of cost-benefit analysis. He views his role as that of a coroner performing an autopsy on resource and welfare economics, as applied to social regulation. His arguments are particularly pertinent in the context of a discussion of psychic spillovers, in that he focuses upon attempts by economists to develop techniques for the quantification of non-material values; to make tangible the intangible.[55] Such techniques have been developed in a bid to counter allegations that an economic perspective on well-being is excessively narrow in its focus upon quantity not quality. Sagoff examines, in particular, a well-known approach to cost-benefit calculation known as 'contingent valuation' or willingness to pay. This approach is conceived as capable of determining *total* economic value in that it permits the aggregation of use, option, bequest and existence value – 'that is, the value placed on the possibility of being able to use the environment in the future, or being able to bequeath it to the next generation, and on the simple existence of the environment irrespective of use'.[56] For Wils also, willingness to pay represents a crucial indicator of the existence of psychic spillovers, and hence of the legitimacy of Community intervention. He notes:

---

[52] Supra, n. 50, p. 223.

[53] Adams, J., 'The Emperor's Old Clothes: The Curious Comeback of Cost-benefit Analysis' (1993) 2 Environmental Values 247.

[54] Supra, n. 35, p. 24. Kaldor-Hicks efficiency is distinguished from Pareto efficiency in that the latter defines as efficient a policy which makes somebody better off and nobody worse off.

[55] On the various methodologies deployed to assist in cost-benefit analysis see supra, n. 24, Ch. 8.

[56] Supra, n. 50, p. 128.

I became aware of psychic spill-overs for the first time on 22 July 1992, when I found on page five of the *Financial Times* a full-page colour-printed advertisement, co-funded by an English animal welfare group, its Scottish and Ulster sister organizations and an international group, which denounced the cruelty of bull-fighting in Spain. The fact that these groups are willing to spend (probably quite a lot of) their money on such actions, shows that bull-fighting in Spain affects the well-being of their members and sympathisers over in the United Kingdom.[57]

While this idea that willingness to pay might represent an appropriate measure of the legitimacy and proper scope of Community action may appear as self-evidently absurd, the credibility of cost-benefit analysis as a basis for public policy should not be underestimated. Leaving aside the plethora of technical difficulties which beset cost-benefit analysis,[58] a number of fundamental conceptual objections may be raised. First, there arises a question of distributive fairness. In Wils's example, the relevant public interest groups were *actually* willing to pay, albeit that their money ended up in the coffers of the Financial Times. However, contingent valuation techniques merely measure *hypothetical* willingness to pay. The victim of a psychic spillover is not required to put her money where her mouth is. The gainer is not required, in practice, to compensate the loser.

Second, cost-benefit analysis, based on a willingness to pay, equates (financial) might with right. It privileges the rich (or the fervent) over the poor (or the passive). It assumes that the credibility of public preferences as to what constitutes a 'good' society is susceptible to measurement rather than political judgment. Sagoff, on the contrary, argues that 'it is the cogency of the arguments, not how much partisans are willing to pay . . . that offers a credible basis for public policy'.[59] Financial might may, on occasion, be equated with right, but may equally favour the obnoxious, the morally repugnant, or the downright stupid. It may therefore be accepted that cost-benefit analysis must operate within certain moral constraints. Yet the development of techniques to 'screen' preferences, with a view to excluding the absurd or the dangerous, undermines the claims of economic reason to objectivity. No

---

57 Supra, n. 32, p. 90.
58 See Jacobs, supra, n. 24.
59 Supra, n. 50, p. 53.

longer the faithful, if amoral, servant of the devil if he should happen to offer the highest wages, cost-benefit analysis transforms the professional economist into an unelected, and frequently inaccessible, politician.

Third, and related to this, cost-benefit analysis not only assumes that it is possible to quantify the value that we place in nature, but also that the task of public policy is to aggregate private preferences which have been formed in a context which is independent of the political process. Our preferences are viewed as pre-political or exogenous. Sagoff, however, argues that:

> A political process – a process of debate and compromise – is supposed to be creative. The ability of the political process to cause people to change their values and to rise above their self-interest is crucial to its legitimacy. Political participation is supposed to educate and elevate public opinion; it is not, like economic analysis, supposed merely to gratify preexisting desires.[60]

In particular, according to Sagoff, it is the task of the political to distinguish between 'consumer' and 'citizen' preferences and to nurture the latter in a context of constructive deliberation and exchange of ideas. Citizen preferences are susceptible to change in the light of the information upon which they based.

What is clear is that this discussion has significant implications for decision-making in the European Union. The concerns of the folk of the Beara peninsula speak not only to the level of governance question, but also to the distance which separates Community law from those whose behaviour it seeks to regulate. The Community today faces pressures which militate in two opposing directions; government by expert in the name of allegedly substantively correct outcomes, and government premised upon popular participation, in the name of responsiveness. At a time when, at last, we are beginning to understand a little more about the Community's labyrinthine 'comitology' structures,[61] the Community is

---

[60] Ibid., p. 96.

[61] This is a topic of crucial importance in EC environmental law. It would not be possible to do justice here to the complexity of the subject and to the excellent work which is currently being undertaken, thus offering us an insight into the possibilities and limitations which are inherent in a committee-based approach to decision-making in technical spheres. For an excellent discussion, see Pedler and Schaefer (eds), *Shaping European Law and Policy: The Role of Committees and Comitology in the Policy Process* (European Institute for Public Administration, Maastricht, 1996).

taking steps to promote participation at a more popular level. This is most readily apparent in the institution of the Committee of the Regions and in the various initiatives encouraging participation by Non-Governmental Organizations, including those active in the sphere of environmental protection.[62] This is a topic which would inevitably take us beyond the parameters of a short introduction to EC environmental law. It is, however, in the context of the European Union's 'quest for legitimacy', a topic which – alongside subsidiarity – is of the utmost importance.[63]

Conclusion

The previous section barely touched upon the complex question of the legitimacy of cost-benefit analysis in environmental law-making. However, it should at least be clear that subsidiarity does not easily lend itself to such a (pseudo) scientific approach. Not only is it the case that the Treaty does not single out efficiency as the ultimate objective of Community level market regulation, but in addition it is neither feasible nor legitimate to capture the level of governance issue purely in the language of economics. The question of whether the Community ought to regulate bull-fighting in Spain, or construction projects on the Beara Peninsula, is necessarily a political question whose resolution depends upon a wide variety of considerations, not least the conception of 'Union' to which one subscribes, and the type of citizenship to which one aspires. Citizenship in a Union necessarily implies, up to a point, a shared sense of identity. In a multinational, multicultural, Union, identity premised upon ethnicity is neither feasible nor desirable. This has led some to propose a 'de-coupling of nationality/*Volk* from citizenship' and toward a conception of 'a polity the demos of which, its membership, is understood in the first place in civic and political rather than ethno-cultural terms'.[64] A civic conception of

---

62 See, especially, Council Decision 93/701 OJ 1993 L328/53, on setting up a general consultative form on the environment, and COM(97) 28 final, *Amended Proposal for a Council Decision on a Community Action Programme promoting non-governmental organizations primarily active in the field of environmental protection.*

63 de Burca, G., The Quest for Legitimacy in the European Union' (1996) 59 MLR 349.

64 Weiler, J.H.H., 'Does Europe Need a Constitution? Reflection on Demos, Telos and the German Maastricht Decision' (1995) 1 ELJ 219, p. 252.

citizenship implies 'a commitment to the shared values of the Union'.[65] The discourse of citizenship, like the discourse of rights in the United States, then emerges as an argument justifying Community intervention in the sphere beyond Wils's 'physicism' and 'economism'. However, only a broad and intense conception of shared 'civic' identity would serve to justify Community regulation of bull-fighting in Spain. This, regardless of how much the animal rights activists are willing (at least in the abstract) to pay.

In a sense, it may be thought that, by focusing upon Wils's little known analysis of psychic spillovers, the latter part of this chapter has been fighting a straw man. However, the economic rationality to which he subscribes in this context, holds considerable sway in the world of environmental law and politics, both in relation to the task of setting environmental standards and in respect of individual project evaluation. While, traditionally, the Community's approach to cost-benefit analysis has been somewhat circumspect, it has more recently come under pressure more fully to rationalize its actions in these terms.[66] This is a theme to which we will return at various times throughout this book. However, the focus in the next chapter is upon means rather than ends, in that it examines the issue of the choice of policy instruments in the Community for environmental protection.

[65] Ibid.
[66] See, for example, the findings of the Molitor group of independent experts, COM(95) 288 final/2.

CHAPTER TWO

Instruments for environmental protection: 'command and control'

The European Community, relative at least to the United States, has been unadventurous in its choice of instruments for environmental protection. Notwithstanding its rhetorical commitment to broaden the range of policy instruments employed,[1] the European Community remains wedded in practice to traditional 'command and control' style regulation. That is to say, simply, that it favours the introduction of legally binding standards which prohibit, constrain and direct the conduct of activities within the Member States. Increasing recourse to the language of command and control has coincided with a decline in support for it as a means of addressing continuing environmental degradation. In a sense, this is hardly surprising. As Jacobs has pointed out, the intention behind the label command and control '. . . is evidently to give the impression of a draconian bureaucracy coercing powerless firms and consumers'.[2] The term is normative rather than merely descriptive. It acts also to conceal the diversity of regulatory forms subsumed within it and the distinct, and sometimes competing, philosophies which these reflect. The aim of this chapter is look behind the label 'command and control'. It seeks, by drawing selectively upon examples in the air quality sector, to exemplify and evaluate the Community's broad approach to environmental regulation and the distinct legal techniques which this embodies. It is intended to provide tools to facilitate the study of Community environmental law, with relevance beyond the environmental medium (air) specifically addressed.

[1] See especially, Fifth Environmental Action Programme, *Towards Sustainability: a European Community Programme of Policy and Action in Relation to the Environment and Sustainable Development* OJ 1993 C138/5.
[2] Jacobs, M., *The Green Economy* (Pluto, 1991), p. 151.

One finds scattered throughout legal literature, environmental and other, various 'taxonomies' used for the classification of regulatory standards.[3] Anthony Ogus, for example, in his book *Regulation: Legal Form and Economic Efficiency*, suggests that 'standards can be subdivided into three categories' – target, performance and specification – the first representing the least, and the last the most, intensive form of intervention through standard setting.[4] Each of these regulatory 'specimens' is currently deployed by the European Community and each will be considered in turn.

Target standards

Target standards, in the environmental sphere, take the form, principally, of ambient quality standards (also known as environmental quality standards or objectives).[5] These establish concentration 'ceilings' for a given pollutant in a given environmental medium. In respect of air quality, these were first introduced at Community level for 'first category' pollutants, namely those characterized by unusually high toxicity or persistence.[6] Subsequently, ambient air quality standards were also introduced in respect of lead[7] and nitrogen dioxide (NO_2).[8] These measures rely upon the twin tools of 'limit' and 'guide' (or 'target') values, and are expressed as microgrammes per cubic metre, in a given area, over a specified reference period. Limit values represent a concentration ceiling which must not be exceeded in accordance with the time scale laid down, subject in some cases to a certain 'margin of tolerance'.[9] Guide values (and target values in the ambient air quality directive) constitute non-binding objectives designed to serve as reference points for achieving longer-term goals in respect of the protection of human health and the environment; the implication being that Member States should strive to meet these values. The ambient air

---

3 See, for example, Winter, G., 'Standard-setting in Environmental Law' in Winter, G., *European Community Law: a Comparative Perspective* (Dartmouth, 1996), p. 109.
4 Ogus, A., *Regulation* (OUP, 1994), pp. 150–1.
5 In German environmental law, these tend to be known as 'immission standards', 'referring to the endpoint where an "emission" arrives'. See Winter, G., supra, n. 3, p. 111.
6 See Council Directive 80/779 on sulphur dioxide (SO_2) and suspended particulate matter. OJ 1980 L229/30.
7 Council Directive 82/884 OJ 1982 L378/15.
8 Council Directive 85/203 OJ 1985 L87/1.
9 See Council Directive 96/62 OJ 1996 L296/55, Article 2(8).

quality directive introduces the notion of 'alert thresholds' which, when adopted for specific pollutants, give rise to an obligation to inform both the public and the Commission in the event that they are exceeded. Target standards adopt a 'once removed' approach in that they impose obligations upon the Member States but do not regulate directly the activities of the polluting entities. As such they constitute Community 'norms constraining the discretion of [national or sub-national] standard setters'.[10]

Performance standards

Performance standards are characterised by Ogus as 'output' standards, requiring 'certain conditions of quality to be met at the point of supply, but leav[ing] the supplier free to choose how to meet those conditions'.[11] For this reason they are also commonly known as 'end-of-pipe' measures, in that they control, by way of *emission* limit values (or outright prohibitions), the quantity of any pollutant entering the environment. Such standards may place specific demands on individual firms or, alternatively, require that Member States ensure that an overall emissions ceiling is not exceeded in a given geographic area. Performance standards may be 'process-' or 'product-' based: the former constraining polluting discharges associated with industrial production processes; the latter regulating the quantity of polluting emissions resulting from the use or consumption of any given product.

Council Directive 84/360 on the combating of air pollution from industrial plants,[12] (a process-based measure) provides a framework for the adoption of emission limit values from industrial undertakings, particularly those listed in Annex 1 attached thereto. Article 8 provides that the Council may, acting unanimously on a proposal from the Commission, fix emission limit values and stipulate assessment and measurement techniques, together with other requirements. As such this measure takes the form of a 'parent' directive. It is not surprising, in the light of the unanimity requirement, and the profound economic consequences associated with regulatory activity in this area, that the Council has proved less than fertile in bearing 'daughter' directives. Indeed,

---

10 Supra, n. 4, p. 208.
11 Ibid., p. 151.
12 OJ 1984 L188/20.

it was not until 1988, following five years of negotiations, that the first offspring was born; taking the form of Council Directive 88/609 on the limitation of emissions of pollutants into the air from large combustion plants.[13] This lays down emissions limit values in respect of sulphur dioxide, nitrogen oxides and dust particulates, for both new and existing combustion plants with rated thermal inputs of at least 50 MW. Performance standards have also subsequently been introduced in respect of emissions from new and existing waste incineration plants.[14]

Product-based performance standards have been adopted primarily in respect of motor vehicles. Council Directive 70/220 provided for the approximation of the laws of the Member States on emissions of unburnt hydrocarbons and carbon monoxide from motor vehicles. The emission limit values laid down therein have been gradually reduced and their scope of application extended to cover emissions of nitrogen oxides,[15] and dust particulates from diesel engines.[16] After more than three decades of negotiation, comparable emission standards are now in place for all categories of vehicle (small, medium and large passenger cars, intermediate vehicles and heavy commercial vehicles).

On 5 June 1997 the Commission adopted an amended proposal for tightening emission standards from motor vehicles.[17] This has been the subject of virulent criticism. On the one hand, the oil industry association, Europia, argues that 'the political views that drove the unnecessary tightening of the fuel proposals do little or nothing for air quality but add approximately 60–70% to the costs', and that the Commission 'had disregarded three years of research carried out under the "Auto-Oil Programme" '.[18] The European Parliament, on the other hand, has indicated dissatisfaction with the proposals, on the basis that they do not go far enough. Particular concern has been expressed over the decision to adopt merely indicative emission standards for 2005, and to delay the in-

13 OJ 1988 L336/1.
14 Council Directive 89/369 OJ 1989 L163/32 (new plants) and Council Directive 89/429 OJ 1989 L 203/50 (existing plants).
15 Council Directive 77/102 OJ 1977 L32/32.
16 Council Directive 88/436 OJ 1988 L214/1.
17 COM(97) 255 final.
18 European Voice on-line: http://www.european-voice.com. See also Commission Communication on a future strategy for the control of atmospheric emissions from road transport taking into account the results from the Auto/Oil Programme, COM(96) 248 final.

troduction of a 'cold-start' test for pollution levels. The proposal looks set to form the subject of Article 189b conciliation talks between the Council and European Parliament. The Council's room for maneouvre, in terms of compromise, is restricted by virtue of a significant North/South split between Member State governments. If the current proposals are to be strengthened, the price to be paid may well be the negotiation of temporary exemptions/derogations for the Community's poorer Member States.

Specification standards

Specification standards take the form of 'input' standards which 'can exist in either a positive or negative form'.[19] Once again, these can be product- or process-based. While the latter may be detailed and specific in nature – as, for example, in the large combustion plant directive discussed above, which requires that waste gases be discharged by means of a stack – they tend more often, in a Community context, to be broadly expressed as 'benefits-based' technology standards. These require that operators comply with the BATNEEC principle by incorporating 'best available technology not entailing excessive cost'[20] or, more recently, introduce the principle of best available techniques (BAT). In the case of the latter, 'available' techniques are defined as 'those developed on a scale which allows implementation . . . under economically and technically viable conditions, taking into consideration the costs and advantages . . .'.[21] In the context of the Integrated Pollution Prevention and Control (IPPC) Directive BAT (unlike BATNEEC in the 1984 'framework' directive) applies, not as a direct means of regulating the behaviour of plants, but rather as a tool to inform the national standard-setter in the formulation of emission limit values (performance standards). Such is the definition of BAT in this directive, and the range of criteria to be taken into account in its application,[22] that BAT-derived emission standards can be anticipated to vary as between both industrial sector and locality.

Product-based specification standards have been widely employed as a means of regulating product quality. Thus, for

---

19 Ogus, supra, n. 4, p. 151. That is to say that they may, alternatively, compel or prohibit certain inputs.
20 See, for example, Article 4(1) Council Directive 84/360, supra, n. 12.
21 Article 2(11), Council Directive 96/61 PJ 1996 L257/26.
22 Ibid., Article 9(4) and Annex IV.

example, directives have been introduced limiting the sulphur content of gas oil for diesel-engined vehicles,[23] and the lead[24] and benzene[25] content of petrol. As with emission standards, the Commission has adopted proposals to tighten existing limits.[26] These are strongly opposed by the Southern Member States who are seeking a delay, where economic circumstances justify this, in the phasing-out of leaded fuel. Europia, the oil industry lobby group, has argued that '[t]he proposed changes would cost – on the fuels side – an extra 50 billion ecu, equivalent to half Europe's exports to the US last year'.[27] The Commission may, in general, be sanguine about the relationship between environment and economic growth,[28] but the tension surrounding the 'Auto-Oil' proposals is indicative of the very real tension to which this gives rise.

Command and control: an assessment

In an age which celebrates economic reason, the future of command and control-style regulation is far from secure. Indicted on a number of serious charges only the complacent, or the unusually robust, are prepared today to speak for the defence. Put somewhat crudely, the case for the prosecution takes the following form.

Command and control regulation is not cost-effective. That is to say, simply, that it does not succeed in minimizing the costs associated with achieving any given environmental objective. Thus, it squanders scarce resources and fails to maximize society's wealth. The principal reasons for this are not hard to ascertain. Command and control regulation is, on the one hand, excessively prescriptive in nature and, on the other, promotes exaggerated uniformity; each of these two characteristics operating, in distinct ways, to preclude 'least cost' solutions in the realization of established environmental goals. In the case of the former, this is due to the tendency of such instruments, on occasion, to designate means as well as ends. In the case of the latter, this reflects the failure of such in-

---

[23] Council Directive 93/12 OJ 1993 L74/81.
[24] Council Directive 85/210 OJ 1985 L96/25 and Council Directive 87/416 OJ 1987 L225/33.
[25] Council Directive 82/806 OJ 1982 L339/55.
[26] Supra, n. 17.
[27] Supra, n. 18.
[28] See Ch. 7.

struments to account for spatial variation in pollution effects and, crucially, to acknowledge significant disparities in pollution abatement costs. '[T]he least-cost solution arises where those for whom cutting emissions is relatively cheap cut them further than those for whom it is more expensive.'[29] By 'commanding' an identical response across all pollution sources, notwithstanding variation in the marginal costs of pollution abatement, attempts to achieve a least-cost solution will inevitably be thwarted.

In its own terms, such a critique is compelling and, the evidence suggests, not without practical consequence.[30] However, it serves to highlight the crucial differences between the various instruments classified collectively as command and control. Not all varieties of standards are equal in their tendency towards excessive prescription and uniformity. From a cost-effectiveness perspective there emerges a clear hierarchy which favours target standards over performance standards; and performance standards – particularly those which institute geographically defined as opposed to firm-specific emissions ceilings – over (non-benefits based) specification standards.

Target standards offer a dual advantage when viewed through the lens of cost-effectiveness. First, they accord considerable flexibility to the Member States in selecting the (most cost-effective) means of ensuring compliance. The world beyond command and control (to be discussed in the next chapter) which is inhabited by new species of environmental protection techniques, may be exploited by the Member States acting in pursuance of their commitment to such Community-level target standards.[31] Second, by focusing upon the overall quality of the receiving environment, even uniform target standards are sensitive to geographic variation in respect of environmental assimilative capacity, and to local, regional and national disparities in terms of the intensity of the environmental problem to be addressed. They thus mitigate the shortcomings inherent in other forms of uniform standards which promote too much protection in some areas, and too little in others. Hence, they better reflect the Treaty commitment to take into account not only the diversity of situations in the various regions of

---

29 Supra, n. 2, p. 155.
30 On the issue of the comparative costs of command and control regulation in the air quality sector, relative to least-cost solutions, see Ackermann and Stewart, 'Reforming Environmental Law' (1985) 37 Stanford LR 1333.
31 Though see discussion of the IPPC directive, supra, n. 21.

the Community, but also the balanced development of the Community's regions.[32] In so far as such standards offer advantages to regions with historically (relatively) low levels of pollution, they may be thought to be more equitable as well as more cost- effective.

Recourse to target standards is also broadly consistent with a number of guiding principles identified in the Community's fifth environmental action programme, and the Commission's more recent report on 'Better Law-Making';[33] notably the principles of proportionality and shared responsibility. Whereas the former, codified in Article 3b EC, regulates the intensity of Community intervention (favouring wherever possible the maximum latitude on the part of the Member States as is consistent with the fulfilment of the Community's objectives), the latter favours 'a mixing of actors and instruments',[34] and a division of responsibilities between different levels of government. Similarly, the recent Molitor Report, endorsed the Community's 'new approach' to environmental regulation 'which stresses the setting of general environmental targets whilst leaving the Member States and, in particular, industry the flexibility to choose the means of implementation'.[35]

It is, therefore, not surprising to find that the Community is moving increasingly in the direction of target standards. This is apparent from two recent Community directives; one regulating air quality[36] and the other, in a bid to promote policy coherence across a number of environmental media, pursuing integrated pollution prevention and control in respect of air, water and soil (IPPC directive).[37] The former provides, in Article 4, that the Commission shall submit proposals, according to the time scale speci-

---

[32] Article 130r EC.

[33] Supra, n. 1 and *Commission Report to the European Council on the application of the subsidiarity and proportionality principles, on simplification and codification.*

[34] Ibid., p. 78.

[35] *Report of the Group of Independent Experts on Legislative and Administrative Simplification* COM(95) 288 final/2, p. 54. This was established in 1994 by the Commission with a view to examining the impact of Community and national legislation on employment and competitiveness. It followed the publication of the Commission's White Paper on *Growth, Competitiveness, Employment: the Challenges and the Ways Forward in the 21st Century* Bulletin of the EC, Supplement 6/93.

[36] Council Directive 96/62/EC on ambient air quality assessment and management OJ 1996 L296/55.

[37] Supra, n. 21.

fied, for the establishment of ambient air quality standards in respect of Annex 1 pollutants. The latter constitutes a 'framework' directive which leaves 'as much freedom as possible for the Member States in its implementation'.[38] Firm-specific emission limit values (performance standards) are to be established at national or local level and implemented by way of a system of prior approval (permits). Such emission limit values are to 'be based on best available techniques, without prescribing the use of one specific technique or technology and taking into consideration the technical characteristics of the installation concerned, its geographic location and local environmental conditions'.[39] 'Additional measures' are required where the attainment of Community level environmental quality standards so demands.[40] The directive thus prescribes the regulatory techniques to be employed by Member States but leaves considerable autonomy to Member States in outlining their substantive implications in any given context. This autonomy is constrained by an obligation to comply with Community target standards. Hence the burden of setting specification and related performance standards shifts largely from the Community to its Member States. The Commission emphasized in its explanatory memorandum to its proposal that 'the setting of emission limit values can generally best be done at local level, taking into account appropriate environmental conditions. The same standards are not always appropriate at each and every location in the Community'.[41] Equally, however, and somewhat paradoxically, the Commission stresses that Community harmonization of emission standards may prove necessary where there is wide variation between national standards, so affecting competitiveness and the functioning of the internal market.[42] Hence Article 18 provides that the Council *will* establish emission limit values for Annex 1 installations and Annex 3 substances where the need for Community action has been identified. To this extent, the Community's conversion to target standards remains equivocal.[43] The relationship between the IPPC directive, the 1984 'framework' directive,

[38] COM(93) 423 final, p. 11.
[39] Supra, n. 21, preamble, para. 17.
[40] Article 10.
[41] COM(93)423 final, p. 12.
[42] Ibid.
[43] For criticism of this and other aspects of this directive see Faure and Lefevere, 'The Draft Directive on Integrated Pollution Prevention and Control: an Economic Perspective' (1996) EELR 112.

and other air quality directives listed in Annex 2, is complex.[44] In respect of new plants, permits are to be issued in accordance with the directive from 30 October 1999, without prejudice to the exceptions provided for in the large combustion plant directive. For existing plants the existing 1984 'framework' directive, and the Annex 2 directives, are to apply until the measures required by the IPPC directive have been implemented in accordance with the time scale laid down in Article 5. At the extreme end of this variable transitional period (30 October 2007) the 1984 'framework' directive is to be repealed. Before this date the other directives are to be amended in order to adapt them to the requirements of the IPPC directive. The material requirements of the large combustion engine directive shall apply until 31 December 2003.

While support for target standards is not universal, the United Kingdom at least, strongly favours this approach. The reasons for this are not hard to ascertain and are both ideological and pragmatic in nature. Ironically, they serve to underline the deficiencies associated with this regulatory approach. Almost two decades of Conservative government placed issues of international competitiveness high on the political agenda. Social regulation, it is assumed, imposes costs upon industry and it is therefore viewed, at best, as a necessary evil to be avoided wherever possible. Cost minimization represents a political priority, as indeed does the preservation of (the appearance of) national sovereignty against encroachment from 'Brussels'. From a UK perspective, environmental target standards are broadly consistent with a strategy of cost minimization. This is due not merely to the advantages which these offer from a perspective of cost-effectiveness. Geographic factors on these islands – strong winds, short and fast flowing rivers, high rainfall, and well-mixed tidal waters – combine to ensure a relatively high environmental assimilative capacity and hence to generate a reduction in the abatement costs associated with target standards. Target standards, unlike specification and performance standards, sanction the translation of natural environmental advantage into comparative (economic) advantage. Geographically differentiated in their impact they are, however, of limited effectiveness as a mechanism for harmonizing conditions of competition

---

[44] See Articles 4, 20 and footnote 1 to Annex 1. Annex 2 refers, *inter alia*, to the large combustion plant directive, the two directives on the prevention of air pollution from new and existing municipal waste incineration plants and Directive 94/67 (OJ 1994 L365/34) on the incineration of hazardous waste.

in the Community and hence of eliminating economic 'spillover' effects. Does this matter? Nigel Haigh[45] puts forward an argument which suggests that it does not:

> Since lemon growers take advantage of the sun that geography brings them, and grow lemons rather than engage in some other activity for that very reason, and since German industrialists benefit from proximity to continental markets as a result of geography, so also it is argued that Britain should quite properly benefit from the ability to locate industries on estuaries or on the coast where acute pollution problems are less likely to arise and where the sea water can assimilate or destroy the pollutants.

Such analogies may not, however, be entirely fair. The United Kingdom's comparative environmental advantage stems not only from the enhanced assimilative capacity of its 'own' natural environment but also from the tendency of such environmental factors to export certain pollution effects, the results of which are felt well beyond its own territorial limits. This can be illustrated by the well-known phenomenon of acid rain. This results from the deposition, in their acidic form (wet or dry), of a number of airborne pollutants: sulphur dioxide, nitrogen oxides and chloride. Its effects are varied and include forest degradation, reduction in crop yield, accelerated decomposition of building materials and the acidification of rivers, lakes and soils with corresponding harm to plant, fish and animal life. The United Kingdom is a net exporter of acid rain. One study[46] suggests that the United Kingdom exports around three-quarters of its sulphur dioxide emissions, and that while it generates around 2.7 million tonnes of nitrogen oxides each year, approximately only 0.3 million tonnes are deposited within its own borders. In this sense, target standards may operate to sanction the emergence of environmental 'free-riders' resulting in an inequitable distribution of the costs associated with compliance – this notwithstanding the exhortations in many Community directives that implementing measures should have no significant effects on the environment in other Member States. Target standards thus sit uneasily with the Treaty principle which provides that the polluter should pay,[47] aptly labelled in the German text (for the purpose of this discussion) as the 'causation' principle.

---

[45] Haigh, N., *EEC Environmental Policy and Britain* (Longman, 1990) p. 22.
[46] Cited in Turner, Pearce and Batemen, *Environmental Economics: an Elementary Introduction* (Harvester Wheatsheaf, 1994).
[47] Article 130r(2) EC.

At any rate, Haigh appears to accept that, in respect of the most toxic and persistent pollutants, such an approach which stops short of demanding 'best discharge abatement technology' is difficult to justify. It remains the case that, at present, emission (performance) standards are deployed by the Community as a means of regulating discharges of the most dangerous substances.[48] The reasons for this are essentially practical and reflect, first and foremost, the difficulties associated with the monitoring of compliance with target standards. Even in the United Kingdom, where support for target standards is strongest, a Royal Commission on Environmental Pollution argued that such standards are 'unenforceable in practice' and hence generate the danger that the law will be brought 'into disrepute'.[49]

In addition, however, it is apparent that target standards have tended, in practice, to 'allow more discharges or emissions to be put into the environment than emission standards'.[50] Why this should be so is not altogether clear, but conceivably the answer is to be found in the observations of Boehmer-Christiansen. She stresses that while an emission standard approach is essentially technology driven, 'promot[ing] the skills of the engineer' (in developing pollution abatement technology), '[r]egulation by EQO [environmental quality objective] represents first of all a scientific challenge'.[51] Consequently:

> Scientifically solvable questions arise over 'how' suspect a substance is and how much reduction is needed before an acceptable level of damage is reached. To prove causal links conclusively, however, is very difficult and time-consuming. The patient may indeed be dead before we know. To base environmental policy on hard fact and proven causality surely represents a very high risk strategy . . . . The preference for quality standards can therefore also serve as a tactic for delaying decisions, or for allowing polluters to clean up voluntarily before the law requires action. Britain is widely suspected of having used this tactic.[52]

---

48 See Kramer, L., *EC Treaty and Environmental Law* (Sweet & Maxwell, 1995), p. 56.

49 Fifth Report of the royal commission on Environmental Pollution (1976, Cmnd. 6371) at paras 182–3.

50 Supra, n. 48.

51 'Environmental Quality Objectives versus Uniform Emission Standards' in Freestone and Ijlstra (eds), *The North Sea: Perspectives on Regional Environmental Co-operation* (Graham & Trotman/Martinus Nijhoff, 1990), p. 140.

52 Ibid., p. 144.

This point is important. It suggests that the close involvement of the scientific community in the formulation of target standards has tended to undermine the stringency of these measures, due to the strict nature of the professional scientist's burden of proof. In practice, target standards may be difficult to reconcile with the application of the precautionary principle.

Moving on; this brief assessment of regulatory technique has been approached from a perspective of cost-effectiveness. Cost-effectiveness considerations are distinct from efficiency considerations in that they offer normative guidance pertaining merely to means rather than ends. While, in the light of the observations put forward in the previous chapter, such a separation between means and ends may be warranted, it does run the 'risk [of] designing the proverbial fast train to the wrong station'.[53] Particular regulatory techniques may represent a cost-effective means of achieving a solution which is itself internally inefficient, in that the costs attached outweigh the benefits derived. This may, in part, be due to the tendency of command and control instruments to stifle technological innovation in that they offer, beyond a given point, no continuing incentive for improved environmental performance. In this sense they fail to exploit potential benefits fully. Command and control-style regulation is not 'technology forcing', in that it provides no motivation for firms to achieve pollution abatement beyond the binding 'bottom line' prescribed.[54] This grievance bites similarly in the context of benefits-based performance (technology) standards; a form of command and control regulation nonetheless highly esteemed in much economic analysis.[55] It might be thought that such standards (BATNEEC or BAT being the Community versions) run a different risk; the risk of designing the proverbial slow train, albeit in the direction of the right station. Both BATNEEC and BAT are predicated upon an acceptance of the legitimacy of cost-benefit analysis. Technological change is to be required by law only where it can be demonstrated that the benefits which will ensue outweigh the costs associated with compliance. Each appears to accept that cost-benefit analysis 'has much to contribute not only in discovering the least costly methods to accomplish

---

53 Hahn and Stavins, 'Incentive-Based Environmental Regulation: A New Era from an Old Idea?' (1991) 18 Ecology LQ 1, p. 30.
54 See also Jacobs, supra, n. 2.
55 See, for example, supra, n. 46.

social goals but also in determining what these goals should be'.[56] It should be evaluated in the light of the difficulties, explored in the previous chapter, attaching to the quantification of costs and benefits.

Uniformity or differentiation in Community environmental law

It was noted above that mistrust of command and control-style regulation derives in part from its putative tendency towards excessive uniformity. Though certain benefits attach to uniformity as a regulatory ideal – they are easier to formulate and cheaper to administer and enforce – cost-effectiveness tends to militate in favour of an approach which endorses differentiation of standards. Differentiation of standards may be justified through recourse to a number of considerations: economic (variation in compliance costs), political (fairness in the distribution of the pollution abatement burden), democratic (differing preferences on the part of the regulated communities), and environmental (variation in assimilative capacity). Uniform standards – of whatever variety – can never fully encompass these, often competing, concerns. Uniform target standards may be cost-effective and environmentally nuanced, but it is not at all clear that they are fair in the face of 'drifting' pollution. Uniform performance and specification standards may be fair in one sense (in that they address the 'free-rider' problem) but not in another (in that they fail to reflect differences in historic pollution levels). Performance standards may be more or less cost-effective, and more or less sensitive to environmental diversity, depending upon whether they impinge at a national or firm-specific level; uniform specification standards are neither. Not one of these three regulatory techniques can, when applied in an absolutely uniform manner, be considered democratic in the sense described above.

It is then not surprising to discover that differentiation has emerged as a key, if multi-faceted, concept in Community environmental law. It is destined to remain so in the context of an expanding Union. A degree of differentiation has been achieved by way of a variety of techniques, each capable of addressing, more or less

[56] Sagoff, M., *The Economy of the Earth* (CUP, 1990), pp. 216–17.

(cost-) effectively, one or more of the above considerations. Such techniques range from the sporadic and *ad hoc*, to the virtually institutionalized. All bar one of the mechanisms deployed may be illustrated through recourse to a single instrument; the large combustion plant directive.[57]

First, the ubiquitous derogation: Annexes 3–7 of this directive establish emission limit values (performance standards) for new combustion plants with a rated thermal input which is equal to, or greater than, 50 MW. Nonetheless, plants burning indigenous solid fuel which cannot meet these standards 'owing to the particular nature of the fuel, without using excessively expensive technology' may exceed the limit values established in respect of sulphur dioxide. It appears that they may do so *ad infinitum*. In the case of Spain, new solid-fuel plants with a rated thermal input of at least 500 MW, may be authorized before the end of 1999, and commissioned before the end of 2005, which will not comply with these standards; subject to the requirement that these installations respect a sulphur dioxide limit value which is some 60% higher than the generally applicable limit and, in the case of plants burning indigenous solid fuel, that they achieve a rate of desulphurization of at least 60% (as opposed to to the 90% reduction generally required by the directive for plants of this size). No minimum requirements are to apply in the case of emissions of nitrogen oxides and dust. Article 5(3) provides that the total authorized capacity of such plants to which this derogation applies must not exceed 2,000 MW in the case of plants burning indigenous solid fuels and, in the case of those burning imported solid fuel, 7,500 MW (or 50% of total new capacity authorized by the end of 1999, where this is lower). If one assumes that such installations enjoy an average life expectancy of around 40 years, this derogation – though temporary – is profoundly important. It would be difficult to justify this country-specific derogation on the basis of any of the considerations outlined above. In view of the dominance of the Council in the Community's legislative process – and the purely consultative role played by the European Parliament in this case – it would be

---

[57] Supra, n. 13. A fourth technique of achieving differentiation involves the geographic 'zoning' of the territory of Member States and the application of differential standards to different zones, defined on the basis of objective environmental considerations, will be exemplified both in ch. 6 in relation to conservation measures, and the final chapter in respect of water quality regulation.

disingenuous to seek to do so in the name of democracy. Such is the price to be paid in the shadow of the veto.[58]

Second, 'shared but differentiated responsibility': the large combustion plant directive institutes separate regulatory regimes for new and existing plants. This, in itself is a common form of differentiation, motivated by political (in terms both of fairness and power) and cost-effectiveness considerations. 'The compliance cost for a firm using alternative equipment will be higher than for a firm which is in the process of constructing a new plant.'[59] The standards introduced in respect of existing plants are shaped by a conception of shared but differentiated responsibility. The regulatory burdens imposed vary considerably between Member States. Take, for example, the ceilings and reduction targets instituted in respect of sulphur dioxide. Relative to a non-adjusted 1980 baseline, Germany, Luxembourg, Belgium, the Netherlands and France were required, by 1993, to reduce emissions by 40%. The Member States retain considerable flexibility in determining how compliance is to be achieved. By contrast, Portugal, Ireland and Greece were entitled to sanction an increase in emissions over this period – equalling 102%, 25% and 6%, respectively. Where the 1980 baseline is adjusted to take into account new capacity added between 1980 and 1987, such differentials are shown to contract, reflecting the more rapid economic expansion experienced by these latter, less economically developed, states.

The directive itself is of limited assistance in seeking to articulate a rationale for this approach. The preamble merely states, laconically, that '. . . due account has been taken of the need of comparable effort, whilst making allowance for the specific situations of Member States'. Equally, so different in nature were the Commission's original proposals for this directive that its explanatory memoranda offer surprisingly little insight into the premises which underpin this form of differentiation. Indeed, such an approach is still exceptional in Community environmental law; although target standards might be thought to pursue such distributive consequences albeit by a different (and, due to the 'free-rider' problem, less equitable) route. It is clear that demand-

---

[58] Even today, measures significantly affecting a Member State's choice between different energy sources and the general structure of its energy supply are to be adopted unanimously, following consultation with the European Parliament. See Article 130s(2).

[59] Ogus, supra, n. 4, p. 168.

ing compliance with a uniform percentile cut in emissions would necessitate a lower overall reduction (in tonnes) on the part of those states in which emissions have been historically low. Yet to do so would be to sanction continuing – though in absolute terms, shrinking – disparities in allowable emissions. Differentiation, in this form it is reasonable to suppose, is designed to achieve progressive equalization in terms of Member State entitlement to pollute. It therefore raises difficult and contentious questions concerning the (equitable) distribution of responsibility for pollution abatement. It represents a radical experiment in addressing the demands of political fairness, and in balancing environmental and economic development concerns; one that might usefully be replicated both within and outside of the European Union. It is consistent with the Treaty requirement that the Community take into account, in preparing its policy on the environment, the need to achieve a balanced development of its regions,[60] and with the Community's task, articulated in Article 2, of promoting economic and social cohesion.

Third, minimum harmonization: in so far as the Community enjoys concurrent competence under Article 130s, it does so only to enact *minimum* harmonization measures. Minimum, in this context, should not be understood to connote 'low' but merely 'bottom-line'. Member States remain free to retain or enact more (but not less) stringent standards, in so far as these are compatible with the Treaty.[61] Such standards are to be notified to the Commission. By way of contrast, the Community is empowered, under Article 100a, to enact 'exhaustive' harmonization measures, thereby occupying the relevant field totally. Increasingly, however, environmental directives adopted on the basis of Article 100a will include a minimum harmonization clause. Even where they do not, Member States retain a limited right to derogate under Article 100a(4). They may do so, *inter alia*, on grounds of environmental protection.

Article 100a being characterized by 'verbose vagueness',[62] the parameters of Article 100a(4) have been contested. It, unlike Article 130t, may be construed as sanctioning merely the *maintenance* of pre-existing national measures, but not the introduction of

---

[60] Article 130r(3).
[61] See Ch. 4 for a discussion of Articles 30–36 EC.
[62] Pescatore, P., 'Some Critical Remarks on the Single European Act' (1987) 24 CMLRev. 9, p. 15.

new measures, subsequent to a Community harmonization measure. That this is the case is set to be confirmed by the Treaty of Amsterdam. It is also significant that this new Treaty would permit the *introduction* of new national measures, where these are based on new scientific evidence, relating, *inter alia*, to the protection of the environment, on grounds of a problem specific (Article 95(5)) to that Member State.

Whereas, under Article 130t, Member States are required merely to notify the Commission of more stringent national measures, Article 100a(4) institutes a more formal Commission control procedure. The national measures are to be notified to the Commission whose task it is to confirm that the measures do not constitute a disguised restriction on trade or arbitrary discrimination. Member States are not authorized to apply the national provisions until such time as it has received Commission confirmation.[63] Under the new Treaty, Member States seeking to derogate, either on grounds of major needs or on the basis of new scientific evidence, would be required to notify the Commission of the national provisions to be applied and of the grounds for maintaining or, in the case of the latter, introducing them. The Commission is required to confirm not only that they do not constitute a disguised restriction or arbitrary discriminaton but also that they do not constitute an obstacle to the functioning of the internal market (Article 95(6)). Were this requirement to be strictly applied by the Commission it would represent a substantial erosion of Member State capacity to derogate.

The Treaty of Amsterdam would further establish a time limit within which the Commission must approve or reject the measures concerned. In the absence of a decision within six months of notification, the measures shall be deemed to have been approved. Inertia, quite properly, is henceforth to be construed as favouring Member State autonomy and hence in favour of regulation, rather than de-regulation. The Commission may, where this is justified having regard to the complexity of the matter, and in the absence of a danger to human health, extend this period for a further six months. That it may only do so in the absence of a threat to human health, and because the new Treaty provides that Community harmonization measures may include a safeguard clause authorizing Member States to adopt provisional measures (Article

---

63 Case C-41/93 *France* v *Commission* [1994] ECR I-829, para. 30.

95(10)), it appears that in normal circumstances national measures may not be applied until such a time as Commission confirmation is granted or deemed to be granted. This point, however, is by no means free from doubt.

It was noted above that in the event of a failure to notify under Article 100a(4), and in the absence of Commission confirmation, national measures may not be applied. What, though, of a failure to notify under Article 130t? Some guidance may be sought from a recent decision of the European Court concerning the application of Council Directive 83/189, laying down a procedure for the provision of information in the field of technical standards and regulations.[64] In the context of the notification system instituted by this directive, a failure to notify was held to deprive national technical regulations of legal effect. A number of factors militated in favour of this conclusion:

> ... the aim of the directive is not simply to inform the Commission ... the directive has, precisely, a more general aim of eliminating or restricting obstacles to trade, to inform other States of technical regulations envisaged by a State, to give the Commission and the other Member States time to react and to propose amendments for lessening restrictions to the free movement of goods arising from the envisaged measure and to afford the Commission time to propose a harmonizing directive. Moreover, the wording of Article 8 and 9 of Directive 83/189 is clear in that those articles provide for a procedure for Community control of draft national regulations and the date of their entry into force is made subject to the Commission's agreement or lack of opposition.[65]

The circumstances pertaining under Article 130t are distinct. In particular, there can be no question, under Article 130t, of any need for Commission ratification of Member State action. Entry into force is not subject to Commission agreement (or lack of opposition) and the aim of the measure cannot be to facilitate Commission participation in the drafting process. Nor can it be to provide the Commission with an opportunity to formulate a harmonizing directive; such a directive being a *sine qua non* for the application of Article 130t. Notification constitutes a legal obligation binding on the Member States. It would, however, be mislead-

---

[64] OJ 1983 L109/8; Case C-194/94 *C.I.A. Security International SA* v *Signalson SA and Another* [1996] ECR I-2211, para. 54.

[65] Ibid., para. 50.

ing to conclude that a failure to comply operates to deprive a national measure of legal effect.[66]

It has nonetheless been argued that, in one respect at least, minimum harmonization is more restrictive in terms of Member State autonomy than derogation under Article 100a(4). 'Minimum harmonization is not a generalization of a right to derogate from a harmonized measure, as in Article 100a(4), but merely establishes a right for the Member States to impose *on their own undertakings* standards which are higher, without the possibility to oppose free movement'.[67] Minimum harmonization proper, on this view, offers the best of all worlds. It walks a politically expedient middle line between the two apparently competing paradigms; 'competition between legal orders' and a 'level playing field' approach – and it does so in a manner which is compatible with the functioning of the internal market. It facilitates legislative agreement in a Community characterized by broad and growing diversity, and yet prevents difference from equalling disruption. All this because Member States are, allegedly, able to impose higher standards on their own undertakings only. To what extent this is true is an issue to which we will return in Chapter 4. Before doing so, however, it is appropriate, first, to examine a number of alternative instruments for environmental protection which take us into a world beyond command and control.

[66] By way of support for this conclusion see also Case 380/87 *Enichem Base and Others* v *Commune Di Cinisello Balsamo* [1989] ECR 2491.
[67] Bernard, N., 'The Future of European Economic Law in the light of the Principle of Subsidiarity' (1996) 33 CMLRev. 633, p. 646.

CHAPTER THREE

Economic instruments for environmental protection

The credibility of command and control regulation is, in academic circles, low. Conceived as 'extraordinarily crude, costly, litigious and counterproductive . . .', attempts to defend the status quo are derided as 'Panglossian' in logic.[1] The aim of this chapter is to enter a world beyond command and control, one which as yet remains largely unexplored by the European Community. It will be concerned exclusively (and even then selectively) with what have come to be called 'economic' instruments for environmental protection. Indicative of the dominance of a 'law and economics' approach in many US law schools, it is this vision of the future which has received resounding, though not invariably uncritical, endorsement in the legal academy.

Economic instruments take a wide variety of forms. As with standards, a number of distinct taxonomies have been proposed. One European Community working group of experts identified the following mechanisms: environmental charges and taxes; tradeable emissions permits; deposit-refund systems; enforcement incentives; financial aid (subsidies); industry agreements; and environmental liability.[2] Such instruments, far from 'commanding' a given response on the part of environmental actors, seek rather to influence their behaviour by, alternatively, imposing economic costs or conferring economic benefits. This chapter will focus in turn

1 Ackerman and Stewart, 'Reforming Environmental Law' (1985) 37 Stanford Law Review 1333; they note that '[i]n 1971, Ezra Mishan brilliantly satirized the views of a Dr. Pangloss who argued that a world of largely unregulated pollution was "optimal" because cleanup would involve enormous transaction costs'. Dr Pangloss, in Voltaire's *Candide*, is renowned for taking an excessively cheerful or over-optimistic view of the world.
2 *Report of the Working Group of Experts from the Member States on the Use of Economic and Fiscal Instruments in EC Environmental Policy* X1/185/90, p. 7.

upon environmental charges and taxes and tradeable emissions permits. Discussion of the former will necessitate consideration of the Community's state aid rules and the legitimacy of environmental subsidies.[3]

Environmental charges and taxes

In July 1995 the European Court annulled Council Directive 93/89[4] on the application by Member States of taxes on certain vehicles used for the carriage of goods by road and tolls and charges for the use of certain infrastructure.[5] This directive provided for minimum harmonization of vehicle taxes, and sanctioned the introduction or maintenance, at Member State level, of certain road tolls or user charges, up to a maximum – in the case of the latter – of 1,250 ECU per year. The judgment of the Court was predicated upon the existence of a breach of an essential procedural requirement, taking the form of a failure to reconsult Parliament following substantial amendment of the earlier proposal. These amendments did not correspond to the wishes of the Parliament. The Court found that the amendments introduced went 'to the very essence of the system',[6] and it was not exaggerating.

Whereas in the version presented to Parliament, the Council was, by the end of 1998, to 'adopt as soon as possible appropriate measures aimed at introducing a harmonised system of road charging which shall include vehicle taxes, excise duty on fuel and charges (user charges and tolls) for the use of certain types of road infrastructure . . .',[7] the revised version provided merely that the Commission present a report to Parliament on the implementation of the directive, accompanied 'if necessary' by proposals for establishing 'cost-charging arrangements . . .'.[8] In relation to the minimum harmonization of vehicle taxes, the directive, as adopted, further departed from the earlier proposal in the range and scope of exemptions encompassed. For example, whereas in the original

3 See Ch. 8 for a discussion of environmental agreements.
4 OJ 1993 L279/32.
5 Case C-21/94 *Parliament* v *Council* [1996] ECR I-1827. The Court, however, decided, in accordance with Article 174(2), to preserve the effects of this directive until such a time as a new measure was adopted.
6 Ibid., para 2.
7 COM(92) 405 final, Article 9(1).
8 Supra, n. 4, Article 12.

proposal Greece and Portugal were authorized on a temporary basis to apply reduced (by up to 50%) rates, this benefit was extended (in a bid to secure agreement), in the final version, to France, Italy and Spain.[9]

The emasculation of the Commission's road taxes initiative, in the course of its adoption, is by no means atypical. Progress in achieving harmonization of Member State environmental taxes and/or charges has been slow. Limited minimum harmonization measures have been introduced in respect of the indirect taxation of mineral oils, providing for the levying of differentiated rates of excise duties on leaded and unleaded petrol.[10] The Community's show-piece initiative – on the basis of which the credibility of its commitment to 'green' taxes will in reality be assessed – has yet to adopted. Its symbolic significance is such, however, that it merits closer analysis.

The proposal for a carbon/energy tax was first presented in 1992, just prior to the conclusion, in the context of the UN Conference on Environment and Development (UNCED), of the Climate Change Convention. Carbon dioxide emissions are widely believed to constitute the most serious threat to climatic stability. The Community is committed to stabalising carbon dioxide emissions by the year 2000 (relative to a 1990 baseline), and to reducing them by 15% by 2010. Nonetheless, 'reliable forecasts suggest that this EU objective cannot be attained [and that in fact emissions would increase by 12%] given anticipated levels of economic growth, if market forces are left to their own devices'.[11]

This proposal was substantially amended in 1995.[12] The proposed tax is to be levied on the products specified in Article 3. This includes solid, viscous and gaseous fossil fuels intended for use as heating or motor fuels, and electricity. Electricity generated from solar, wind, tidal and geothermal power, or from biomass transformation (renewables) is excluded.[13] The energy component of the tax is to be charged according to the energy content (calorific

---

9   Supra, n. 4, Article 6(2). See also Articles 6(3) and 6(5).
10 Council Directive 92/82 OJ 1992 L316/19. This provides for limited exceptions in respect of Luxembourg and defined parts of the territories of Portugal and Greece.
11 Opinion of ESC on carbon/energy tax proposal OJ C174/47.
12 See COM(95) 172 final for the text of both proposals.
13 Ibid. See also Article 3(2)(b) noting that electricity generated in hydroelectric installations with a capacity of over 10 MW is to be taxed. Nuclear energy is thus subject to the energy component of the tax.

value) of the product, except where these are used to generate electricity in which case the chargeable unit is to be the megawatt hour. The carbon dioxide component will be determined according to the volume of carbon dioxide emitted upon combustion.[14]

In the Commission's original proposal, the tax was to be levied, in the first instance, at (as a minimum) the rate laid down in Article 9. This was to be increased by one-third, on an annual basis, for seven years, starting from the date at which the tax arrangements were to take effect.[15] The Commission estimated that the tax would, were the entire cost borne by consumers, generate a price increase of 6% in respect of petrol and 14% in respect of natural gas. At 1991 prices, the tax would, at the outset, represent a cost of \$3 per barrel of oil equivalent, rising to \$10.[16]

The amended proposal, by way of contrast, provides that Member States shall, during a four-year transitional period, set a single rate of tax per product specified.[17] They are to *endeavour* to make their rates converge towards target rates established in the directive.[18] Not later than one year before the end of the transitional period the Commission shall present a report on the implementation of the directive, accompanied by proposals laying down rules for the application of harmonized rates of carbon dioxide/energy tax. By the day following the end of the transitional period the Council is, acting *unanimously*, to adopt measures necessary for the introduction of harmonized rates of tax.[19] In this respect the revised proposal represents no more than an agreement to disagree and a decision to delay, indefinitely until even this proposal is adopted, the task of reaching agreement as regards the rates of tax to be levied.

The watering down of the Commission's proposals is indicative of the competitiveness concerns associated with environmental taxes. In the original proposal these were addressed directly by way of a 'conditionality' clause. This provided that, even following adoption of the directive, the introduction of the tax in the Community was to be contingent upon 'the introduction by other member countries of the OECD of a similar tax or of measures having

---

14 Ibid., Article 8(2).
15 Ibid., Article 9(3).
16 Johnson and Corcelle, *The Environmental Policy of the European Communities*, (Kluwer, 1995) p. 176.
17 Supra, n. 12, Article 8(1).
18 Ibid., Article 8(3).
19 Ibid., Article 12.

a financial impact equivalent to those provided for in this directive'.[20] Though this has been deleted from the revised proposal, such competitiveness concerns are exemplified and, at least partially, addressed by a variety of mechanisms still contained therein.

First, Article 4 defines the 'chargeable event' as 'the extraction or manufacture of the products specified . . . on the territory of the Community . . . *or their importation into that territory*'. Similarly, Article 5 provides that the tax shall become chargeable upon the release for consumption of the product to be taxed, or when shortages are recorded. Hence the proposed directive provides for a system of border tax adjustment in that they:

> put into effect, in whole or in part, the destination principle . . . [enabling] exported products to be relieved of some or all of the tax charged in the exporting country in respect of similar domestic products sold to consumers on the home market and . . . [enabling] imported products sold to consumers to be charged with some or all of the tax charged in the importing country in respect of similar domestic products.[21]

The directive therefore sanctions the levying of taxes on imported products (including, it appears, those imported from other Member States during the transitional period, as well as from third countries) and, unless shortages are recorded, the remission of taxes on exports. A more difficult question arises in relation to the role of border tax adjustment in respect of those products which have been manufactured through recourse to a taxable product but do not, in their final form, physically incorporate that product. Düerkop offers the example of steel, a commodity 'whose production process involves a high consumption of products which bear the tax' but which nonetheless is not integrally comprised of any one of these products. The directive, in its current form, does not provide for border tax adjustments in such situations. To this extent, the destination principle can appease only partially, competitiveness concerns.[22]

[20] Ibid., Article 1(2).
[21] OECD definition, cited by Düerkop, M., 'Trade and Environment: International Trade Law Aspects of the Proposed EC Directive Introducing a Tax on Carbon Dioxide Emissions and Energy' (1994) 31 CMLRev. 807, p. 820.
[22] See Demaret and Stewardson, 'Border Tax Adjustments under GATT and EC Law and General Implications for Environmental Taxes' (1994) 28 JWT 5 and Düerkop, ibid. See also the new Uruguay Round Agreement on Subsidies and Countervailing Measures OJ 1995 L336/156.

To this, however, it is necessary to add the provisions of Article 9(2). This provides, in so far as it is compatible with the Community's international commitments and the rules of Community law, for a graduated reduction in respect of the tax payable 'in the case of firms with high energy consumption, where these are seriously disadvantaged on account of an imbalance in trade from other Member States, or an increase in imports from third countries'; and the possibility of a full, though temporary, exemption where the firms have made 'substantial efforts to save energy or to reduce carbon dioxide emissions'. Whereas previously this was to apply only in the case of trading partners which had not introduced a similar tax or measures with equivalent effect, this qualification no longer explicitly applies. Equally, the concept of 'high' is no longer defined (previously it was fixed at 8% of cost of production), thus leaving substantial autonomy to the Member States. Article 9(3) goes on to sanction tax reductions or refunds equal to the cost of any new investment undertaken during the transitional period, designed to promote either the efficient use of energy or to limit carbon dioxide refunds.

Finally, on the competitiveness issue, it is important to stress that any harmonized Community tax introduced at the end of the transitional period is to respect the principle of tax neutrality and shall not result in an increase in the overall tax burden.[23] This principle is not binding upon the Member States during the transitional period.

It would be wrong to conclude, on the basis of the above discussion, that environmental charges and taxes currently play a negligible role in promoting protection of the Union's environment. It is simply the case that, to date, recourse to such instruments has remained largely the preserve of the Member States. Denmark, the Netherlands and Sweden, for example, levy a tax on carbon dioxide emissions, and waste and water charges are widely deployed in a variety of forms. The Community's proposed directive, and experience at the national level, raise a wide variety of issues in Community (and international trade) law. Many of these have been considered by the Commission in its recent Communica-

---

[23] Article 12. The Commission estimates that this should reduce 'quasi-tax' pressure on unskilled labour by 1% and create an extra 2.5% more jobs. See Opinion of the ESC on direct and indirect taxation OJ 1996 C82/49.

tion on Environmental Taxes and Charges in the Single Market.[24]

The next section of this chapter will focus upon only one contentious issue, namely the application of the Community's state aid rules in the context of environmental taxes. Two principal issues arise, the first relating to the manner in which revenue generated is used, where this is deployed to support environmental investment or activities, and the second to legality of partial or total exemptions from standard charges or taxes. These will be discussed within the framework of a broader discussion of the environmental dimension of Community law and practice in relation to subsidies.

Environmental subsidies and Community law

In 1994 the Commission issued new guidelines on state aid for environmental protection.[25] These outline the circumstances in which state aid, granted pursuant to an environmental objective, may benefit from one of the exemptions to the basic prohibition on state aids contained in Article 92 EC. The legal status of the guidelines is unclear and, as in national legal orders, policy-making by guideline raises difficult issues in administrative law, relating above all to legal certainty and the protection of legitimate expectations.[26]

The first category of aid covered by the guidelines relates to aid granted for investment.[27] This covers aid for investment in land, buildings, equipment and plant in so far as this is necessary to meet environmental objectives. The proportion of investment costs which may be met through aid depends upon a number of considerations. It depends, for example, upon whether the aid is designed, on the one hand, to assist firms adapt to new mandatory environmental standards[28] or, on the other, to improve upon exist-

---

24 COM(97) 9 final. See also Case C-13/96 *Bic Benelux* v *Belgian State* judgment of 20 March 1997, where the European Court found that national rules requiring the labelling of products (in this case disposable razors) subject to an environmental tax, constitutes a technical specification within the meaning of the Community's notification directive (83/189 OJ 1983 L109/8).

25 OJ 1994 C72/3.

26 This is a fascinating issue but not one which falls within the scope of this chapter. See the contributions by Rawlinson, F., and della Cananea, G., in Harden, I., *State Aid: Community Law and Policy* (Trier Academy of European Law/Bundesanzeiger, 1993).

27 Supra, n. 25, section 3:2.

28 Firms which have been in existence for less than two years prior to the introduction of the mandatory standards are not entitled to such assistance.

ing standards or to improve environmental performance in the absence of any mandatory standards. As regards the former, an aid ceiling of 10% (20% in the case of small and medium-sized enterprises – SMEs) of eligible costs is imposed, rising to 30% (40% for SMEs) in the latter case. Higher limits are set in respect of investment in the Community's poorer regions. These limits apply cumulatively to aid deriving from all sources, national and Community, where this is combined with national aid.

It is thus not at all clear that the Article 9(3) exemption contained in the carbon/energy tax proposal is (or is not) consistent with existing Commission practice concerning state aid, providing as it does for 100% relief; this though it is granted for a limited (transitional) period, as required under the guidelines. Article 92 applies to aid granted by a Member State or through state resources. It does not apply where the benefit is granted out of Community resources. Nonetheless, the revenue generated by the new Community tax is to accrue at national level. Any tax relief therefore deprives the national exchequer of tax revenue, and is therefore to be viewed as national as opposed to Community aid. That tax relief may constitute a state aid within the meaning of Article 92 is established beyond doubt.[29]

However, it may well be that Article 9(3) does not attain the necessary degree of specificity to give rise to a state aid issue. Article 92 defines state aid in terms of assistance which favours *certain* undertakings, or the production of *certain* goods. The Article 9(3) benefits are available, in principle, to all undertakings and are generally available. They are not inherently sector specific. They are, however, to be granted on an optional, as opposed to a mandatory, basis and consequently their legality hinges upon Member State practice in the granting such relief.

The situation under Article 9(2) may be thought to be even more dubious, not least because it expressly provides that this exemption is to be applied only in so far as it is consistent with the Treaty,[30] as well as favouring a particular sector of industry. This

---

[29] See Case 30/59 *Steenkolenmijnen* v *High Authority* [1961] ECR 1 and supra, n. 25, footnote 10.

[30] Even though Article 9(3) does not provide this, a directive cannot undermine the state aid procedures laid down in Articles 92–94 of the Treaty. The EC institutions, including the legislator, are bound by Treaty rules (See Case C-114/96 *Kieffer & Thill* 25 June 1997) and the only way for the legislator to declare an aid to be compatible with Article 92 is to follow the decision-making procedure laid down in Articles 93 and 94.

takes the form of an 'operating aid which relieves firms of costs resulting from the pollution or nuisance they cause'.[31] The Commission guidelines provide that the Commission would not normally approve such aid. They go on, however, to note that it may make an exception in certain well-defined circumstances, and that it has, in the past, done so in respect of the granting of relief from environmental taxes.[32] In this case strict criteria are to be applied; the aid must not more than compensate for the additional costs associated with this tax, it should be temporary and, in principle, degressive. It is not entirely clear in the guidelines whether these criteria are also to apply in the case of temporary relief from environmental taxes, including those introduced pursuant to EC legislation, in so far as this is necessary to offset losses in competitiveness, particularly at the international level.[33] In this context the guidelines note that a further factor is to be taken into account, namely 'what the firms concerned have to do in return to reduce their pollution'.[34] While, in the case of full (but temporary) relief, the Commission's proposal for a carbon/energy tax demands that a degree of environmental attainment must be demonstrated, this is not true of a partial reduction in tax payable. In the latter case there is nothing in the proposal to suggest that the relief is to be granted on a temporary basis, and, though graduated, it is not degressive.

The Commission guidelines on environmental aid acknowledge that, from the perspective of the polluter pays principle, subsidies may represent a 'second-best solution'.[35] They 'aim to strike a balance between the requirements of competition and environment policy .... Such [environmental] aid is normally only justified when adverse effects on competition are outweighed by the benefits for the environment'.[36] They seek to strike a balance between the demands of market integration and the public interest in rapid environmental modernization. This while recognizing international

---

31 Supra, n. 25, section 3:4.
32 For details see the State Aid (Horizontal Aid: Environmental Protection) section of the Commission's annual Reports on Competition Policy. The Commission has emphasized, in exempting aid in the form of tax relief, the temporary nature of the relief, and the competitiveness concerns associated with the unilateral introduction of such a tax. It recognized that in the absence of such relief, taxes of this kind would be politically unachievable.
33 Supra, n. 25, para. 3.
34 Ibid.
35 Ibid., para. 1.4.
36 Ibid., para. 1.6.

competitiveness concerns, together with the unequal starting point of the Community's various regions and of the particular difficulties faced by SMEs. They represent an important acknowledgement of the obligation to integrate environmental concerns, horizontally, across other areas of Community policy-making. Yet such integration demands more than merely providing a framework for *environmental* subsidies.

Many national aid plans which have in the past received Commission approval have subsidized activities, particularly in the energy sector, with negative environmental consequences. It has been estimated that 63% of national aid to the energy sector has accrued in favour of fossil fuels, and 28% to the nuclear industry. Such aid measures tend to have been exempted as being in the common European interest, understood in terms of security and diversity of energy supply. A report submitted to the Commission in 1992 suggested that 'security of supply' has been deployed as a catch-all for a variety of diverse interests, including employment and regional policy objectives.[37] From the perspective of the integration obligation, it is crucial that the environmental impact of all state aid be taken into account in assessing the applicability of the Article 92 exemptions.

On a related note, it is the case that the Community today finances, out of its own resources, a large number of projects and programmes in the area of environmental protection.[38] However, experience demonstrates that, equally, Community subsidies have been made available in such a manner as to exacerbate environmental degradation. The case of regional policy will be discussed in Chapter 7. The Community's Common Agricultural Policy (CAP) provides the most striking (both in qualitative and quantitative terms) evidence of this. By linking level of subsidy to agricultural output, it is often claimed that this policy serves to reward the Community's most efficient farmers. However, that it has tended to subsidize environmental destruction, by militating in the direction of the intensification of farming, has been well documented.[39]

---

[37] Report by independent consultants, 'Mesures Nationales Pour la Sécurité d'Approvisionnement en Energie' (1992), cited in Hancher, L., in Harden, supra, n. 26, p. 141.

[38] See Ch. 7 and Council Regulation 1973/92 establishing a Community Financial Instrument of the Environment (LIFE) OJ 1992 L206/1.

[39] See Elworthy, S., 'Legal Obstacles to Integrating Environmental Concerns in the CAP' in Van Dael (ed.), *Recente Ontwikke-Lingen in het Europees Milieurect* (Kluwer, 1997).

The introduction of agri-environmental measures, under the guidance section of the European Agricultural Guidance and Guarantee Fund, has done little to mitigate the adverse environmental impact of the CAP, particularly because of the limited amount of funding dedicated to such programmes.[40]

In December 1995 the Commission presented an Agricultural Strategy Paper to the Madrid European Council. This stressed the need for an integrated rural policy which, *inter alia*, would more fully reflect the important environmental and recreational functions which such areas serve. Subsequently, in its voluminous 'Agenda 2000' report, the Commission calls for a more prominent role for agri-environmental instruments, and for increased budgetary resources to be dedicated to these.[41] It emphasises, in particular, Community co-financing in respect of organic farming, maintenance of semi-natural habitats, traditional orchards or hedgerows, continuation of alpine cattle-keeping and upkeep of wetlands. It also stresses the need for environmental considerations to be more fully integrated into the market support systems of the CAP. It intends to forward a proposal enabling Member States to make direct payments to farmers conditional upon compliance with environmental quality criteria. To an extent the report provokes a sense of *déjà vu*. The year of 1992 was, according to the Commission, to:

> mark a decisive turning-point in the development of the common agricultural policy and European agriculture ... [and] the break between the old development model of European agriculture, which was principally an intensive one, and the more extensive model the reform of the CAP should encourage in the future.[42]

Nonetheless, the Community is currently facing an unusual constellation of circumstances; expansion eastwards as well as preparation for a new round of multilateral trade negotiations, due to commence in 1999. In its current form, the CAP is neither financially viable, nor politically acceptable at an international level. It is significant that, for the purposes of the Uruguay Round Agreement on Agriculture, direct payments to farmers for environmental purposes, de-coupled from production levels, were classified as

---

[40] See Council Regulation 2078/92 OJ 1992 L215/85.
[41] COM(97) 2000 final.
[42] *The Agricultural Situation in the Community* (Commission of the European Communities, 1992) p. 31.

'green box' measures which were exempt from the usual rules governing overall reductions in levels of domestic subsidies payable.[43] It remains to be seen whether Franz Fischler, bucolic Commissioner with responsibility for agriculture, will succeed where his predecessor MacSharry failed.

Tradeable emissions permits

The concept of tradeable emissions permits – still a twinkle in the Commission's eye[44] – finds its clearest concrete expression in an EPA (United States Environmental Protection Agency) inspired, court-sanctioned, reading of the Clean Air Act (CAA). Central to this regime is the principle of aggregation – over space and time – of polluting emissions. Aggregation implies a (variable) degree of agnosticism, on the part of the state, as regards the specific source of polluting emissions, in favour of an approach which focuses, within a given area, upon total emissions loading. Trading (and hence aggregation) takes a variety of forms and serves a number of distinct functions within the framework of the CAA. Four mechanisms, conceptually closely related, are central to an understanding of this system: bubbles, netting, offsets and banking. Brief analysis of these will serve to illustrate both the principle of aggregation, and the relationship between this and more conventional forms of command and control style regulation.[45]

The language of bubbles denotes the existence of an imaginary dome suspended from the air to cover a given geographic space. Within this space there may exist merely one plant incorporating a number of polluting units, or a group of plants each constituted by distinct units. Such domes are constructed against a backdrop of binding performance standards requiring a percentage reduction in emissions of a given substance. It provides a degree of flexibility in the achievement of this reduction by existing sources, as the pollution abatement burden may be distributed unevenly between those

---

[43] *Agreement on Agriculture* OJ 1995 L336/22, Annex 2:12.

[44] See Fifth Environmental Action Programme, OJ 1993 C138/5, p. 69.

[45] Few statutory regimes are as complex as the CAA. For a full analysis of its operation see Menell and Stewart, *Environmental Law and Policy* (Little, Brown & Co., 1994), and on emissions trading see *Emissions Trading Policy Statement: General Principles for the Creation, Banking and Use of Emission Reduction Credits* EPA, 51 Federal Regulation 43,814 (1986).

units which together comprise a single plant (internal bubbles), or even between entirely separate plants (external bubbles).

The concept of netting is closely related, though functionally distinct. The CAA institutes a burdensome system of preconstruction review and permitting in respect of new polluting sources. 'New' in this context extends to major modifications to existing sources. A modification will not, however, be construed as major for the purpose of certain preconstruction permit requirements, where its net effect, in terms of total plant emissions, is neutral; an increase in emissions from one unit might be offset by a concomitant decrease in emissions from another. Netting is, by definition, internal (intra-plant).

The concept of 'offsetting' evolved in the context of strategies to balance economic and environmental interests in so-called non-attainment areas; namely areas which fail to comply with federal ambient air quality standards (target standards). In the absence of such trading, economic growth would be sacrificed on the altar of environmental rigidity. Offsetting applies to both new and (modi-fied) existing sources and may be internal or external. In order that 'reasonable progress' toward attainment be achieved, offsetting requires that new emissions be *more than* compensated for by reductions elsewhere. To this end an 'offset ratio' must be established, its precise terms reflecting the light of the intensity of the attainment deficit.

Aggregation of pollution generates the existence of private markets in pollution rights – hence the terminology 'market-based instruments'. Permanent emissions reductions (where these are quantifiable and enforceable) are awarded credits. Such credits may be deployed in the manner described above under the various regimes. They cannot, however, be used to circumvent technology-based standards applicable in the case of new or modified sources. Since 1979 the EPA has sanctioned the 'banking' of credits, either for later use by the same firm (aggregation over time), or for sale or lease according to the rules governing the operation of the market. Emissions 'banks' may be established at state or local level in order to facilitate trading by reducing the transaction costs associated with locating serviceable emission credits.

It will be apparent from the above that emissions trading has, in the United States, accompanied rather than superseded command and control regulation. To a degree this coupling is inevitable. Trading presupposes the existence of defined emission limits, but operates to mitigate the worst excesses (from an economic perspective) of uniform performance standards by permitting burden sharing which is guided by differentials in pollution control costs. It is by virtue of this coupling that trading retains that element of predictability, and certainty of environmental outcome, which is forfeited in the case of taxes and charges. Business does not invariably act in a manner which is economically rational.[46] Where it fails to do so, in a context of tradeable emissions as opposed to taxes, it is the economy and not the environment which is the loser. Yet, in the United States trading has operated against a backdrop of arguably excessive 'regulatory overhang'. One of the consequences of this, and especially of the continuing emphasis upon a variety of more or less cost-sensitive forms of technology standard, is that demand for emission reduction credits is suppressed. This may be one reason why emissions trading transactions (above all, external trading) are less frequent than might have been anticipated.[47]

Yet the difficulties which inhere in emissions trading are not merely pragmatic; not merely a reflection of the less than enthusiastic response which it has elicited in practice. The concept of emissions trading begs a host of difficult – and in some cases morally loaded – questions. There arises first the issue of the initial allocation of the pollution quota both between and within Member States. 'Grandfathering', whereby entitlement is calculated according to existing output and is, up to this level, free of charge, may avoid the 'excess burden' problem associated with environmental taxes, whereby each and every unit of pollution incurs a charge, not merely those above a level which is deemed to be sustainable. It may, however, in the absence of adjustment, be inequitable in a Union currently characterized by vastly uneven economic development.

Two further related issues arise: the geographic boundaries of the trading space(s), and the principles governing the acquisition of

---

[46] For concrete examples, see Jacobs, M., *The Green Economy* (Pluto, 1991), p. 156.

[47] See Dwyer, J.P., 'The Use of Market Incentives in Controlling Air Pollution: California's Marketable Permits Program' (1993) 20 ELQ103, and Turner, Pearce and Bateman, *Environmental Economics: and Elementary Introduction* (Harvester Wheatsheaf, 1994), pp. 185–6, where they suggest other reasons for the limited amount of trading, especially external trading. The hoarding of permits has often been cited. This may be motivated by a concern to hold on to a security blanket for the future or in terms of anti-competitive behaviour (barriers to new entrants). Hoarding would become an issue to be dealt with under Article 86 EC, relating to abuse of a dominant position.

banked emission reduction credits. Bigger may be better from an economic (cost-savings) perspective in relation to the first, while environmental considerations (the danger of pollution 'hot spots') and policy concerns may militate in favour of more spatially restricted markets. Recent experiences in the functioning of the Common Fisheries Policy, and the negative political consequences associated with quota transfers between Member States (from the United Kingdom to Spain, for example), are illustrative of the credibility gap which may be generated by the operation of supranational markets. Against a backdrop of Community inspired emissions trading, economic stagnation in one region or Member State may, in a world of 'sound bites' and 'blame Europe' politics, do little to enhance the social legitimacy of the European Community. Such concerns may be capable of being addressed through political screening of transfers, at which point a system apparently predicated upon market logic would be transformed into an instrument of industrial policy.

One final concern which arises in respect of both emissions trading and taxes is ethical in nature. There are those who have argued that such instruments are morally offensive. The nature of such concerns is captured well by the following scenario:[48]

> SCENE: The new Federal Licensing Bureau. A bored clerk is approached by a middle-age applicant who looks nervous.
>
> *Applicant*: I'd like to apply for a licence to emit sulphur oxides. I have this small backyard smelter . . .
> *Clerk*: Okay. That'll be $10,000.
> *Applicant*: Did you say $10,000? That's exorbitant!
> *Clerk*: Look Mac, sulphur oxides aggravate lung diseases, dissolve nylon stockings, peel paint, and create killer fogs. The right to do all that doesn't come cheap.
> *Applicant*: I'm sorry I didn't realise . . .
> *Clerk*: Remember, it's high fees that reduce damage to health and property. Now if you want something cheap I can let you have a licence good for tossing three beer cans and a sandwich wrapper out of your car window. That's only ten bucks.
> *Applicant*: Littering? I don't know, there doesnt seem to be much profit in it.
> *Clerk*: Ah, you're looking for a profit? Confidentially I think our

---

48 Hoppe, 'A Licence to Steal' *San Francisco Chronicle* 8 February 1971, cited in Menell and Stewart, supra, n. 45, pp. 381–2.

best buy is a Mugging licence. It entitles you to hit three old ladies over the head in the park of your choice and snatch their purses. Most guys come out ahead on this one.

Applicant (surprised): Hitting old ladies over the head? That sounds anti-social somehow.

Clerk (shrugging): It's no different than a licence to poison people's lungs. And it only costs $100.

Applicant (indignant): That's highway robbery!

Clerk: Nope. Highway robbery is $200. But it's a non-renewable, non-transferable, one-shot deal.

Applicant: I'd hate to risk that kind of money.

Clerk: Tell you what. Get a group of your friends together and take out a licence to Riot. You can burn and loot five stores in the ghetto of your choice. The fee's relatively low because it's part of our Urban Renewal Program.

Applicant (shaking his head): It seems like these days people are getting away with murder.

Clerk: Not unless they got 50,000 bucks buddy. Remember, we got to keep the charges sufficiently high to encourage control of everyone's criminal instincts.

Applicant (appalled): What kind of concept is this? It just means the rich can get away with crimes like poisoning people's lungs that the poor can't afford to commit.

Clerk (yawning): So what else is new? Next.

The message which this exchange imparts is powerful and it appears, intuitively, effectively to expose the ethical shortcomings inherent in economic rationality as applied to the protection of the natural environment. The premises upon which it rests are closely related to those discussed in Chapter 1 in the context of cost-benefit analysis; the social acceptability of polluting activity is to be assessed in the light of willingness to pay. Back again to '. . . and how much for your grandmother?' logic.[49] A particular activity, whether mugging old (or young) ladies, burning or looting, or generating nylon-dissolving polluting emissions, is simply morally wrong, regardless of the degree of satisfaction (in material or non-material terms) which ensues and regardless of attempts to quantify the associated costs.

It is clear from Chapter 1 that this is an argument which is, in this writer's view, compelling. However, it is not one which is

---

[49] Adams, J.G.U., '... and how much for your grandmother?' (1974) Environment and Planning A,6.

equally applicable in respect of both taxes/charges, and emissions trading. On the contrary, it appears to militate in favour of the latter. Whereas the former sanctions a given activity so long as there is willingness to pay, the latter assesses the legitimacy of that activity in economic terms, but only within prescribed parameters. To the extent that financial might equals right, it does so only up to a point – and that point depends, in part, upon arrangements for the initial distribution of credits. Parameters may be drawn on the basis of considerations which are not based on the application of economic reason. In the case of the latter, willingness to pay is relevant only in articulating the means of achieving an established objective and not in the definition of that objective itself, a question of 'means and ends in social regulation'.[50] 'Markets in pollution "rights", offsets, and similar schemes do not necessarily replace ethical thinking with economic thinking, moral norms with economic principles'.[51] To this extent tradeable emissions merely render explicit that which is perhaps hidden in a command and control context; namely that there is a point at which pollution control may be deemed to be 'good enough'. Emissions trading, unlike taxes, leaves space not merely for economic rationality in the delineation of this point, but also for ecological and ethical reason.

Conclusion

In the first chapter of this book the rationale for environmental law was presented in terms of a 'social cost' approach. Economic instruments, such as taxes and charges, or emissions trading, constitute means of forcing the polluter to 'internalize' costs which previously have been borne by society as a whole. They emerge as a logical response to an economic analysis of the causes of pollution; a means of correcting market failure by artificially constructing a market in public-type goods in respect of which markets will not naturally develop. Cost-effective, and compatible with the dominant ideology of market liberalism, such instruments enjoy widespread support. In the European Community, however, academic enthusiasm has not been matched by political action. In part

---

50 Sagoff, M., *The Economy of the Earth* (CUP, 1990), p. 210.
51 Ibid.

this may be explicable on the basis that such instruments render explicit the very substantial costs inherent in pollution control. Their implications, in terms of competitiveness, are more immediately apparent.

There are, however, some very real problems and dilemmas associated with the use of economic instruments. These may be understood, on the one hand, in terms of effectiveness and, on the other, in terms of fairness or equity. As to the former, these arise in particular in markets which may be classified as broadly inelastic; that is to say, in which demand for the product remains relatively stable regardless of an increase in price. In such circumstances the increased costs associated with production can be passed on to the consumer with relative impunity. The polluting activity may continue on the same scale; business as usual. While in economic terms this may be taken to imply that the value of the goods exceeds the full cost of production (including social costs) and that this activity does not, therefore, lead to a misallocation of society's resources, in environmental terms intervention provokes limited results. As was noted above, this criticism bites more strongly in the case of taxes or charges, when compared with tradeable emissions. In the latter case, a degree of effectiveness is guaranteed by the establishment of overall emission limits. Tradeable emission permits, like taxes, also give rise to the danger of the emergence of pollution 'hot spots'.[52] To this extent it may be thought necessary to deploy such instruments alongside, rather than instead of, environmental quality standards.

In terms of fairness, economic instruments may be thought to be problematic. These imply that those who can pay may continue to pollute. In a European Community characterized by vastly uneven development at a regional level, and broad disparities in terms of individual income, this equation between financial might and right may be thought to be unacceptable. Distributive concerns represent one important reason for continuing political antipathy to the introduction of economic instruments. So strong were these concerns in the wake of the indirect taxation of gas and electricity in the United Kingdom, that the new Labour government has taken steps to reverse this development. It may well be that at a political level, taxes and charges may be most readily justified in the case of

---

52 See Boucquey, N., 'Hot Spots in the Bubble: Ecological Liability in Markets for Pollution Rights' in Teubner, Farmer and Murphy (eds), *Environmental Law and Ecological Responsibility* (Wiley, 1994).

products which may be considered as non-essential or luxuries; where private motor cars fit into this picture is a matter of considerable debate.

More generally, economic instruments give rise to a variety of ethical concerns, the distribution of the costs of pollution abatement being only one. The earlier extract from the San Francisco Chronicle exemplifies these well. The problem is not that it is not fair that not all of us can afford to buy a permit to mug an old lady; it is that any of us should be entitled to do so, thus receiving official sanction to engage in an activity which is fundamentally wrong. In so far as pollution, unlike mugging, may be regarded as a necessary evil – to sustain the consumption habits of a modern industrial society – it may be thought that there are better ways of allocating entitlement than on the basis of willingness/ability to pay. It may also be argued that the extent to which it ought to be considered a necessary evil is ultimately a question of politics and not economics.

Notwithstanding the limited success of the European Community in realizing its commitment to the introduction of economic instruments for environmental protection, this topic is of considerable importance for the Community lawyer. Recent years have seen a proliferation of such instruments at Member State level, as is apparent from the Commission's recent survey.[53] In themselves such national initiatives, often taken within the framework of Community environmental quality standards, raise questions of compatibility with Community internal market law. This chapter has sought to exemplify this through discussion of the issue of subsidies. Regard should also be had to Community law in so far as it pertains to the free movement of goods (Articles 9–12 and 30–6 EC) and internal taxation (Article 95). Tradeable permits, in view of the permit hoarding experiences of the United States, also raise questions about Community competition law. The determination of certain Member States to pursue an economic instruments-based approach, and the danger of market fragmentation to which this gives rise, will certainly ensure that this topic remains on the Community's political agenda for years to come. In a book of this size it not possible to analyse in detail the Treaty constraints on Member State action in the environmental sphere. However, one subject has emerged as deeply controversial

[53] Appendix to COM(97) 9 final, supra, n. 24.

and of very real practical importance. It is to the relationship between trade (in goods) and environment that the next two chapters
will turn.

CHAPTER FOUR

Trade and environment: an internal market perspective

The trade/environment debate in the European Union takes shape against a backdrop of 'shared responsibility' for environmental protection. Community competence notwithstanding, the regulatory sovereignty of Member States, though diminished in this sphere, remains substantial. Such are the implications of the classic doctrine of preemption in areas of concurrent jurisdiction that Member States may, until such a time as the Community has acted, retain or introduce such measures as they deem appropriate for the protection or conservation of the physical environment. Indeed, such is the Community's nuanced conception of preemption that the Community may endeavour merely to occupy partially a given regulatory 'space'. 'Minimum' harmonization is emerging as the rule rather than the exception, with the Community rule prescribing the 'bottom line' below which the regulatory practices of the Member States may not sink. The precise scope of the Member States' residual competence will depend ultimately upon both the legal basis of the Community act, and the wording of that act.

To stop here, however, would be to tell only half the story. Community law comprises more than the sum of the legal acts adopted by the Community institutions. It encompasses also the Treaty establishing the European Community (the EC Treaty) on the basis of which these institutions derive their power to act. If Community legislation, increasingly, establishes a 'floor' of rights and duties, this Treaty represents a 'ceiling' beyond which neither the Community, nor its Member States may lawfully venture.[1]

---

[1] See Weatherill, S., 'Beyond Preemption? Shared Competence and Constitutional Change in the European Community' in O'Keefe and Twomey (eds), *Legal Issues of the Maastricht Treaty* (Wiley/Chancery, 1994), p. 25, where he notes that '[w]hereas, under old-style preemption, the Community rules provided both floor and ceiling, now, under minimum harmonization, the rule provides the floor but Articles 30–36 the ceiling'.

Consequently, even in the absence of exhaustive Community harmonization the regulatory sovereignty of the Member States should not be regarded as absolute. This chapter is concerned to explore the limits to Member State regulatory autonomy in the environmental sphere, arising from the application of Articles 30–36 EC.

For most students engaged in the study of EC environmental law, the nature of the Community rules relating to the free movement of goods will be well known.[2] Articles 30–36 have evolved in a manner which is tolerant of regulatory diversity. From the point of view of the internal market project and the free circulation of goods, difference (in terms of national standards) does not necessarily equal market fragmentation. Application of the principle of 'mutual recognition' succeeds, in an overwhelming majority of cases, in reconciling regulatory diversity with the demands of market integration. It does so by instituting a rebuttable presumption of 'equivalence' in respect of Member State regulatory regimes. Born of pragmatism and expediency, mutual recognition and an ethos of 'live and let live', have emerged as defining (and increasingly celebrated) features of the Community integration dynamic.

Such an ethos of 'live and let live' should not, however, be regarded as problem-free in a context of intense market ('negative') integration and, consequently, profound transnational interdependence. The *de jure* sovereignty of the Member States may emerge as largely unscathed – at least in the absence of Community norms – while, *de facto*, their effective regulatory autonomy may, in practice, be severely diminished. Free trade may render it physically impossible or economically untenable for Member States to achieve or even pursue certain environmental policy objectives – other than by way of concerted action at Community level ('positive' integration measures). This, then, brings us to the nub of the trade/environment debate. To what extent, and under what circumstances, may a Member State restrict trade in the Community in order to reinforce (or render effective) domestic environmental policy preferences? The range of situations in which a Member State may seek to assert (more or less credibly) a legitimate interest in doing so is broad; the nature of the interdependence arising out of trade may be physical, economic or even

---

2   For those to whom this does not apply see Weatherill and Beaumont, *EC Law*, (Penguin, 1995), chs 15–16 and Craig and de Burca, *EC Law: Text, Cases and Materials* (OUP, 1995), Ch. 14.

'psychic' (psychological),[3] and it may originate in product quality or production process. As will become apparent as we turn to examine these issues in more detail, the existing jurisprudence of the Court does little to clarify the norms applying in situations which may be characterized as 'non-paradigmatic'; where interdependence is other than physical in nature, and/or arises out of production process not product quality.

Trade in goods: the jurisprudence of the European Court

Article 30 prohibits 'quantitative restrictions' on imports and 'all measures having equivalent effect'.[4] Its scope is notoriously broad and yet, at the penumbra, ill-defined. It extends not only to import bans and quotas, but to 'all trading rules enacted by Member States which are capable of hindering, directly or indirectly, actually or potentially, intra-Community trade'.[5] It applies both to rules which discriminate between domestic and imported products, and to those which apply equally to both, regardless of origin. In the language most commonly deployed, both 'distinctly' and 'indistinctly' applicable measures are capable of hindering intra-Community trade. Hence, Article 30 prescribes an 'effects' as opposed to discrimination-based approach.[6] The famous *Danish Bottles*[7] case may serve to illustrate the notion of an indistinctly applicable measure, arising in the environmental sphere.

In 1981 Denmark introduced legislation requiring that beer and

---

3   See Ch. 1.
4   Article 34 imposes an equivalent prohibition in respect of exports. However, discrimination between goods destined for the domestic market and those to be exported, is a *sine qua non* in the application of Article 34. See Case 15/79 *Groenveld* v *Produktschap voor Vee en Vlees* [1979] ECR 3409. It might be anticipated that this may change in the light of the Court's decision in Case C-384/93 *Alpine Investments BV* v *Minister van Financien* [1995] ECR I-1141, which concerned an indistinctly applicable restriction on the export of services.
5   Cases 8/74 *Procureur du Roi* v *Dassonville* [1974] ECR 837, para. 5.
6   Marenco, G., in 'Pour une interprétation traditionnelle de la notion de mesure d'effet équivalent' (1984) Cahiers de Droit Européen 291, argues, contrary to received wisdom, that the jurisprudence of the Court can be understood in terms of discrimination. Rejected as 'unconvincing' by Weatherill and Beaumont, supra, n. 2, p. 504, Marenco's analysis merits serious consideration in the wake of *Keck & Mithouard* (Cases C-267 & 268/91 [1993] ECR I-6097), discussed below.
7   Case 302/86 *Commission* v *Denmark* [1988] ECR 4607.

soft drinks be marketed within its territory in returnable containers, of a type authorized by the relevant Danish authorities. The use of metal cans was prohibited. In 1984 this legislation was amended in such a way as to permit the marketing of up to 3,000 hectolitres (per producer, per year) in returnable but non-approved containers (other than metal cans); subject only to the proviso that in such cases a deposit and return scheme be established. These rules were indistinctly applicable, in that they applied equally to domestic and imported goods. In so far as they did differentiate on the basis of the origin of the product, they did so by condoning a partial relaxation of the rules for importers seeking merely to test the Danish market. In this sense they discriminated in favour of importers, giving rise to 'reverse' discrimination of a kind which is tolerated by Article 30. The Court, in assessing the legitimacy of these rules, found that:

> ... by restricting ... the quantity of beer and soft drinks which may be marketed by a single producer in non-approved containers to 3 000 hectolitres a year, the Kingdom of Denmark has failed, as regards imports of those products from other Member States, to fulfil its obligations under Article 30 of the EEC Treaty.[8]

The remainder of the application was dismissed. Hence, it condemned, as contrary to Article 30, the rule requiring the use of specifically approved containers (over and above the 3,000 hectolitre limit). It upheld, however, the norm relating to the institution of deposit/return arrangements. On what basis might this distinction be explained?

The European Court has consistently held that the mere existence of disparities between national laws is capable of generating obstacles to intra-Community trade.[9] The application of Danish rules on packaging of imported goods would restrict trade and impede market penetration. This does not imply, according to the jurisprudence of the Court, that these rules must be set aside as incompatible with Community law; but rather that a Member State may not insist upon compliance with them, in the case of imported goods, *except*, in so far as they are 'necessary' in order to satisfy a 'mandatory requirement' recognized by Community law. In so far

---

[8] Ibid., para. 22.
[9] For the seminal judgment in this area see Case 120/78 *Rewe-Zentrale AG* v *Bundesmonopolverwaltung fur Branntwein* (Cassis de Dijon) [1979] ECR 649, para. 8.

as they are not necessary, such rules will, in their application to imported goods, be incompatible with Article 30. In the *Danish Bottles* case the Court acknowledges the existence of a mandatory requirement relating to environmental protection. It accepts, furthermore, that the Danish rule relating to deposit and return is indeed necessary to satisfy this imperative requirement. The same, however, the Court held, could not be said for the rule necessitating the use of approved containers.

Article 36 and 'mandatory requirements'

It is, then, apparent that the Court, in construing Article 30, has sought to strike a balance between market integration and sometimes competing societal interests, such as the protection of the environment. Significantly, recourse to this mandatory requirements 'exception' is permitted only in the case of indistinctly applicable measures. These may be *prima facie* contrary to Article 30 but capable of being 'saved' by mandatory requirements. Distinctly applicable measures, on the contrary, are *per se* incompatible with Article 30 and are susceptible to justification only on the basis of the explicit treaty-based exception laid down in Article 36.[10] Article 36 is substantively more narrowly defined than the concept of mandatory requirements, and less fluid in its application; the list of headings which it encompasses is regarded as exhaustive. While it may serve to justify measures which are necessary to protect the life or health of humans, animals or plants, it does not extend to environmental protection objectives more broadly defined.[11] That said, 'Article 36, on the one hand, and the mandatory require-

---

10 Though Article 36 can be invoked in defence of both indistinctly and distinctly applicable measures, in the case of the latter the discrimination should not be 'arbitrary' (see the final sentence of Article 36). Hence it will be crucial to inquire into whether the Member State has taken effective steps within its jurisdiction to regulate production or marketing of the product which forms the subject of the import restriction. See, for example, Case 42/82 *Commission* v *France* [1983] ECR 1013.

11 Article 130r(1) provides a broad definition of the objectives of Community policy on the environment. This is to contribute to the pursuit of a number of objectives, including the protection of human health, but extending to preservation, protection or improvement of the quality of the environment, promotion of the prudent and rational utilization of natural resources and of measures at international level to deal with regional or world-wide environmental problems.

ments, on the other, share several common features. This reflects their functional similarity as expressions of the residual competence of the member states to impose obstacles to interstate trade'.[12] In particular, in the case of each, scrutiny of national measures is predicated upon the application of three related concepts: necessity, proportionality and least restrictive means. Though arguably conceptually distinct, these three tools tend, in practice, to coalesce at the hands of the Court. In the *Danish Bottles* case, the deposit/return system was accepted by the Court as 'an indispensable element of a system intended to ensure the re-use of containers', and 'therefore' as necessary. 'That being so' it could not be regarded as disproportionate.[13]

Necessity speaks to cause and effect; to the existence of a genuine threat to a societal interest deemed, in the circumstances, to be worthy of protection by Community law, and to the capacity of the measure at hand to address that threat effectively. Closely related to this is the concept of least restrictive or alternative means. In *Commission* v *Germany*[14] the Court 'rejected forthwith' the argument that a total import ban on live freshwater crayfish (subject only to limited derogations) could be considered indispensable to the objective of protecting native crayfish from disease. The Court concluded that this aim could be just as effectively attained by measures having less restrictive effects on intra-Community trade; by way, for example, of health checks and certification, regulation of the marketing of crayfish and the imposition of certain health measures on those importing crayfish into Germany.[15]

Proportionality proper speaks, on the one hand, to the intensity of a measure in terms of the degree of restraint of trade which it implies and, on the other, to the degree of protection which it is capable of achieving. It demands a balancing of one against the other. It was on this basis that the Danish rule relating to the use of approved containers (over and above the 3,000 hectolitre limit for importers) fell. The Court did not doubt that this measure

---

[12] Weatherill and Beaumont, supra n. 2, p. 506.

[13] Supra, n. 7, para. 13.

[14] Case C-131/93 [1994] ECR I-3303.

[15] Ibid., paras. 18–27. In respect of the mandatory requirement relating to consumer protection, the Court has consistently adopted the view that consumers derive adequate protection from a system of compulsory labelling and hence that more restrictive impediments to trade cannot be justified. Even such labelling requirements must be deomonstrated to be necessary and proportionate.

would contribute to the protection of the environment. Indeed, it acknowledged that it operated to guarantee a maximum degree of re-use and hence a 'very considerable degree of protection of the environment'.[16] In this sense it was strictly necessary in order to achieve this very high level of protection. Equally, there was no suggestion that less restrictive alternative means would be sufficiently potent to achieve the same degree of protection. Nonetheless, having regard to the limited quantity of imported beverages sold, or likely to be sold, in Denmark, the additional degree of environmental protection ensured by this measure was, in practice, marginal. Balancing the intensity of the restriction against the intensity of the benefit, the Court found that the measure was 'disproportionate to the objective pursued'.[17] Consequently, a measure may be strictly necessary to achieve that 'extra inch' in terms of environmental protection; nonetheless in the absence of a reasonable relationship between the extra restriction on trade implied by the measure, and the extra protection achieved, such rules will be sacrificed in the name of proportionality. Proportionality, however, should be viewed as art not science.[18] It demands not only a necessarily subjective assessment of the degree of environmental worth attaching to Member State action, and of the costs associated with this in terms of market fragmentation, but also a balancing of competing, and arguably incommensurable, goals (integration and environment). Intensely value-laden, Member States must be permitted a wide margin of appreciation.

Such language of necessity, proportionality and alternative means sounds, or ought to sound, warning bells in the minds of environmental lawyers. It appears to be predicated upon a naïve faith in the revelationary potential of science, and an assumption of knowledge, pertaining especially to the existence, magnitude and origins of environmental risk. In the absence of certainty regarding, for example, the causal relationship between certain substances and their alleged effects, and/or the intensity of the risk associated with a given activity, it is not at all apparent that attempts to apply these principles will be meaningful at all. How, in

16 Supra, n. 7, para. 20.
17 Ibid., para. 21.
18 Viewed by some as a form of cost-benefit testing, proportionality is approached by the European Court in an intuitive as opposed to technical manner. On proportionality before the German courts in the environmental sphere see Rose-Ackerman, S., *Controlling Environmental Policy: The Limits of Public Law in Germany and the United States* (Yale University Press, 1995).

the face of scientific uncertainty, can the necessity or sufficiency of a measure be authoritatively assessed? How, in the face of conflicting evidence as to the magnitude of environmental risk, might the proportionality of a measure be evaluated?

While, contrary to certain 'absolutist' constructions of the precautionary principle, the Court continues to insist that it is for the importing state to discharge the burden of proof implicit in these free movement exceptions,[19] the evidential stringency of this burden declines sharply in the face of evidence of scientific uncertainty. It does appear, at least in respect of the protection of health and life of humans, that, in such circumstances, Member States are entitled to err on the side of caution. Evidence of scientific uncertainty, as a minimum, is, however, required. Hence, in the *German Beer*[20] case, the German rules on the use of additives in beers were rejected as incompatible with Article 30 and not susceptible to justification under Article 36. Significantly, the German government failed to adduce evidence to counter the claims of the Community's own Scientific Committee for Food, as well of those of the Food and Agricultural Organisation's *Codex Alimentarius* Committee and the WHO, that such additives did not present a risk to public health and met a real need, especially a technical one.[21]

In the area of public health the Court has demonstrated a willingness to adopt a broadly precautionary approach. What remains unclear is whether this approach is to apply regardless of the intensity of the putative risk arising. The subject of numerous, often inconsistent, formulations in international law,[22] the precautionary principle is thought by many to apply only in the face of a threat of 'serious' or 'irreversible' damage. In the area of public health which 'rank[s] first among the property or interests protected by

---

19 See, for example, Case 227/82 *Van Bennekom* [1983] ECR 3883, para. 40, where the Court notes that 'it is for the national authorities to demonstrate in each case that the marketing of the product in question creates a serious risk to health'. In Case 174/82 *Officier van Justitie* v *Sandoz BV* [1983] ECR 2245, para. 24, the Court rejected an attempt to reverse the burden of proof by requiring that the importer demonstrate that a particular additive was safe from the perspective of public health.

20 Case 178/84 *Commission* v *Germany* [1987] ECR 1227.

21 See generally, Hession and Macrory, 'Balancing Trade Freedom with the Requirements of Sustainable Development' in Emiliou and O'Keefe (eds), *The European Union and World Trade Law* (1996, Wiley, 1996), pp. 198–202.

22 See Sands, P., *Principles of International Environmental Law* (MUP, 1995), pp. 208–13 for an overview of these.

Article 36',[23] every risk may properly be characterized as serious, even where it attaches only to a small number of particularly vulnerable and sensitive consumers.[24] Hence in this area the Court, unsurprisingly, appears to have adopted a liberal conception of risk and to have defined broadly the scope of application of the precautionary principle. To what extent it would be prepared to adopt a comparable approach in the face of insufficient, or less than conclusive, evidence of environmental risk remains, for the present, a matter of speculation.

While on the subject of risk it is useful also to highlight the approach of the Court to the ongoing BSE (mad cow disease) crisis. Though not concerned with the intepretation of Article 36, its reasoning is highly pertinent nonetheless. In 1996 the United Kingdom government brought an Article 173 action seeking the annulment of Commission Decision 96/239 on emergency measures to protect against bovine spongiform encephalopathy.[25] At the same time it sought interim suspension of the operation of this decision.[26] The decision prohibited the export of bovine animals and beef and veal (or derived products) from the United Kingdom, both to other Member States and to third countries. The United Kingdom argued that the products concerned posed no danger to human health and that the ban was not supported by scientific evidence. It alleged that the ban had been introduced solely or primarily to reassure consumers and to protect the beef and veal markets; this due to a rather inopportune statement to this effect by agriculture Commissioner, Franz Fischler.

The European Court, having regard to the preamble to the Commission Decision, concluded that the Commission had based its decision above all on considerations relating to the protection of public health. It emphasized that continuing scientific uncertainty notwithstanding, 'the transmissibility of BSE to humans had ceased to be a theoretical hypothesis and was now regarded as the 'most likely explanation of the new variant of Creutzfeldt-Jakob disease recently detected in a number of people'.[27] The Com-

---

[23] Case 104/75 *De Peijper* [1976] ECR 613, para. 16.

[24] See, for example, Case 97/83 *Criminal Proceedings against Melkunie BV* [1984] ECR 2367, para. 19.

[25] OJ 1996 L 78/47.

[26] Case C-180/96R *United Kingdom and Northern Ireland* v *Commission* [1996] ECR I-3903.

[27] Ibid., para. 60. See also paras 73–8 on the application of the proportionality principle.

mission had taken this 'particularly serious' information into account in adopting its decision. Notwithstanding scientists' imperfect knowledge of Creutfeldt-Jacob disease, but in view of its fatal consequences and the fact that the most likely explanation . . . is exposure to BSE . . . the Court cannot but recognize the paramount importance to be accorded to the protection of public health'.[28]

Distinguishing distinctly and indistinctly applicable measures

Notwithstanding the conceptual similarity between Article 36 and mandatory requirements, it remains important to distinguish their relative spheres of application. The substantive scope of the latter is more broadly defined and the headings incorporated thereunder more fluid. Environmental protection may be invoked in respect only of indistinctly applicable measures.[29] Classification is consequently of the essence and yet, in several important respects, far from straightforward. There is, in the free movement literature, and in the case law of the Court, a tendency to conflate 'distinctly applicable' with 'discriminatory' and to insist that mandatory requirements may be invoked only in the absence of discrimination. Yet it is not altogether clear that these two terms may properly be regarded as synonymous. Discrimination may be direct or indirect. It remains far from clear whether a measure which is indirectly discriminatory is to be regarded as distinctly or indistinctly applicable, and hence whether it is susceptible to justification through recourse to the concept of mandatory requirements.

The concept of indirect discrimination finds its clearest expression in the law relating to sex discrimination. It is said to pose 'two essential questions'; 'is there a "neutral" requirement or condition which has an adverse impact upon members of one sex? If so, can the employer justify the use of this criterion?'[30] Hence, inherent in

---

[28] Ibid., para. 93.

[29] Public health, on the contrary, falls within the scope of both Article 36 and mandatory requirements. Strictly, the Court ought to consider mandatory requirements first in that a measure justified in this way is deemed to fall outside of the scope of Article 30 altogether. In practice, however, the Court tends to consider public health claims in the light of Article 36. That it does so serves to exemplify the broadly similar conceptual underpinnings of the two exceptions.

[30] Rubenstein, M., *Equal Pay for Work of Equal Value* (Macmillan, 1984), p. 90.

the concept of indirect discrimination is the possibility of 'objective justification'. For some, mandatory requirements represent the 'functional equivalent' of objective justification. Thus, 'considering that the mandatory requirements exception does not apply in the case of indirectly discriminatory measures makes no sense'.[31] For others, the two concepts (objective justification and mandatory requirements) are to be regarded as distinct. Weatherill and Beaumont conclude, having regard to the case law of the Court, that mandatory requirements cannot be invoked in respect of measures which are either directly or indirectly discriminatory. They rely, *inter alia*, upon *Commission* v *United Kingdom*[32] in support of this conclusion. Nonetheless, they accept that 'if it can be shown that there are objectively justifiable reasons for the rules in question unconnected with nationality, then the rules will be considered lawful'; but concede that '[p]erhaps surprisingly, this argument has rarely been advanced'.[33] Craig and de Burca propose a third approach, equating distinctly applicable not simply with discriminatory but with *deliberately* discriminatory. They thus attach considerable importance to a subjective test in the case of indirectly discriminatory measures, having regard to the purpose or intent of the regulating state.[34] Hence, a superficially indistinctly applicable measure, which is purposively distinctly applicable, cannot be justified by way of mandatory requirements.

It is perhaps surprising that in an area as apparently well trodden as free movement of goods there remains such scope for legitimate debate even as regards the 'basics'. Certainly, the case law of the Court is far from conclusive. It is far from being clear that the Court, in *Commission* v *United Kingdom*,[35] does in fact exclude, as a matter of principle, the application of mandatory requirements to a rule which is indistinctly applicable only in form but not in substance. Its conclusion that 'the protection of consumers is sufficiently guaranteed by rules which enable the use of false indications of origin to be prohibited [and that] [s]uch rules are not called into question by the EEC Treaty',[36] may be construed as im-

---

31 Bernard, N., personal e-mail. See also his 'Discrimination and Free Movement in EC Law' (1996) 45 ICLQ 82.
32 Case 207/83 [1985] ECR 1202.
33 Supra, n. 2, p. 445.
34 Supra, n. 2, p. 636. For similar arguments in relation to workers and services see ibid., pp. 659 and 767 respectively.
35 Supra, n. 32.
36 Ibid., para. 21.

plying simply that the more general rules on indication of origin were not truly 'necessary' in this case to satisfy any imperative requirement relating to protection of the consumer. Were mandatory requirements to be precluded in the case of indirectly discriminatory measures it does appear strange that the (according to Weatherill and Beaumont) ostensibly separate objective justification defence has been so rarely (if ever) advanced. Equally, it appears strange that in cases in which it is acknowledged that national legislation generates protective effects there has been so little effort to demonstrate that this 'protective effect'[37] has its origins in indirect discrimination. In many of the cases arising before the Court in which mandatory requirements have been invoked, the measure in question, though on the surface equally applicable, is such that in practice it is 'satisfied entirely or mainly by domestic products rather than imports'.[38] It would be strange were it otherwise, given that such national rules are constitutive of, and hence reflect, national traditions. Think, for example, of the infamous *German Beer* case.[39]

Craig and de Burca's analysis may not be incompatible with this conclusion if one accepts that 'the concept of intentional indirect discrimination . . . is a contradiction in terms'.[40] Paraphrasing Rubenstein, if a Member State intends to differentiate on grounds of nationality, that is not indirect discrimination. It constitutes less favourable treatment on grounds of nationality, namely direct, albeit disguised, discrimination. Evidence of *male fides* (discriminatory intent) hence remains relevant in the application of Articles 30-36; both in determining the scope of application of mandatory requirements and in assessing the credibility of claims under Article 36.[41]

What, however, of the relatively recent judgment of the Court in *Keck and Mithouard*?[42] This case, as he himself notes, appears to offer sustenance to the Bernard approach to classification, an

---

37 See, for example, Case 788/79 *Gilli and Andres* [1980] ECR 2071 and Case 16/83 *Prantl* [1984] ECR 1299 (Weatherill and Beaumont, supra, n. 2, argue that *Prantl* represents merely an anomaly in the case law of the Court).

38 Wyatt and Dashwood, *European Community Law* (Sweet & Maxwell, 1993), p. 220.

39 Supra, n. 20.

40 Supra, n. 30, p. 135.

41 For examples of its relevance in respect of the latter, see Case 40/82 *Commission v United Kingdom* [1982] ECR 2793 (French poultry) and *Commision v Germany* supra, n. 20.

42 Supra, n.6.

approach which accepts that indirectly discriminatory measures may be vindicated through recourse to mandatory requirements. Yet, as will be seen, the significance of this case extends beyond classification and merits analysis, albeit brief. The facts are straightforward. Keck and Mithouard were prosecuted in France for reselling goods (picon beer and sati rouge coffee) at a loss. They argued that the French law prohibiting this practice was contrary to Article 30. The European Court accepted that such legislation may restrict the volume of sale of these products, including those imported from other Member States, but found that this, in itself, was insufficient to 'characterize the legislation in question as a measure having equivalent effect to a quantitative restriction on imports':[43]

> ... contrary to what has previously been decided the application to products from other Member States of national provisions restricting or prohibiting certain selling arrangements is not such as to hinder directly or indirectly, actually or potentially, trade between Member States ... provided that those provisions apply to all affected traders operating within the national territory and provided that they affect in the same manner, in law and in fact, the marketing of domestic products and those from other Member States.[44]

While the judgment is laconic ('reasoning was renounced on the altar of expediency'[45]), it may be read as an endorsement of the 'dual burden/equal burden' distinction, long favoured by certain academic commentators.[46] The Court appears to distinguish between two categories of rules; those regulating intrinsic product character (relating, for example, to composition or packaging) and those regulating selling arrangements (relating, for example, to shop opening hours, retail licensing requirements or advertising).[47]

---

43 Ibid., para. 13.

44 Ibid., para. 16.

45 Gormley, L., 'Reasoning Renounced? The Remarkable Judgment in *Keck & Mithouard*' (1994) European Business Law Review 63, p. 67.

46 See, especially, White, E., 'In Search of the Limits to Article 30 of the EEC Treaty' (1989) 26 CMLRev. 235.

47 Post-*Keck*, rules relating to composition (Case C-17/93 *Openbaar Ministerie* v *Van der Veldt* [1994] ECR I-3537) and designation (Case C-315/92 *Verband Sozialer Wettbewerb* v *Clinique* [1994] ECR I-317) have been held to fall within this first category, and those relating to shop opening hours (Cases C-69 and 258/93 *Punto Casa Spa* v *Sindaco del Commune di Capena* [1994] ECR I-2355), advertising restrictions (Case C-412/93 *Leclerc-Siplec* v *TF1 Publicité and Another* [1995] ECR I-179) and licensing requirements for retail outlets (Case C-140-42/94 *DIP SpA* v *Commune Di Bassano Del Grappa* [1995] ECR I-3257), to fall within the second.

The former may be thought to impose a dual burden on importers in that 'these rules will have to be satisfied by the importer *in addition* to any such provisions existing within his or her own state'.[48] They oblige importers to jump through one regulatory hoop at home, in accordance with the principle of home country control, and another in the destination state. The latter, on the contrary, appear to impose a truly equal burden on all those seeking to market goods within a given territory. They are assumed to be genuinely even-handed in their implications and hence, in the absence of evidence of discrimination (direct or indirect), to fall entirely outside of the scope of Article 30.

In terms of the classification issue the significance of this judgment lies in its propensity to resurrect discrimination as a defining characteristic of Article 30. It is at least arguable that, in its wake, Article 30 no longer self-evidently takes us 'beyond discrimination'. Measures imposing a dual burden are discriminatory in effect. Those imposing an equal burden are not, in the absence of specific evidence to the contrary. Discrimination arguably emerges as a *sine qua non* in the application of Article 30. If so, it would be nonsensical to equate distinctly applicable with discriminatory. To do so would render the concept of mandatory requirements nugatory.[49]

Moving on, this issue of classification logically precedes consideration of the substantive merits of a Member State's defence under Article 36 or mandatory requirements. Yet, on at least one occasion, (*Commission* v *Belgium*[50]) the Court appears to have been influenced in performing this task by the merits (as it saw it) of the rule in question, and by its desire to achieve a 'correct' policy outcome, having regard to the facts of the case before it. This case arose out of a decision of the Wallonian regional government to prohibit, in its territory, the storage, tipping or dumping of

---

[48] Supra, n. 2, Craig and de Burca, p. 628 (emphasis added).

[49] In *Keck* and subsequent case law, the Court places considerable emphasis upon the purpose of the rule at hand in that it was not intended to regulate trade between Member States. Analysis of purpose appears to be significant in the Court's determination of whether the measure falls within Article 30, rather than merely in relation to the question of justification under Article 36 and mandatory requirements. In this it exacerbates confusion surrounding the Court's approach to discrimination and the issue of whether it adopts an essentially intention or effect based approach. See generally, Dine and Watts, *Discrimination Law* (Wiley, 1996) and especially the chapters by Bernard and Barnard therein.

[50] Case C-2/90, [1992] ECR I-4431.

waste originating outside of the region. This prohibition applied both to hazardous and non-hazardous waste and followed 'an abnormal, massive influx of waste' into the region.[51]

In so far as the ban related to trade in hazardous waste, the Court found that this matter had been the subject of exhaustive Community-level harmonization, and hence that autonomous Member State action going beyond the requirements of the Community directive was precluded. In so far as the regional prohibition applied to trade in non-hazardous waste, the regulatory autonomy of the Member States was preserved, subject of course to the requirements of Articles 30–36.[52] Were the measure to be classified as distinctly applicable it could be saved only by virtue of Article 36. Yet this exception appeared to offer little succour to the Wallonian government. It would scarcely have been credible to invoke requirements relating to the protection of public health in respect of a measure regulating the movement of *non-hazardous* waste. The Court, however, accepted that the measure was indistinctly applicable in nature, and hence susceptible to justification on the basis of considerations relating to the protection of the environment. The Court's reasoning is somewhat strained ('exotic' according to one author[53]) and not entirely convincing.

The measure in question appeared to discriminate directly between Wallonian waste and waste originating outwith the region. Admittedly, the measure was equally applicable as regards a substantial proportion of Belgian (non-Wallonian) waste and 'foreign' waste. Nonetheless, in its earlier jurisprudence the Court had confirmed that such regionally specific restrictions should be viewed as distinctly applicable.[54] The Court sought to justify its (unacknowledged) departure from its earlier case law in the following terms:

> ... having regard to the differences between waste produced in one place and that in another and its connection with the place it is produced, the contested measures cannot be considered to be discriminatory.[55]

---

51 Ibid., para. 31.

52 The decision of the Court was, of course, taken prior to the entry into force of Council Regulation 259/93 OJ 1993 L30/1, which regulates transfrontier shipments of all kinds of waste.

53 Oliver, P., *Free Movement of Goods* (Sweet & Maxwell, 1995).

54 See, especially, Case C-21/88 *Du Pont de Nemours Italiana SpA* v *Unita Sanitaria Locale No 2* [1990] ECR I-889.

55 Supra, n. 50, para. 19.

A measure is discriminatory in a formal sense where it treats like situations differently (or in a material sense where it treats unlike situations in the same way). Viewed through an environmental lens, having regard to the principle that environmental damage should as a priority be rectified at source,[56] domestic and 'external' waste are not 'alike' in terms of their environmental effects and consequently differential treatment cannot be equated with discriminatory treatment.[57] Indistinctly applicable in nature, the measure was found to be justified because of the mandatory requirement relating to environmental protection.[58] The Court offers little by way of supporting analysis of the principles of necessity, proportionality and alternative means. While the basic framework of the Community's rules on free movement emerge unscathed from this case, it does demonstrate that application of these rules owes much to political expediency. It is anomalous that environmental protection, 'one of the Community's essential objectives',[59] to 'be integrated into the definition and implementation of other Community policies'[60] has not been included, by way of Treaty amendment, in the list of societal interests deemed worthy of protection under Article 36. This would remain the situation even following the entry into force of the Treaty of Amsterdam.

Beyond the 'paradigm' in the Community's free movement rules

Each of the cases discussed above may be viewed as 'paradigmatic' in the sense referred to in the introduction to this chapter. They arise against a backdrop of physical interdependence, originating in intrinsic product quality. Each measure under consideration

---

56 A principle laid down in Article 130r(2) EC.

57 The Court bolsters its conclusions in this respect by having regard to the Basle Convention on the Transboundary Movement of *Hazardous* Waste and the principles of self-sufficiency and proximity which it sets out, an international agreement not yet in force at the time of the judgment, and to which the Community had not yet become a party.

58 The Advocate-General offered two separate opinions in this case. On each occasion he accepted at the outset that the measure was distinctly applicable in nature and hence that the measure was incompatible with Community law.

59 Case 240/83 *Procureur de la République* v *Association de Défense des Bruleurs de l'Huiles Usagées* [1985] ECR 531, para. 13.

60 Article 130r(2) EC.

aims at the protection of the environment of the importing state.[61] Moreover, each measure is allegedly necessary to address a threat arising out of the physical characteristics of the goods in question. There remains considerable uncertainty as to the proper application of the Community's free movement rules in 'non-paradigmatic' or atypical situations. A scenario may be characterized as such where it exhibits one or both of the following features:

(a) it aims at the protection of an environmental resource which is located outside of the territorial jurisdiction of the importing state;
(b) the environmental threat to be addressed is associated, not with the goods themselves and manifest upon consumption, but with the production processes or techniques employed in their manufacture.

Turning first to the question of 'extra-territoriality'. The Court has studiously avoided engagement with this issue, though it might have been anticipated that some guidance would have been forthcoming in *Gourmetterie van den Burg*.[62] This case arose out of the activities of a Dutch poultry and game undertaking (Gourmetterie van den Burg) which offered for sale, in the Netherlands, 'dead, red, grouse'. The bird species in question was not native to the Netherlands and had, in this case, been imported from the United Kingdom, where they had been hunted in accordance with both domestic and Community law. Trade in this species was, however, prohibited under Dutch law and, in the course of criminal proceedings against Gourmetterie van den Burg, the Dutch High Court requested a preliminary ruling of the European Court pertaining to the construction of Council Directive 79/409 (Wild Birds)[63] and Articles 30–36.

For reasons which, as will be seen, are somewhat surprising, the European Court concluded that recourse to Article 36 was precluded in the circumstances of this case. The wild birds directive

---

[61] In the *Danish Bottles* case it is, admittedly, not entirely clear whether the primary objective of the measure was to reduce the quantity of waste to be disposed of in Denmark and hence to protect the domestic environment, or to conserve those natural resources utilised in the production of containers, thus contributing to environmental protection in the exporting state.
[62] Case C-169/89 [1990] ECR I-2143.
[63] OJ 1979 L103/1.

was deemed to regulate exhaustively the Member States' powers with regard to the conservation of wild birds. '[T]he Court has consistently held ... that a directive providing for full harmonization of national legislation deprives a Member State of recourse to that article [Article 36]'.[64] The Community was deemed, through legislation, to have 'occupied the field' and hence to have preempted Member State action in so far as it was incompatible with that directive. Having regard to the terms and objectives of the wild birds directive, the Court found that a prohibition on the importation and marketing of 'dead, red, grouse' could not be justified.

The Court's reasoning in respect of the wild birds directive and, relatedly, the scope of application of Articles 30-36, is somewhat strained. Article 14 of that directive explicitly authorizes Member States to introduce stricter protective measures than those for which it provides. The directive appears to take the form of a minimum, not exhaustive, harmonization measure.[65] It might therefore have been anticipated that the directive would constitute merely the 'floor' to Member State action (below which they are not permitted to sink) and Articles 30-36 the 'ceiling'.[66] Indeed, this is the approach endorsed by Advocate-General van Gerven in this case. Yet the Court specifically cites Article 14 as evidence of the exhaustive nature of the directive. '[T]he fact remains that Article 14 authorizes the Member States to introduce stricter protective measures ... . The directive has *therefore* regulated exhaustively the Member States' powers with regard to the conservation of wild birds'.[67] Ultimately, the Court concludes that Article 14 sanctions the adoption of more stringent measures only in respect of certain species of birds; those which are endangered, migratory or occurring within the territory of the regulating state. This, according to Kramer, 'seems to be a contradiction':[68]

> ... insofar as Article 14 does not apply, it cannot exclude the application of Article 36 of the EEC Treaty. Since the Court gives a limited field of application to Article 14, it cannot, at the same

64 Supra, n. 62, para. 8.
65 On minimum harmonization see Weatherill, S., *Law and Integration in the European Union* (OUP, 1995).
66 Supra, n. 1.
67 Supra, n. 62, para. 9 (emphasis added).
68 Kramer, L., *European Environmental Law: Casebook* (Sweet & Maxwell, 1993), p. 153.

time, argue that Article 14 is of general application to all birds and thus exclude the application of Article 36 to any bird.[69]

This point is not entirely convincing. One may argue equally that it is only through a reading of Article 14 which is such as to confine its application to particular bird species, that the Court may conclude that the directive is exhaustive in respect at least of those other species to which it does not apply. Read in this way, Article 14 precludes the adoption of stricter measures in relation to a residual category of birds (into which the red grouse falls) and is consequently exhaustive in respect of this residual category.[70] This, nevertheless, does not diminish the force of Kramer's arguments relating to the substantive scope of Article 14. The Court's construction is artificial, and there is little by way of sustenance for it in either the wording or the objectives of the directive. Yet it is this very artificiality which facilitates the Court's apparent endeavour to avoid addressing the sensitive issue of the territorial scope of Article 36.

Gourmetterie van den Burg, in this sense, represents a missed opportunity. No more so, however, than proceedings before the French *Cour de Cassation* in *Vituret et Chambon.*[71] Here the French Court sanctioned, under Article 36, a French prohibition on the importation of 'woodcock paté' from Belgium. The issue of extra-territoriality is simply not addressed by this Court, and no preliminary ruling requested. Like the red grouse, however, the woodcock is neither migratory or endangered, nor (in the case of those birds used in the production of the pâté) occurring within France. Notwithstanding the French court's somewhat spurious findings on Article 6(4) of the directive,[72] the European Court again might have been inclined to neatly side-step the Article 36 issue, in favour of a ruling premised solely upon a construction of the wild birds directive.

[69] Ibid.
[70] Though it is possible, in this way, to impose a certain logic on the Court's approach, it is important to remember that the Court reaches its conclusions regarding the exhaustive nature of the directive even before it turns to consider the substantive scope of Article 14.
[71] *The State (France)* v *Vituret and Chambon* [1995] 1 CMLR 185.
[72] Article 6(4) permits Member States to continue to apply existing national rules in relation to species listed in Annex 3/3. This is, however, a transitory provision with effect only until such time as the Commission adopts a decision on the transfer of such species to Annex 3/2; a decision which is to be adopted within four months of the implementation deadline laid down in the directive (two years after notification).

In the absence of a direct ruling on this point, the significance of a territorial nexus in the application of Article 36 and mandatory requirements remains uncertain. One recent decision of the Court, though arising in a different context, may be cited as offering tentative support to those who argue that Member States may deploy trade related environmental measures only with a view to protecting 'their own' environment. In *Alpine Investments*[73] the Court emphasised that 'the protection of consumers in the other Member States is not, as such, a matter for the Netherlands authorities'.[74] Hence the interests of these 'foreign' consumers could not in itself constitute a justification for an indistinctly applicable Dutch measure prohibiting 'cold-calling' by firms established in the Netherlands. Equally, in *Gourmetterie van den Burg* it should be recalled that the Court, in construing the wild birds directive, sanctions the adoption of stricter measures in respect of, on the one hand, birds occurring within the territory of the regulating state, and on the other, those species which are migratory or endangered. Territoriality may be thought to provide the rationale for each of these categories, even the latter. Endangered species, conceived as part of the Community's 'common heritage', constitute a shared resource forming part of the global (or Union) commons. While not directly on point, this case may be thought to offer a hesitant insight into the mind-set of the Court on this issue, revealing an inclination to endorse territoriality while, at the same time, conceding a broad (to include the global commons) construction of the parameters of the territorial reach of the Member States.

Were the Court in fact to adopt such an approach, it would not only preclude the application of Article 36 and mandatory requirements in 'type a' non-paradigmatic situations, but also in the majority of 'type b' scenarios (where the environmental or other threat originates in production processes rather than in intrinsic product quality). Except where the environmental hazards associated with production or manufacture 'spillover' physically to the territory of the importing state (or perhaps the global commons), trade restrictions instituted on this basis would by definition be 'extra-territorial' in nature. Yet would such physical spillover effects, arising out of production techniques, be such as to justify recourse to Article

[73] Supra, n. 4.
[74] Ibid., para. 43.

36 or mandatory requirements? Once again, speculation is the order of the day.[75]

Application of the established principles of necessity and proportionality might tend to militate in favour of a negative response. Necessity, as was noted above, speaks in essence to cause and effect. It pertains to the sufficiency and effectiveness of a measure. In the case of trade restrictions motivated by concerns about production processes, such measures are largely contingent in their effect. In so far as such measures fail to exert sufficient pressure (economic or moral) to affect a change of policy on the part of the exporting state, their capacity to contribute to the protection of the environment is marginal, at best; and only that where the magnitude of the risk associated with production is proportionate to the scale of output, and the trade restriction in question is capable of ensuring an overall reduction in production, rather than merely a deflection in terms of patterns of trade. Even where it might be demonstrated that such restrictions are marginally beneficial – in a direct sense – and hence strictly necessary, such is the degree of market fragmentation engendered by them that they may only rarely, if ever, be viewed as truly proportionate.

This space, beyond the paradigm in the trade/environment debate, is of profound importance to the future of environmental regulation in the European Union. The arguments in favour, and against, the application of the free movement exceptions in such situations are finely balanced; in essence 'green imperialism' versus 'the race to the bottom'. The Court has demonstrated a marked reluctance to sanction recourse to trade mechanisms, even in order to promote compliance with objectives established in Community legislation. In *Hedley Lomas* it places emphasis upon the importance of mutual trust between the Member States.[76] It is not hard to appreciate that the economically more powerful Member States might seek, beyond the paradigm, to employ the free trade rules as a means of imposing their own standards on their unwilling, but ultimately dependent, trading partners; or that economic 'might' would come to signal 'right' though, in some cases, barely concealed beneath a surface of parochial protectionism. Yet the cries

---

75 See Ch. 5 for a discussion of this issue in international law.
76 Case C-5/94 *R* v *Ministry of Agriculture, Fisheries and Food,* ex p *Hedley Lomas (Ireland) Ltd* [1996] ECR I-2553, para. 19.

of 'sovereignty' which accompany such concerns merit closer analysis.[77]

Sovereignty, though established in law, may be illusory in practice. An ethos of 'live and let live' may offer small comfort to a state whose *de facto* regulatory autonomy is undermined by virtue of 'economic' as opposed to 'physical' spillover effects. To the extent that environmental regulation may be thought to impose significant costs upon industry – and to what extent this is in fact true is a matter of considerable debate[78] – de-regulation may be the only viable alternative to trade restrictions beyond the paradigm. In the face of intense 'competition between rules', sovereignty may emerge as a slim defence against powerful (and mobile) economic actors, well versed in a strategy of Member State 'divide and rule'. Such issues arise not only in respect of intra-Community trade, but, *a fortiori*, in the context of the Community's external trade relations with third countries.

---

[77] For a fuller discussion see Scott, J., 'The GATT and Community Law: Rethinking the "Regulatory Gap"' in Shaw and More (eds), *New Legal Dynamics of European Union* (OUP, 1995).

[78] See Stewart, R., *Environmental Regulation and International Competitiveness* (1993) 102 Yale LJ 2039, for an overview of the literature on this topic.

CHAPTER FIVE

Trade and environment: an external relations perspective

The previous chapter focused upon Articles 30–6 EC and the trade/environment debate in the context of the Community's internal market. It was seen that the principle of the free movement of goods is not absolute and that Member States may, in strictly controlled circumstances, restrict the importation of goods from other Member States with a view to protecting the environment. This chapter will move on to consider a distinct, though related, issue, viz. the relationship between trade and environment in the Community's external relations with third (non-Community) countries. This topic raises a host of important legal questions, associated, for example, with the issue of choice of legal basis and the division of competence as between the Community and its Member States. It highlights further questions pertaining to the role and status of the World Trade Organization Agreement (WTO) in the Community legal order, and the substantive constraints which this imposes on the Community in contemplating recourse to external trade related environmental measures (TREMs).

The issues arising are by no means hypothetical. A substantial body of Community law has emerged regulating the environmental dimension of the Community's external trade relations. Among the most important are those relating to trade in certain wildlife and plant species and derived products,[1] and those regulating trade in waste and dangerous substances, including chemicals.[2] These

---

[1] See Council Directive 83/129 OJ 1983 L91/30 (seal pups); Council Regulation 3254/91 OJ 1991 L308/1 and Commission Regulation 35/97 OJ 1997 L8/2 (leghold traps); and Council Regulation 3387/97 OJ 1997 L61/1 (wild flora and fauna).

[2] Council Regulation 259/93 OJ 1993 L30/1 (waste); Council Directive 92/3/Euratom OJ 1992 L35/24 (radioactive waste); Council Regulation 2455/92 OJ 1992 L251/13 (dangerous chemicals); and Council Regulation 594/91 OJ 1991 L67/1 (ozone depleting substances).

measures make use of a broad array of trade-related instruments, ranging from a straightforward import/export ban[3] or quantitative restrictions,[4] to systems of licensing,[5] notification or prior informed consent (PIC).[6] The legislation is, in certain cases, gratifyingly straightforward. The seal pups directive extends to a mere four articles, with a single short annex. In others, especially those concerned with waste and flora and fauna, it is mind-numbingly complex. This chapter will not examine these various regimes in any great detail. It should, however, be read alongside the primary legislation concerned.

Much, though not all, of the Community legislation in this field has emerged after a pre-existing international agreement. Of particular importance are the Montreal Protocol to the Vienna Convention on substances that deplete the ozone layer, the Basel Convention on the control of transboundary movements of hazardous wastes and their disposal,[7] and the Washington Convention on international trade in endangered species of wild fauna and flora (CITES). Each of these agreements specifically requires the introduction of TREMs, though in certain respects, especially with CITES, the Community has introduced more far-reaching measures than those provided for under the Convention.

In certain cases the Community has enacted TREMs with a view to protecting the Community environment. It should be recalled that the concept of environmental policy in the Treaty is broadly defined, to include protection of public health. Other legislative enactments are concerned principally with preserving and improving environmental quality in the 'global commons'; the ozone depleting substances regulation being the clearest example. A third category of measure is characterized by the fact that the object of protection (seal pups or furry animals, for example) is situated in a third state. This is true of the waste regulation and

---

3   For example, supra, n. 1, seal pups and leghold traps.
4   For example, supra, n. 2, ozone depleting substances.
5   Ibid., chemcials and waste. PIC refers to the consent of the party whose territory the product is to be introduced into.
6   For example, supra, n. 1, flora and fauna.
7   The Community regulation on the transfrontier shipments of waste is intended to implement three international agreements; the Basel Convention, the Lomé Convention, and a 1992 OECD Decision on the control of transfrontier movements of waste destined for recovery operations. Thus, different rules apply to different groups of countries and also according to whether the waste is destined for recovery or disposal. Hence the complexity of this regime.

the chemicals directives, in so far as they restrict exports from the Community to third states. It is also true, in part, of the flora and fauna regulation, implementing the CITES Convention. Before turning to consider the substantive implications of those parts of the WTO Agreement pertaining to trade and environment, it is necessary to examine the legal questions surrounding Community competence to enact TREMs.

Trade or environment: the classification conundrum

Paul Demaret published a seminal paper in 1993 on the subject of external Community TREMs.[8] In it he stated emphatically that '[a]s a matter of Community law, the *Chernobyl 1* and *GSP 1* judgments seem to settle the issue: TREMs should be based on Article 113. This is indeed the right solution'.[9] The problem for which this solution was propounded relates to the legal classification of TREMs. These take shape at the interface between trade and environment, pursuing environmental objectives through recourse to instruments of international trade. The Community enjoys competence both in the sphere of external trade under Article 113 (common commercial policy), and in relation to environmental policy by virtue of Article 130s. Under each it enjoys power both to enact legislation and to enter into international agreements. Yet the competence which it can claim in respect to each is qualitatively different.

The Community enjoys *a priori* exclusive competence in respect of common commercial policy.[10] That is to say that Member States are, even in the absence of Community measures, precluded from entering this sphere except in so far as they are specifically authorized to do so by the Community.[11] This reflects the identity of the Community as a customs union in which goods, having lawfully entered the territory of a single Member State, are put into

---

8 'Environmental Policy and Commercial Policy: The Emergence of Trade-Related Environmental Measures (TREMs) in the External Relations of the European Community' in Maresceau, M., *The European Community's Commercial Policy after 1992; the Legal Dimension* (Martinus Nijhoff, 1993).

9 Ibid., p. 352.

10 For judicial authority for this proposition, see Case 41/76 *Donckerwolcke* v *Procureur de la République* [1976] ECR 1921.

11 Ibid., para. 32.

free circulation and assimilated with goods originating within the Community.[12] The Community, on the contrary, enjoys merely concurrent competence in respect of environmental policy. That is to say that, in the absence of Community measures, Member States retain autonomy to regulate this sphere. Community measures, once enacted, take the form of minimum harmonization measures and, as was seen in Chapter 2, Member States may maintain or enact more stringent protective measures. Hence, the choice of legal basis for TREMs impinges not only at the level of legislative procedure, but also in terms of the residual autonomy of Member States.

Such is the nature of Community law that, with the passage of time, Demaret's certitude appears surprising. He is not necessarily wrong but it is by no means clear that he is right. There is some support for his proposition in the case law of the Court. The Court has favoured an expansive interpretation of the concept of common commercial policy; this with a view to ensuring that it does not become 'nugatory' over time.[13] It has adopted a dynamic interpretation 'in order to take account of any changes of outlook in international relations'.[14] In the *Chernobyl*[15] case, the contested measure regulated imports of agricultural products in the wake of the nuclear accident. This aimed both to safeguard the health of consumers and to maintain the unity of the Community market, by preventing deflections of trade (as between Member State) while avoiding 'unduly adverse effects on trade between the Community and third countries'.[16] The Court, purporting to have regard to the regulation's objective and content, concluded that it was intended to regulate trade between the Community and third countries, and hence fell within the scope of Article 113.

More recently, in *Werner*[17] and *Liefer*,[18] the Court held that national measures restricting the export of so-called dual-use goods (goods with the potential to be deployed for military purposes) fell within the scope of Article 113, notwithstanding that they pursued foreign policy and security objectives. Here, the Court emphasized

12 Ibid., para. 25.
13 *Opinion 1/78* [1979] ECR 2871, p. 2913.
14 Case 45/86 *Commission* v *Council* (GSP) [1987] ECR 1493, para. 19.
15 Case C-62/88 *Greece* v *Council* [1990] ECR I-1527.
16 Ibid., para. 14.
17 Case C-70/94 [1995] ECR I-3189.
18 Case C-83/94 [1995] ECR I-3231.

that the 'effects' of the national measures was to prevent or restrict exports, and that consequently they could not be treated as falling outside the scope of the common commercial policy. Such measures were permissible only in the event that they were specifically authorized by the Community.

Nevertheless, recent legislative practice leans in the direction of a preference for Article 130s. Whereas the leghold trap regulation was adopted upon a dual legal basis (113 and 130s), Community legislation pertaining to waste, flora and fauna and ozone depleting substances took, as its legal basis, Article 130s alone. In *Parliament* v *Council*,[19] the Court found that the Community's regulation on transfrontier shipments of waste had been correctly based upon Article 130s. However, this judgment is predicated exclusively upon a consideration of the European Parliament's arguments that the regulation, in so far as it governed movements of waste *within* the Community, should have been based upon Article 100a. That part of the application, pertaining to Article 113 and the external dimension of the waste regulation, was declared inadmissible, as having no bearing upon the prerogatives of Parliament in the legislative process.[20] Nevertheless, this judgment ought not to be dismissed as entirely irrelevant to this discussion.

First, taking us back to Chapter 1, it reminds us that *Chernobyl* is a product of the *Titanium Dioxide* age. Times have changed. The Court now seeks out the centre of gravity of a measure, be it in terms of its objectives or its effects. It no longer exhibits the same automatic preference for Article 100a, wherever there is so much as a hint of a relationship to the Community's internal market objective. Second, if one accepts as Demaret, like Eeckhout, has argued, that Article 113 should be viewed as the flipside of Article 100a, and that 'Article 113 should therefore be used as the legal basis for measures regulating [external] trade matters which, in the Community's internal relations, would come under Article 100a',[21] then *Parliament* v *Council* emerges as important indeed. As recourse to Article 100a, as a legal basis for internal market

---

19 Case C-187/93 [1994] ECR I-2857.
20 See Article 173 on Parliament's standing to bring actions for annulment. At the time the waste regulation was adopted Article 113, unlike Article 130s, did not even provide formally for consultation with Parliament. Even today, and post-Amsterdam, the European Parliament enjoys substantially greater powers under the latter.
21 Supra, n. 8, p. 353. See also Eeckhout, P., *The European Internal Market and International Trade: A Legal Analysis* (OUP, 1994) pp. 256–8.

harmonization, diminishes, so too the role of Article 113, as a legal basis for what Eeckhout calls 'external harmonization' may be anticipated to contract, though certainly not to vanishing point.

This, as was noted above, would imply a relative shift from exclusive to concurrent competence. Yet the implications of this in terms of Community coherence in relation to third countries may be less dramatic than they first appear. This might be illustrated by reference to a proposal currently pending before the Lower House of the Dutch Parliament. This aims to prohibit, at the end of a transitional period, the importation into the Netherlands of wood which has been harvested in a non-sustainable manner. Were the proposal to be adopted (which, by all accounts, seems unlikely) the resulting ban would apply both to goods originating in the other Member States and in third countries. Legal analysis of the Dutch proposal is complicated by the considerable uncertainty which surrounds the question of its 'identity', and the classification conundrum addressed above.

Assuming an absence of specific Community legislation on this topic, it would still be open for the Dutch government to argue, were this viewed as a commercial policy measure, that it is compatible with the Treaty and in keeping with the principle of exclusivity which underpins Article 113. Council Regulation 3285/94[22] laying down common rules for imports within the framework of the CCP, provides, in Article 24, that Member States are not precluded from restricting the entry of goods from third countries, on the basis of the grounds listed in Article 36 of the Treaty. Demaret accepts that '[t]o these grounds, the mandatory requirements in the meaning of the *Cassis de Dijon* case law should be added for reasons of consistency'.[23] This may be construed as constituting a specific authorization in terms of the *Donckerwolcke* formula. Hence, subject to the principles of necessity and proportionality,[24] and pursuant to an obligation to inform the Commission of such measures, Member States have, even in the context of Article 113, retained the freedom to restrict the entry of third country goods.

---

22 OJ 1994 L349/53.
23 Supra, n. 8, p. 347. He made this argument at a time when the previous import regulation (288/82) was still in force. As a matter of logic this argument remains convincing but, given that the 1994 regulation remains unaltered in this respect, it is by no means certain that the Court would accept this interpretation.
24 See *Werner* and *Liefer*, supra, nn. 17 and 18, where the Court construes the equivalent exception in Council Regulation 2603/69 laying down common rules for exports.

To deny this possibility would lead to the absurd conclusion that Member States are authorized 'to restrict the movement of goods within the internal market more than movement between themselves and non-member countries'.[25] Hence, while the Court has clung steadfastly to the principle of exclusivity underlying Article 113,[26] it has interpreted the concept of specific authorization in such a way as to soften the blow it delivers to Member State competence.

Were this measure to be classified as environmental in nature, it is readily apparent that *de jure* the Dutch governments room for manoeuvre on the external plane would be more substantial. The discipline inherent in Article 36 and mandatory requirements would not bite.[27] That said, the Dutch government would not be entirely unconstrained. The *de facto* effectiveness of any measure falling outside of Article 36 or the mandatory requirements doctrine would be diminished by virtue of the phenomenon of trade deflection. In so far as the measure relates to imports from other Member States, regardless of the origin of those goods, it would be incompatible with Article 30. Hence, timber harvested in a non-sustainable manner could enter the Dutch market, via another Member State. The introduction of an external TREM, in this situation, would be of limited utility.

One final question remains as to the autonomy of the Dutch government in such circumstances. Demaret expresses concern about the implications of recourse to Article 130s from the perspective of the Community's participation in GATT. It will be seen that TREMs are regulated within the framework of the GATT 1994 and other associated agreements on trade in goods. In the case of the WTO agreements on trade in goods, it is the Community, rather than its Member States, which are answerable before the WTO dispute settlements bodies in the event of a complaint by another contracting party. This gives rise to the possibility that the Community will be condemned, under GATT law, for the wrong-doing of a Member State. Yet, in so far as the

---

25 Ibid., *Werner*, para. 25.
26 See Gilsdorf, P., 'Portée et délimitation des compétences communautaires en matière de politique commerciale' (1989) RMC 195, for a suggestion that the Court should abandon exclusivity in relation to those parts of commercial policy which may be considered marginal.
27 This may be of considerable importance depending upon whether Articles 30–36 are ultimately construed as sanctioning trade restrictions which seeks to protect an environmental resource situated outwith the territory of the regulating state. See Ch. 4.

WTO Agreement constitutes a part of Community law, it is binding also upon the Member States. It is for the Community to take
steps, according to its own enforcement procedures, to ensure that
the Member States respect the terms of this agreement. There are,
however, substantial difficulties associated with the enforcement of
WTO/GATT in the Community legal order. In the case of Member
States, the Commission has been reluctant to pursue Article 169
actions in the case of an alleged infringement of the GATT. Ehlermann, formerly head of the Commission Legal Service, argues that
the Commission 'dislikes the idea of using specifically Community
provisions to do non-member countries' business for them'.[28] As
will be seen, these difficulties also extend to enforcing
GATT/WTO against the Community's own institutions.

The WTO Agreement and Community law

On 20 September 1986 the Punta del Este Ministerial Declaration
launched the Uruguay Round of Multilateral Trade Negotiations.
Eight years later the Uruguay Round Final Act was signed at Mar-
rakesh. By adopting the Final Act, signatories agreed to submit for
approval, to the competent national authorities, the World Trade
Organization Agreement (WTO). Annexed to this agreement, and
integral to it, are a number of multilateral trade agreements, including, in the area of goods, the GATT 1994, the Agreement on
Technical Barriers to Trade (TBT), and the Agreement on Sanitary
and Phytosanitary Measures (SPS). The European Court, in its
WTO Opinion,[29] accepted that the European Community, on the
basis of Article 113, was exclusively competent to enter into these
(and other) agreements regulating trade in goods. The Community
is a party to these agreements and they are binding upon the institutions of the Community.[30] The significance of this for the evolution of the Community's environmental policy – and not merely
in its specifically external manifestations – should not be underestimated.

That said, for reasons which have been fiercely criticised by aca-

---

28 Ehlermann, C.-D., 'Application of GATT Rules in the EC' in Hilf, Jacobs and
Petersmann, (eds) *The European Community and the GATT* (Kluwer, 1986),
p. 139.
29 Opinion 1/94 [1994] ECR I-5267.
30 See Council Decision 94/800 OJ 1994 L336/1.

demic commentators, the European Court has denied – in relation to the earlier GATT 1947 – the capacity of this agreement for direct effect.[31] Consequently, national courts are precluded from relying upon this agreement in actions before them,[32] and the European Court, when faced with an Article 177 reference concerning the validity of a Community act, has consistently refused to assess validity in the light of the GATT. Similarly, in the context of Article 173 direct actions for annulment, the European Court has denied the justiciability of the GATT except in so far as the Community act under attack was intended to implement the GATT or explicitly refers to it.[33] Though it has been argued that objectively the 'new' GATT may, by virtue of its characteristics, be considered suitable for adjudication before courts – national and Community – Council Decision 94/800 expressly provides, in the preamble, that the agreement is not suitable for application before either the national or the Community courts.[34]

One argument which has been put forth as militating in favour of the direct effect of GATT 1994 relates to the new Understanding and Rules and Procedures Governing the Settlement of Disputes annexed to the WTO Agreement.[35] If, in the past the 'dispute settlement procedure of the GATT ... constitutes one of the obstacles to its direct effect',[36] the new procedures laid down are characterized by a 'significant legalization' and 'quasi-judicialization' of the dispute settlement procedures.[37] In particular, it is no longer possible for the party whose actions form the subject matter of a complaint, to veto the adoption of either a GATT panel report, or the findings of the newly established Appellate Body constituted to hear appeals on points of law. Regardless of whether,

31 For critical analysis see Petersmann, E.-U., 'Application of the GATT by the Court of Justice of the European Communities' (1993) 20 CMLR 1147 and Eeckhout, P., 'The Domestic Status of the WTO Agreement: Interconnecting Legal Systems' (1997) 34 CMLRev. 11.
32 Case 2-4/72 *International Fruit Company* [1972] ECR 1219.
33 Case C-280/93 *Germany* v *Council* [1994] ECR I-4973.
34 The Court, having regard to GATT's general spirit, scheme and terms, emphasized the flexibility of the GATT particularly as regards the possibilities of derogation and to adopt safeguard measures, and the nature of the dispute settlement mechanism, as militating against its justiciability. On the significance of the Uruguay Round changes in this respect see Eeckhout, supra, n. 31.
35 Annex 2.
36 Maresceau, M., 'The GATT in the Case-Law of the European Court of Justice' in Hilf, Jacobs and Petersmann, supra, n. 28, p. 105.
37 See Lowenfeld, A., 'Remedies Along with Rights: Institutional Reform in the New GATT' (1994) 88 AJIL 477.

ultimately, this will be sufficient to persuade the European Court to reassess its position on the justiciability of the GATT, it marks a transition, in international law, toward a 'GATT with teeth', a GATT which neither the Community, nor its Member States, can afford to ignore.[38]

The WTO and TREMs

The GATT is, first and foremost, premised upon the principle of non-discrimination. Article III establishes the concept of national treatment as regards internal taxes, charges and regulations. National measures may be applied to imported products provided that they are accorded treatment which is no less favourable than that accorded to 'like' domestic goods, and that national measures are not applied in such a manner as to afford protection to domestic production. Article II lays down the most favoured national principle (MFN) which precludes discrimination as between contracting parties. Thus, the GATT, when compared to to Article 30 EC, appears rather tame. Though it prohibits, in Article XI, quantitative restrictions on imports and exports, it is predicated upon the principle of non-discrimination as opposed to mutual recognition. Nonetheless, upon closer analysis, it is apparent that the autonomy of WTO contracting parties is quite dramatically circumscribed. This is due to a number of factors, notably the manner in which the concept of 'like' products has been construed under Article III, the narrow parameters of the GATT, Article XX, exceptions, and the additional discipline inherent in the TBT and SPS Agreements.

Turning first to Article III: in assessing the lawfulness of a national measure under GATT, it is necessary first to determine whether it is protected under Article III. The blanket of protection which this offers is more limited than it may at first appear. This is due, in particular, to the fact that the concept of 'like' products is adjudged on the basis of the intrinsic characteristics of the products in question. For the purpose of comparison, production process is not relevant. Production processes do not, according to this construction, serve to differentiate domestic and imported goods

---

[38] Montana I Mora, M., 'A GATT with Teeth?: Law Wins Over Politics in the Resolution of International Trade Disputes' (1993) 31 CJIL 103.

under Article III.[39] Differential treatment, on the basis of differences in production process, will amount to discriminatory treatment. The example of the Community's leghold trap regulation serves to exemplify this.

Council Regulation 3254/91 (the basic regulation)[40] prohibits, as of 1 January 1995, the use of leghold traps in the Community; these being defined as a device designed to restrain or capture an animal by means of jaws which close tightly upon one or more of the animal's limbs, thereby preventing withdrawal of the limb or limbs from the trap. It was further to prohibit, by virtue of Article 3(1), the introduction into the Community of pelts (undressed skins) and manufactured goods of certain fur bearing mammals, unless these originate in a country which has banned the use of such traps or uses methods which meet internationally agreed humane trapping standards. It was for the Commission, acting in accordance with a regulatory committee procedure, to draw up a list of countries satisfying one of these criteria. The ban was to come into effect on 1 January 1995, with the possibility of a one-year suspension for those countries deemed to be making sufficient progress in developing humane methods of trapping. On 19 July 1994 the Commission adopted Regulation 1771/94,[41] which provided that the ban would enter into force on 1 January 1996, and that the Commission was to determine, before 1 September 1995, which countries satisfied the conditions specified in Article 3(1) of the basic regulation. Although the Commission did, in late 1995, submit a draft list of countries, it wrote to Member States on 8 December 1995, informing them that implementation of the prohibition was for the time being impracticable, and asking them to refrain from customs action which would be likely to disrupt trade in the goods concerned.[42] It also stated its intention to submit a proposal for the amendment of the basic regulation. The basic problem facing the Commission appeared to be a delay in the formulation, within the International Standards Organization, of in-

---

[39] This interpretation is supported by the following GATT 'case law': *Belgian Family Allowances* (1953) 1 BISD supp. 59; *United States Restrictions on Imports of Tuna* 33 ILM 839 (1994), pp. 889–90; *United States Standards for Reformulated and Conventional Gasoline* 35 ILM (1996), p. 274 (panel report), p. 603 (Appellate Body Report).

[40] OJ 1991 L308/1.

[41] OJ 1994 L184/3.

[42] Case T-228/95 *Lehrfreund* v *Council and Commission* [1996] ECR II-111, para. 9.

ternationally agreed humane trapping standards. As a result, the new Commission proposal militated in the direction of a bilateral, as opposed to multilateral, approach, whereby framework agreements on humane animal trapping standards would be negotiated as between the Community and third states.[43] In the absence of a ban on leghold traps, a formal commitment on the part of third states to implement such agreements would suffice for such a state to be excluded from the Commission's list of non-approved countries. At this time the Commission also proposed to exempt pelts and goods resulting from trapping activities carried out by indigenous peoples, a source of considerable acrimony between the Community, and the United States and Canada. Although this proposal has not been adopted, the Council authorized the Commission to negotiate a framework agreement with Canada, the United States, the Russian Federation, and other interested parties. The resulting proposal for a Council Decision concerning the signing and conclusion of this agreement (based upon Articles 113 and 100a) claims, in its preamble, that 'it satisfies the concept of internationally agreed humane trapping standards referred to in the second indent of Article 3(1)' of the basic regulation.[44] Agreement was reached, as between the Community, Russia and Canada, on 20 June 1997. This was opposed by the United Kingdom, Austria and Belgium and has been the subject of fierce criticism by the European Parliament.[45] Finally, Commission Regulation 35/97 lays down provisions for the implementation of the basic regulation, for the certification of products. This is to apply from the first day of the third month following the publication of an Article 3(1) list of 'approved' countries. This list was published in the official journal on 4th September 1997.[46] As things currently stand, the United States is excluded from this list (but see COM97 726 final).

This Community regime for leghold traps is unlikely to derive protection from Article III. According to this, one otter pelt is to be regarded as 'like' any other, regardless of the manner in which the animal was trapped, and regardless of the regulatory framework prevailing in the state in which it was caught. To permit the

---

[43] COM(95) 737 final.

[44] COM(97) 17 final.

[45] See European Voice on-line: http://www.european-voice.com

[46] OJ 1997 L8/2. This also provides that animals born and bred in captivity may be imported into the Community. See Council Decision 97/602 OJ 1997 L242/64 for the Article 3(1) list.

marketing of domestic goods, but to prohibit the importation of 'like' goods from certain third countries, on the basis of differences in production process, will amount to less favourable treatment under Article III. Having failed the national treatment test, the measure will fall for consideration under Article XI. Such an import ban, clearly being a quantitative restriction, is to be evaluated in the light of the Article XX exceptions, which provide:

> Subject to the requirement that such measures are not applied in a manner which would constitute a means of arbitrary or unjustifiable discrimination between countries where the same conditions prevail, or a disguised restriction on international trade, nothing in this Agreement shall be construed to prevent the adoption of enforcement by any contracting parties of measures:
>
> . . . .
>
> (b) necessary to protect human, animal, or plant life or health;
>
> . . . .
>
> (g) relating to the conservation of exhaustible natural resources if such measures are made effective in conjunction with restrictions on domestic production or consumption.

These provisions have been strictly construed by GATT panels, and more recently by the WTO Appellate Body. For example, the term 'necessary' has been interpreted to necessitate the application of a least restrictive means test. '[A] contracting party is bound to use, among the measures reasonably available to it, that which entails the least degree of inconsistency with other GATT provisions'.[47] Hence, in the first Tuna/Dolphin panel report, significance was attached to the fact that '[t]he United States had not demonstrated . . . that it had exhausted all options reasonably available to it to pursue its dolphin protection objectives . . ., in particular through the negotiation of international cooperative arrangements'.[48] This approach to the concept of necessity has been condemned by Schoenbaum as according neither with the 'grammar and syntax' of the paragraph in which the term is contained, nor with the structure of Article XX as a whole.[49] So strict is that, according to Schoenbaum, it 'leads to the quiet demise' of the 'chapeau' to this article which comprises a more tolerant standard of review.

---

[47] Tuna/Dolphin 2, supra, n. 39, pp. 896–7.
[48] (1992) 30 ILM 1598, para. 5.28.
[49] Schoenbaum, T.J., 'International Trade and Protection of the Environment: The Continuing Search for Reconciliation' (1997) 91 AJIL 268, pp. 276–7.

Similarly, the terms 'relating to' and 'in conjunction with' in Article XX(g) have been construed by a number of GATT panels as requiring an assessment of the primary aim of the measure, having regard both to its purpose and effect. A national measure is to be exempted only where it is 'primarily aimed' at the conservation of natural resources, and 'primarily aimed' at rendering effective the restrictions on domestic consumption or production.[50] More recently, the Appellate Body has adopted a more circumspect approach in its construction of Article XX(g), emphasising that the term 'primarily aimed' does not derive from the text of the Treaty and cannot be viewed as a 'simple litmus test for inclusion or exclusion from Article XX(g)'.[51] The Appellate Body, in examining US rules relating to the annual baseline to be deployed in the calculation of the composition of gasoline, accepted that the measures did relate to conservation and that they were made effective in conjunction with domestic restrictions. The panel emphasized that the baseline establishment rules could not be regarded as 'merely incidentally or inadvertently aimed' at conservation', applying a test which appears to be the inverse of that favoured by the panel.

Moreover, it argued that the phrase 'made effective in conjunction with . . .' should not be read as establishing an 'empirical "effects test" ', due to difficulties associated with determining causation, particularly when the observable effects may be distant in time. While this phrase requires a certain 'even-handedness' in the treatment of domestic and imported products, it does not require identical treatment. However, where '*no* restrictions on domestically-produced like products are imposed at all, and all limitations are placed upon imported products *alone*, the measure cannot be accepted as primarily or even substantially designed for implementing conservationist goals. The measure would simply be naked discrimination for protecting locally-produced goods'.[52]

The approach of the Appellate Body meets many of the criticisms put forward by Schoenbaum. In particular, in view of this body's lighter interpretative touch, it falls to the 'chapeau' to screen for 'abuse or illegitimate use' of the Article XX exceptions.[53] Three concepts are inherent in this: arbitrary discrimination, unjustified discrimination, and disguised restriction on trade.

50 Supra, n. 39 (Tuna), p. 893.
51 Supra, n. 39 (Gasoline), p. 19.
52 Ibid., p. 21.
53 Ibid., p. 25.

These, the Appellate Body stresses, are to be read 'side-by-side', as imparting meaning to one another. The report makes it plain that subterfuge, in terms of an attempt to conceal the nature of a restriction or the existence of discrimination, is not a prerequisite for the application of the chapeau. In assessing whether discrimination is arbitrary and/or unjustifiable, and hence whether there is a disguised restriction on trade, the Appellate Body adopts what looks very like a least restrictive means test. In condemning the United States, it observes that there were a number of alternative courses of action available to it, at least one of which would have entirely avoided discrimination. The United States failed to establish 'what, if any, efforts had been taken by [it] to enter into appropriate procedures in cooperation with the governments of Venezuela and Brazil so as to mitigate the administrative problems [associated with existing alternatives] pleaded by the United States'.[54]

As yet, no opportunity has arisen for the new Appellate Body to comment authoritatively upon what is perhaps the most well known, and controversial, aspect of GATT panels' approach to the construction of the environmental exceptions. Through recourse to the language of necessity, in paragraph b, and 'relating to' (primarily aimed at) in paragraph g, and having regard to the objectives of the GATT Agreement, the second tuna/dolphin panel concluded that:

> ... measures taken so as to force other countries to change their policies, and that were effective only if such changes occurred, could not be primarily aimed either at the conservation of an exhaustible natural resource, or at rendering effective restrictions on domestic production or consumption, in the meaning of Article XX(g). [Nor could they be considered 'necessary' for the protection of animal life or health in the sense of Article XX(b).][55]

Hence, while this panel did not accept that there was any territorial limitation inherent in Article XX, and held that parties *are* entitled to seek to protect an environmental resource situated beyond its territorial jurisdiction, it posited the need for a direct causal connection between the measure and the environmental objective pursued. Where a measure is capable of achieving its desired effect only were it to be followed by changes in the policies and practices of exporting states, it cannot fall within the parameters of Article

54 Ibid., p. 27.
55 Supra, n. 39, pp. 894 and 898.

XX. Thus, one state may not restrict the entry of goods, originating in the global commons or in another state, on the basis of the manner in which that good has been produced; at least so long as the importing state does not enjoy jurisdiction over the party procuring the goods. The same cannot be said where the environmental hazard is associated with intrinsic product quality. Here, a trade restriction is capable of directly protecting the environment of the importing state, and is consequently not contingent upon a change of policy on the part of a third state. More often than not, in practice, territoriality is going to define the limits to Article XX, albeit that extra-territorial jurisdiction is accepted, up to a (by no means certain) point in international law.

Returning to the example currently under consideration, namely the Community's leghold trap regulation, this may be argued to be necessary to protect the health of the animal species concerned – even though it aims to do so just as the animals are about to die![56] It is just possible that this measure would be deemed to comply with the least restrictive means test. Time and time again, introduction of the ban has been delayed while the Community has sought to enter into agreements on the subject with its trading partners, or pursuant to the formulation of internationally agreed standards. Were such an agreement to be concluded it would, in principle, take precedence over the GATT, as between parties to both. However, it is notable that the agreement with Canada and Russia provides that it is to apply without prejudice to the parties obligations under the WTO Agreement. Where a state is not party to an agreement, or where a multilateral agreement predates the GATT/WTO,[57] the latter will prevail.

However, there is almost certainly a problem. As in the case of the tuna ban, the leghold trap regulation prohibits the importation of *all* pelts and relevant manufactured goods from countries not included on the Commission's list, other than those which are

---

[56] It is because this regulation only regulates methods of trapping, and pertains purely to quality and not quantity, that it would, in this writer's view, be difficult to argue that it relates to the conservation of an exhaustible resource. This, notwithstanding that the resource need not be endangered to fall within Article XX(g) and also the language of the preamble to the regulation which provides that the abolition of the leghold trap will have a positive effect on the conservation status of threatened or endangered species.

[57] Article 11(4) of the WTO Agreement provides that the GATT 1994 is legally distinct from GATT 1947. Hence it is now the later agreement in relation to a multitude of multilateral environmental agreements, and hence formally takes priority, even as between parties to both.

farmed, regardless of the methods of trapping deployed in relation to a specific consignment of goods. In this it is broadly comparable to the US tuna ban and, as in the tuna case, this factor may be anticipated to alert the WTO dispute settlement bodies to the fact that its aim is to exert pressure upon third countries, with a view to inducing a change of policy on their part. The leghold trap regulation emerges as an ideal candidate to test the new Appellate Body's attitude to extra-jurisdictional measures which are contingent in their environmental effect.[58]

As was noted above, the WTO Agreement, even in so far as it regulates trade in goods, encompasses more than merely the GATT 1994. Annex 1A includes 12 additional multilateral agreements whose status is defined in a General Interpretative Note, which provides that:

> In the event of a conflict between a provision of the General Agreement on Tariffs and Trade 1994 and a provision of another agreement in Annex 1A, the provision of the other agreement shall take precedence to the extent of the conflict.

In other words, both the GATT 1994 and another Annex 1A agreement, may be simultaneously applicable, in so far as they are not incompatible, and in so far as the relevant agreement does not explicitly provide otherwise.[59] Of particular importance to the environment are the SPS and TBT Agreements.[60] These are mutually exclusive in their scope of application. The former covers measures aiming at the protection of animal or plant life or human health, including those regulating *inter alia*, the risks arising from additives, contaminants, toxins or disease-carrying organisms, in food, beverages and feedstuffs. The latter covers all other product standards,[61] which may be applied in so far as they are non-discrimina-

---

58 Relevant here is a case pending before a GATT panel concerning a US import prohibition on certain shrimp and shrimp products which are caught without the use of turtle protection devices.

59 See, for example, Article 2(4) of the agreement on the application of sanitary and phytosanitary measures which provides that SPS measures which conform with this agreement are presumed to be in conformity with the GATT 1994 and in particular Article XX(b).

60 OJ 1994 L336/40 and L336/86.

61 The agreement distinguishes between technical regulations, compliance with which is compulsory and standards, which are voluntary. The term product standards is used here to refer to both. In addition it should be noted that standards pertaining to production process are covered, in so far as production process 'relates' to intrinsic product quality; i.e. where there is a link between method of production and product characteristics.

tory, necessary to fulfil a legitimate objective (including protection of the environment) and do not create unnecessary obstacles to trade. It is thus apparent that WTO law will extend to internal measures, including those which are not specifically designed to regulate trade between parties. Thus, for example, the Community's controversial packaging directive[62] would have to be assessed in the light of the TBT Agreement.

Space precludes a full analysis of these agreements.[63] Of particular significance, however, is the emphasis they place upon scientific reason and evidence. The SPS Agreement, for example, provides that Members are to ensure that any measures applied be based on scientific principles and are not maintained in the absence of sufficient scientific evidence. This is qualified to the extent that where relevant scientific evidence is insufficient, a Member may provisionally adopt SPS measures on the basis of available pertinent information, including that from international organizations and in the light of the measures applied by other Members. This reflects a commitment to the precautionary principle. This commitment notwithstanding, a dispute settlement panel has recently condemned the Community's ban on the introduction of hormone treated meat and meat products.[64] The panel concluded *inter alia* that the community had failed to justify its departure from international standards. The Community had neither based its decision upon a proper risk assessment nor demonstrated scientifically the existence of an identifiable risk to humans. This is an important report and currently the subject of an appeal.[65]

This example of hormone-treated beef raises one final question of considerable importance. The European Community decided to appeal the findings of the panel (see report of the WTO Appellate Body of 16 January 1998), rather than merely accept that a second best solution is to permit the introduction of such meat into the territory of the Community, but to insist that it be labelled as to methods of production. The Community is already contemplating this option in relation to genetically modified wheat. The SPS Agree-

---

62 Council Directive 94/62 OJ 1994 L365/10.
63 See Schoenbaum, supra, n. 49 and Rege, V., 'GATT Law and Environment-Related Issues Affecting the Trade of Developing Countries' 28 (1994) JWT 95.
64 Council Directive 96/22 OJ 1996 L125/3.
65 See EC measures concerning meat and meat products (hormones); http://www.wto.org/

ment extends to measures regulating the packaging and labelling of products in so far as they relate directly to food safety. Again, however, these must be demonstrated to be necessary, having regard to scientific principle and reason. More generally, 'eco-labelling', as it has come to be called, is permitted under the GATT, subject to the MFN principle, and the national treatment standard. This is true both in relation to labelling requirements pertaining to product characteristic and to production process. The former are subject also to the discipline of the TBT Agreement.

Conclusion

The subject of trade and environment, in international law, is as complex as it is controversial. There are few subjects in the environmental sphere about which more has been written.[66] This short chapter aims merely to highlight some of the principal issues arising in so far as they impinge upon the sovereignty and autonomy of the Community, both in regulating its own market and as an international actor. Two factors emerge as of particular importance. First, the Community may not, in general, lawfully demand on the part of imported products, compliance with its own production process standards. In principle, it may not even demand compliance with those process standards which are enshrined in multilateral agreements except in so far as these post-date the WTO Agreement, and the goods originate in a state which is party to the environmental agreement. The WTO Agreement is premised upon an acceptance of the principle of regulatory competition in so far as this relates to the circumstances surrounding the production of goods, rather than the goods themselves. The concept of 'eco-dumping' is not one which is recognized in international law.

Second, even in the case of product standards, the WTO is lurching in a direction which takes us beyond discrimination. For such standards to be lawfully applied to imported goods, these must be justified as being necessary to pursue a legitimate objective. Both the SPS and TBT Agreements are premised upon a clear preference for the application of internationally agreed product standards, and the latter subscribes to the principle of equivalence (mutual recognition) although, at this time, it is not binding upon

---

66 For an up-to-date overview, see the various contributions to (1997) 6 RECIEL.

Members. Each time that the Community enacts measures regulating the quality of goods to be placed on its market, it must consider not only whether these afford protection to domestic goods, but also whether the justification for such measures would stand up in WTO dispute settlement proceedings, and before scientists drafted in to assist the dispute settlement bodies. WTO law impinges upon the Community's sovereignty not merely in respect of TREMs as traditionally conceived, but also in the sphere of internal market harmonization.

It should thus be apparent that Community environmental law and policy cannot be viewed in isolation from WTO law. The latter is no longer the preserve of the international trade specialist. Community law and WTO law are, as Eeckhout expresses it, 'interconnecting legal systems', and they meet at an ever greater number of points.[67]

[67] Supra, n. 31.

CHAPTER SIX

Nature conservation and environmental impact assessment

Who had ever heard of Newbury's terrestial pulmonate snail (*vertigo moulinsiana*) until the United Kingdom government announced plans to construct a by-pass around the town? Perhaps I exaggerate – who has heard of it even now? Then again, how deeply embedded in the psyche of the American public was the fate of the now legendary snail darter until the Supreme Court of the United States ruled that its preservation legally precluded the completion of the multi-million dollar Tellico dam? Moreover, who could have believed that the Texas Blind Salamander would be capable of mounting 'an attack' on the people of Texas, threatening (according at least to the Mayor of San Antonio) to destroy the economy of that vast state?[1] A vision of the future for the European Union or a salutary lesson from America?

The nature conservation law of the European Community is premised principally upon two related legal instruments: Council Directive 79/409[2] (wild birds) and Council Directive 92/43[3] (habitats). It is these measures that this chapter will consider first. They serve to exemplify a number of issues endemic in Community environmental law. In so far as they pursue an 'enclave' strategy, premised upon the designation of areas enjoying special conservation status, they represent but one (though in some ways distinct) manifestation of the Community's 'framework' approach. In so far

---

1 On this occasion the Texas Blind Salamander joined forces with the San Marcos Salamander, the Fountain Darter, the San Marcos Gambusia and Texas Wild Rice, all species listed as endangered or threatened under the (federal) Endangered Species Act (ESA). See Albritton, E., 'The Endangered Species Act: The Fountain Darter Teaches What the Snail Darter Failed to Teach' (1994) 21 ELQ 1007, for a more realistic assessment of the implications of the ESA in the Texas Edwards Aquifer debacle.
2 OJ 1979 L103/1.
3 OJ 1992 L206/7.

as they threaten, in the name of conservation, to obstruct initiatives brought forth in the name of development, they constitute an unusually stark illustration of the contested nature of the interface between ecology and economics. The first part of this chapter will focus upon the environmental 'enclave' approach embodied within these directives, considering the rules governing both designation and management of sites. It will also examine (schematically) the rules relating to the protection of species. It will then consider the role of environmental impact assessment (EIA) in Community law, examining the recently amended EIA directive,[4] as well as the Commission's proposal for a directive on strategic impact assessment.[5]

Natura 2000: towards 'a coherent European ecological network'?

In 1991, in a seminal essay, Joseph Weiler explored the shifting relationship between what he called 'exit' and 'voice' in the European Community.[6] 'Crudely put', he argued that, 'a stronger "outlet" for [Member State] Voice reduces pressure on the Exit option . . .'.[7] He proposed a 'tentative thesis' whereby '[t]he "harder" the law in terms of its binding effect both on and within states, the less willing states are to give up their prerogative to control the emergence of such law . . .'.[8] Conceived as a means of analysing the evolution of the Community's constitutional order, from inception to Single European Act, Weiler's thesis nonetheless constitutes a useful heuristic device capable of being deployed to more modest ends. Specifically, in the context of this chapter, it offers an analytical framework within which the two nature conservation directives (wild birds and habitats) may be explored and contrasted. To this end, the concept of 'voice' may be viewed as speaking to the autonomy of the Member States in designating environmental 'enclaves'; and the concept of 'exit' as pertaining not (as in Weiler's thesis) to the capacity of Member States to violate or disregard the

---

4   Council Directive 85/337 OJ 1985 L175/40, as amended by Council Directive 97/11 OJ 1997 L73/5.
5   Com(96) 511 final. Proposal for a council Directive on the assessment of the effects of certain plans and programmes on the environment.
6   'The Transformation of Europe' (1991) 100 Yale Law Journal 2403.
7   Ibid., p. 2411.
8   Ibid., p. 2426.

substantive obligations imposed, but rather to their capacity to delineate their scope of application by virtue of the existence of exceptions, the parameters of which may be more or less fluid and more or less broadly defined.

Article 3(1) of the habitats directive provides for the establishment of 'Natura 2000', a 'coherent European ecological network of special areas of conservation' (SAsC). Parasitic, in part, upon the achievements of the earlier wild birds directive, Natura 2000 is to include Special Protection Areas (SPAs) designated thereunder, as well as Special Areas of Conservation to be classified according to a new and distinct procedure laid down in the habitats directive.

Wild birds

The procedure for the classification of SPAs under the wild birds directive is straightforward though by no means uncontested. Responsibility rests with the Member States upon whom it is incumbent to 'classify in particular the most suitable territories in number and size' for the conservation of those species of birds listed in Annex 1 to the directive.[9] Member States 'shall also take similar measures for regularly occurring migratory species not listed in Annex 1, bearing in mind their need for protection ... Member States shall pay particular attention to the protection of wetlands and particularly to wetlands of international importance'.[10] The directive appears, in this respect, to confer substantial discretion upon the Member States, thus ensuring the audibility of their 'voice'. Recourse to concepts such as 'the most suitable', and to a range of factors simply to be 'borne in mind' or 'taken account of', serves to underline this.

It is against such a backdrop that the willingness of the Member States (acting unanimously under Article 235 EEC) to sanction a closure of the 'exit' option in relation to SPAs can be understood. Among the substantive obligations imposed upon Member States pertaining to the management of SPAs is the duty outlined in Article 4(4), wild birds. This provides that Member States 'shall take appropriate steps to avoid pollution or deterioration of habitats or any disturbances affecting the birds, in so far as these would be significant having regard to the objectives of this Article', thus

9 Supra, n. 2, Article 3(1).
10 Supra, n. 2, Article 3(2).

appearing to preclude recourse to any form of cost-benefit analysis such as might permit the introduction of arguments of an economic nature. Recourse to the language of 'significant' pollution, deterioration or disturbance in Article 4(4) may be thought to offer an escape route for Member States. In *Commission* v *Spain*[11] the European Court stressed that the proposed activities would produce 'significant deterioration' and cause 'considerable damage'.[12] Advocate General van Gerven has argued that Article 4(4) should not be read as prohibiting 'all deleterious action', but equally that a 'minimalist' approach, precluding only those measures which endanger the survival or reproduction of the species, should be rejected. He maintained that it is for the Member States to 'determine what specific measures must be taken to ensure the most suitable living conditions in the designated areas and to prevent pollution, deterioration and disturbances which would significantly affect those circumstances'.[13]

Notwithstanding continuing uncertainty as to the concept of significant pollution, the Court has adopted a strict approach to the interpretation of Article 4(4). In the *Leybucht dyke* case,[14] it found that Germany was permitted to reduce the extent of an SPA only on exceptional grounds, corresponding to a general interest which is superior to the general interest represented by the ecological objective of the directive. Economic and recreational requirements, of the type referred to in Article 2, may not be cited to this end. Article 2 does not represent an autonomous derogation.[15] Works undertaken in order to offset the danger of flooding and to ensure coastal protection were sanctioned in this case, subject to the proportionality proviso that they be 'confined to a strict minimum'.[16] The Court accepted that economic considerations could be taken into account in determining the line of the new dyke, but only because at the same time the line chosen could be justified in environmental terms as producing 'offsetting ecological benefits, *and only for that reason*'.[17] The restrictive approach of the Court

---

11 Case C-355/90 [1993] ECR I-4221.
12 Ibid., paras. 46 and 52. See Freestone, D., 'The Enforcement of the Wild Birds Directive: a Case Study' in Somsen, H., (ed.), *Protecting the European Environment: Enforcing EC Environmental Law* (Blackstone, 1996).
13 Case C-57/89 *Commission* v *Germany* [1991] ECR I-883, p. 918.
14 Ibid.
15 Ibid., para. 22.
16 Ibid., para. 23.
17 Ibid., para. 26 (emphasis added).

may be understood in terms of 'exit' and 'voice'. It has emphasized that Member States 'do not have the same discretion under Article 4(4) of the directive [as compared to the degree of discretion which they appear to enjoy at the designation stage] . . . since they themselves acknowledged in their declarations that those areas contain the most suitable environments for the species listed in Annex 1 to the directive'.[18] Their voices having been heard, exit is precluded.

Although the decision of the Court in *Leybucht* appears to represent a resounding endorsement of the original equilibrium between exit and voice constituted by the wild birds directive (promoting the closure of exit and the audibility of voice), in practice it serves to promote a diminution of Member State voice (discretion) in the designation of SPA. By confirming that Article 2 (which refers to economic and recreational requirements) 'does not constitute an autonomous derogation from the general system of protection established by the directive', the Court prepared the ground for its subsequent, more explicit, finding that economic considerations have no part to play in the designation of SPAs.[19] On the contrary, in designating such areas, Member States are obliged to apply (only) certain ornithological criteria, determined by the directive, such as the presence of Annex 1 species (Article 4(1)) or the qualification of a habitat as a wetland (Article 4(2)).[20] These criteria are viewed by the Court as sufficiently objective and precise in nature to permit the condemnation of a Member State for its failure to fulfil these obligations, at any rate in a case concerning one of the most important ecosystems in the Iberian peninsula, home to various endangered species and a resting and feeding ground for a variety of migratory species. Moreover, crucially, in this case the Court found that the obligations inherent in Article 4(4) apply not only to sites designated as SPAs but also to sites which *ought*, in the light of of the relevant ornithological criteria, to have been so designated.[21] As such, the closure of exit could no longer be viewed as contingent upon the audibility of Member State voice.

18 Ibid., para. 20.
19 See supra, n. 11 and Case C-44/95 *R* v *Secretary of State for the Environment, ex p RSPB* [1996] ECR I-3805. On the contrary the Advocate-General in *Leybucht* considered that such requirements may be taken into account in the context of Article 4(4).
20 Supra, n. 11, *Commission* v *Spain*, para. 26.
21 Ibid., paras. 20–2.

This judgment has generated debate as to the capacity of Articles 4(1) and 4(2) for direct effect. Wils has argued that, since the Court has held that these provisions are based on the application of certain objective ornithological criteria, they are susceptible to application by national courts.[22] Somsen, on the contrary, has argued that:

> even though the obligation to protect certain birds by means of the classification of special protection areas appears to be an absolute one, the exact form these measures must take (such as the location and size of site) is largely left open by the Directive. Under these circumstances, it is difficult to see how Article 4(1) could produce direct effect.[23]

In a more recent, high profile, case the European Court, while confirming that economic considerations have no role to play in the designation of SPAs, did not confront the question of direct effect.[24] The case arose in the context of judicial review proceedings brought by the RSPB, challenging a decision of the Secretary of State to designate the Medway Estuary and Marshes as an SPA, but to exclude from it an area of inter-tidal mudflat known as Lappel Bank. The basis of this decision was to enable the expansion of the Port of Sheerness, having regard to its economic significance, at national and local level. The port is a significant employer in an area with high unemployment. It was accepted that exclusion of this area would 'probably result in a reduction in the wader and wildfowl populations of the Medway Estuary and Marshes'.[25]

Though the RSPB did not succeed before the Divisional Court or the Court of Appeal, the findings of these courts were predicated upon an analysis of the substance of the case, and not on the basis that the relevant provisions were incapable of direct effect. The House of Lords commented with surprise on the decision of the Court of Appeal not to refer the relevant questions to the European Court, on the basis that they could be considered *acte claire*.[26] It is of considerable importance to observe that, while

[22] Wils., W.P.J., 'The Birds Directive 15 Years Later: a Survey of the Case Law and a Comparison of the Habitats Directive' (1994) 6 JEL 218, p. 230.

[23] Somsen, H., 'Member States' Obligations under Directive 79/409' (1993) Water Law 209, p. 212.

[24] Supra, n. 19 (RSPB).

[25] Ibid., para. 12.

[26] (1995) 7 JEL 245.

legal proceedings were pending, the site was destroyed, raising crucial questions surrounding the availability of interim relief.[27]

Habitats

In the light of the above, it may come as no surprise to discover that the habitats directive institutes a revival of the exit option in the face of a judicially ordained diminution of voice. The first sentence of Article 4(4) (obligation to avoid pollution or deterioration etc.) is to be replaced by those obligations enshrined in Articles 6(2)–(4) of the habitats directive, concerning the management of the Natura 2000 network as a whole.[28] Natura 2000 comprises both SPAs and SAsC. The procedure as regards designation of SPAs, and the criteria governing selection, are to remain unchanged.[29]

Consequently, from the date of implementation of this directive[30] or, if later, the date of establishment of an SPA, Member States may authorize plans or projects with a deleterious effect on such an area where this can be justified by 'imperative reasons of overriding public interest, including [contrary to what was previously decided in *Leybucht*] those of a *social or economic* nature',[31] a slap in the face for the European Court. For SAsC hosting a priority species and/or a priority habitat type, only those imperative reasons relating to human health, public safety or ecological interests may be considered, subject to the proviso that, 'further to an opinion from the Commission', other imperative reasons may be taken into account. While the established jurisprudence of the Court in other areas of environmental law suggests that such an opinion must be sought prior to the granting of approval for a plan or project, there is nothing to suggest that the Commission's opinion is in any way binding.

The Commission issued such an opinion in the context of German plans to build a motorway (A20) which would intersect the Peene Valley, which included two SPAs and hosting priority habi-

---

27 See Ch. 8.
28 Supra, n. 3, Article 7.
29 This was confirmed in supra, n. 23.
30 Two years after its notification.
31 Supra, n. 3, Article 6(4) (emphasis added). See, for example, Case 187/87 *Saarland and Others* v *Ministry of Industry and Others* [1988] ECR 5013.

tat types. The Commission accepted that the intersection would 'create a new artifical obstacle for the migration of species in the Peene valley and [would] create disturbances to other habitat types important for the species listed under the Birds and Habitats Directive'.[32] However, it concluded that the construction project was justified on the basis of imperative reasons of overriding public interest, relating to employment, economic and social cohesion and, because the A20 would form part of a trans-European road network, the establishment of the internal market. It emphasized that the route chosen represented the least damaging alternative, and that Germany had agreed to take steps both to mitigate, and compensate for, the damage caused. By agreeing to create or restore 'seven different habitat types in an area of nearly 100 hectare[s] in the Peene valley', the global coherence of the Natura 2000 network would be preserved.

If the habitats directive serves to facilitate Member State 'exit', what of Member State 'voice' in relation to the classification of SAsC? The procedure laid down in the habitats directive is far from straightforward, comprising three distinct stages, the first of which constitutes the clearest embodiment of Member State 'voice'.[33] This first stage represents the defining moment in shaping the first pillar of the 'voice'/'exit' relationship and in view of its political poignancy the ambiguity which characterizes it is readily explicable. What at least is clear is that the Member States are required to 'propose a list of sites' indicating which natural habitat types of Community importance (listed in Annex 1) and species of Community importance (listed in Annex 2), native to its territory there are, which these sites host. They are to propose this list on the basis of the scientific criteria set out in Annex 3 (stage 1) to the directive which speak to the relative importance of sites for the conservation of habitat types and species of Community importance. Annex 3 (para. C) provides that the Member States are, on the basis of these criteria, to classify sites which they propose on the national list as sites eligible for identification as sites of Community importance. It appears, therefore, contrary to first impressions, that national lists need not include all sites hosting relevant habitat types or species but only those which are deemed to be 'high value' in terms of the conservation effort. Thus, the relatively

---

[32] Commission Opinion 95/15 OJ 1996 L6/14. See also OJ 1995 C178/3 for an earlier opinion relating to this motorway construction project.

[33] Supra, n. 3, Articles 4 and 5.

open-ended nature of the Annex 3 criteria – which identify the factors to be taken into consideration but not the precise thresholds to be applied – accords substantial 'voice' to the Member States. The data gleaned from the application of these criteria is, together with the proposed list of sites and additional information specified in Article 4(1), to be transmitted to the Commission within three years of the notification of the directive. Member States do not appear to be obliged to forward data collected in respect of sites not ultimately included on the national list.[34]

The second stage in the identification of SAsC takes the form of a Community procedure whereby the Commission, acting in accordance with the procedure laid down in Article 21, adopts (by June 1998) a list of sites of Community importance, to be designated by Member States (during the third stage) as SAsC. For sites included in a national list hosting one or more priority natural habitats or priority species, Member State voice is all but excluded during this second stage. The list of sites of Community importance is to be drawn up on the basis of the scientific criteria laid down in Annex 3 (stage 2). This provides that all such sites will be considered sites of Community importance.[35] It is no doubt in the light of this that the question of which sites housing priority habitat types and species are included on national lists is of such importance and sensitivity; hence the rationale for the special procedure laid down in Article 5 of the habitats directive. This permits the Commission to institute bilateral consultations with a Member State where, in exceptional circumstances, it finds that a national list fails to include a site housing a priority natural habitat type or species which the Commission considers, on the basis of relevant and reliable scientific information, to be essential for the maintenance of that habitat type or the survival or that species. Ultimately, where the dispute cannot be resolved amicably, the Commission may place a proposal before the Council that the site be selected as a site of Community importance, notwithstanding its exclusion from the national list. The Council shall act *unanimously.*

---

34 This is indicated also by Article 5(1), supra, n. 3.

35 Nevertheless, Article 4(2) provides that Member States in which such areas comprise more than 5% of their territory may, in agreement with the Commission, request that the Annex 3 (stage 2) criteria be more flexibly applied in relation to *all* sites of Community importance, hence including those hosting priority natural types or species.

Outside of areas hosting such priority resources the Commission shall, in agreement with each Member State, draw up a draft list of sites of Community importance on the basis of the Annex 3 (stage 2) criteria.[36] It shall forward this draft to a committee consisting of representatives of the Member States and chaired by the Commission, which shall deliver an opinion on the draft, acting by a qualified majority.[37] The Commission may adopt the measures if they are in accordance with the opinion of the Committee. Otherwise, the Commission is to submit a proposal to the Council which may adopt the measures by a qualified majority.[38] Hence, the original draft list drawn up by the Commission, in agreement with each Member State, may undergo revision on the basis of the support of a (qualified) majority of the Member States. Member State voice is consequently diminished during this second stage. From the moment a site is included on the Community list it is to be subject to the substantive management obligations attaching to SAsC, regardless of whether a Member State formally designates the area as such (within six years at most) in accordance with Article 4(5). Hence, whereas under the birds directive obligations attach to areas which merely ought to have been designated as SPAs, under the habitats directive obligations arise only once an area has been included on the Community list. Which ever way this is considered, inclusion on the Community list is contingent upon the acquiescence of the relevant Member State.

It is then apparent that the adoption of the habitats directive represents a dramatic reassertion of Member State sovereignty over 'their' natural resources; facilitating the expression of voice (in relation to SAsC) and engendering enhanced opportunities for exit (in relation to SPAs and SAsC). In this it mirrors developments on the international plane. 'One of the most striking results of the Rio Declaration is its reaffirmation of traditional "sovereignty" in the face of an appeal for a new globalism called forth by the dominant environmental motif of the conference'.[39] Nevertheless, sovereignty often has its price and its revival during this period has coincided with the proliferation of mechanisms for the trans-

---

[36] Supra, n. 3, Article 4(2).
[37] Ibid., Articles 20 and 21(1). The Commission representative does not vote.
[38] Ibid., Article 21(2).
[39] Porras, I. M., 'The Rio Declaration: a New Basis for International Cooperation' in Sands, P., *Greening International Law* (Earthscan, 1993).

national transfer of financial resources.[40] The habitats directive likewise takes a tentative step in this direction providing, in certain circumstances, for Community co-financing of conservation measures undertaken by Member States pursuant to Article 6(1).[41]

Protection of species

The habitats directive adopts an approach to the protection of (plant and animal) species which differs significantly to that espoused by the wild birds directive. Each contains a network of rules regulating the hunting, taking, disturbance, keeping, transport, sale and exchange of species.[42] In the case of the latter these apply to all birds species naturally occurring in the European territory of the Member States (and to their eggs, nests and habitats) with Annexes 2 and 3 identifying those species in relation to which a more liberal regime is to apply. In the case of the former a more permissive approach is adopted, the application of the rules being contingent upon the inclusion of a given plant or animal species in Annexes 4 or 5. In essence, the effect of the habitats directive is to shift the burden of proof. In the face of institutional inertia, whereby a given species is not included in the relevant annex, the wild birds directive presupposes a need for strict protection, whereas the habitats directive condones exploitation of that resource. Practical considerations aside, the former may be thought to be more consistent with a precautionary approach to environmental management. Member States may derogate from the rules regulating the protection of species where there is no other satisfactory solution (wild birds) or satisfactory alternative (habitats).[43] They may do so only on the basis of the reasons listed which, in the case of the habitats directive, include those of a social or economic nature. In respect of the habitats directive, however, derogation is made conditional upon 'the maintenance of the population of the species concerned

---

40 See Sands, P., *Principles of International Environmental Law: Volume 1* (MUP, 1995), Ch. 19.
41 Supra, n. 3, Article 8.
42 See supra, n. 2, Articles 5–8 and supra, n. 3, Articles 12–15.
43 Supra, n. 2, Article 9 and supra, n. 3, Article 16.

at a favourable conservation status in their natural range'.[44]

As would be expected, the Article 9 wild birds derogation has been strictly construed by the Court. It has, in particular, emphasized the importance of the criteria laid down in Article 9(2), relating to the kind of detailed information which must be included in a decision to derogate. The purpose of these 'is to limit derogations to what is strictly necessary and to enable the Commission to supervise them'.[45] Most recently, the Court has held that a Member State may not permit the capture, even on a decreasing basis for a limited period, of certain protected species in order to enable bird fanciers to stock their aviaries. It insisted that breeding and reproduction of the species in captivity was a satisfactory alternative solution, even though the bird fanciers 'would be compelled to alter their installations and change their habits'.[46] However, a derogation designed to avoid problems of consanguinity (in-breeding) was permitted subject to the proviso that there be no other satisfactory solution, and that the number of birds permitted to be captured be fixed at the lowest possible level necessary to guarantee a solution to the problem, and at any rate be 'small' within the meaning of Article 9(1)(c).[47]

Environmental impact assessment

In the previous section we deployed the concepts of 'exit' and 'voice' as a means of analysing the obligations incurred by the Member States under the wild birds, and the more recent habitats, directives. These concepts provided a convenient framework for analysis, due principally to the 'enclave' approach which these directives pursue, requiring as they do the designation by Member

---

[44] Supra, n. 3, Article 16(1). The definitions in Article 1 provide that conservation status will be taken as favourable when population dynamics data indicates that it is maintaining itself on a long-term basis as a viable component of its natural habitats and the natural range of the species is neither being reduced nor is likely to be reduced for the foreseeable future and there is, and will 'probably' continue to be, a sufficiently large habitat to maintain its populations on a long-term basis. Recourse to the language of probability in this context is interesting. In the face of a degree of scientific uncertainty exit may nonetheless be sanctioned.

[45] Case 412/85 *Commission* v *Germany* [1987] ECR 3503, para. 18.

[46] Case C-10/96 *Ligue royal belge pour la protection des oiseaux ASBL and Another* v *Région Wallonne* [1996] ECR I-6775, para. 22.

[47] Ibid., para. 27.

States of sites of unusual ecological importance. In addition, these directives impose certain substantive constraints upon Member States, such as may require a particular outcome in relation to a project (road building, for example) under consideration. The EIA directive,[48] by way of contrast, is not premised upon an 'enclave' strategy, and the obligations which it imposes are of a purely procedural rather than a substantive nature:

> Environmental assessment sets procedural requirements for decision making rather than containing specific standards. Environmental assessment rules relate to the style and structure of decision making. The element of legal control is indirect: environmental assessment provides a conduit by which information may enter decision making procedures, but in theory at least, will not determine the outcomes of these procedures.[49]

The objective underlying the directive is to ensure that those national authorities with responsibility for planning will take decisions on the basis of full knowledge of the environmental impact of the proposed project. As an idea, the directive is broadly consistent with the concept of preventive action enshrined in Article 130r(2). With a view to understanding some of the difficulties associated with this directive, two questions will be addressed.

When is an EIA required?

The directive applies to public and private projects likely to have a significant effect on the environment.[50] In more concrete terms, Article 4 is predicated upon a distinction between Annex I and Annex II projects, assessment being mandatory in the case of the former, and at the discretion of the Member States in the case of the latter, depending upon the characteristics of the proposed project in question. Whereas the former are assumed to have 'significant effects' on the environment, the latter require assessment only where Member States consider that they are likely to do so. In *Commission v Belgium*[51] the Court held that Belgium was in breach of its obligations under the directive, by virtue of the introduction of

---

48 Supra, n. 4.
49 Elworthy and Holder, *Environmental Protection: Text and Materials* (Butterworths, 1997), p. 390.
50 Supra, n. 4, Article 1.
51 Case C-133/94 [1996] ECR I-2323.

criteria and quantitative thresholds to be applied in determining whether integrated chemical installations were to be subject to assessment, pursuant to Article 4(1) (annex I). The question of 'whether a chemical installation is integrated does not depend on its processing capacity or on the type of chemical substances processed in it but on the existence of interlinked production units constituting in terms of their operation a single production unit'.[52]

Article 4(2) provides, in respect of Annex II projects, that Member States may specify certain types (categories) or projects for which EIA will be required, or may establish criteria and/or thresholds for determining which projects falling within the Annex II categories will be subject to EIA. The European Court has found that Member States are not entitled to exempt a whole category of Annex II projects in advance. 'Article 4(2) does not empower the Member States to exclude generally and definitively from possible assessment one or more classes mentioned in Annex II.'[53]

Recent amendments to the EIA directive have sought to further circumscribe the degree of Member State discretion as regards Annex II. It has done so, first, by transferring a number of project categories from the second to the first annex,[54] and also through the introduction of a 'screening' procedure in respect of Annex II. Whether the need for EIA is determined on a case by case basis, or on the basis of thresholds and/or criteria, Member States are (from 14 March 1999 at latest) obliged to take into account the selection criteria laid down in Annex III. These cover the characteristics of the project and of its potential impact, and its location. In essence, Annex III seeks to clarify and strengthen the Article 2(1) obligation on Member States, in assessing effects, to have regard *inter alia* to the projects's nature, size and location. An Article 169 case currently pending against Ireland exemplifies the kind of shortcomings which the recent amendments seek to address.[55] First, the 'salami' effect: the Commission is concerned that the Annex II thresholds set in Ireland fail to take adequate account of the incremental or cumulative effects of a number of separate projects. As Meldon puts it:

[52] Ibid., para. 27.
[53] Ibid., para. 43.
[54] Annex 1 now contains 21 as opposed to nine categories of projects; Annex 2, 13 as compared to the previous 12.
[55] Case C-392/96 *Commission* v *Ireland* action brought on 5 December 1996, OJ 1996 C40/12.

The problem has arisen in Ireland in relation to forestry where most projects fall into the category of less than 200 hectares and therefore do not require the submission of an EIS [Environmental Impact Statement]. Yet the cumulative impact of a number of smaller forestry projects may be quite significant ... The problems of cumulative effect also arises in the case of roads covered by Annex 2 of the Directive where roads of a specified would only require an EIS where the length exceeds certain parameters. The need for an EIS can be avoided altogether by the construction of roads in section.[56]

Hence, by breaking down a development scheme into a number of distinct component projects, Member States have been able to evade the procedural demands of the EIA directive. Advocate-General Gulman has advocated a purposive approach to the interpretation of the concept of a project in order to prevent this occurring. The purpose of the directive 'entails that as far as practically possible account should also be taken in the environmental impact assessment of any current plans to extend the specific project at hand'.[57] This is not an issue which the European Court has addressed. A similar question arose before the English High Court in *R v Secretary of State for the Environment and Others, ex p Greenpeace and Others,*[58] though in that case the government was accused of lumping together two allegedly distinct projects in order that both could benefit from the fact that the earlier of the two projects had been commenced prior to the entry into force of the EIA directive, and hence was not subject to EIA. The Court accepted that the two measures – construction of the THORP thermal nuclear reprocessing plant at Sellafield, and the subsequent emission of radioactive substances to the atmosphere (for which separate permission was required under statute) – represented a single project and hence was able to benefit from the 'project in the pipeline' defence.[59]

56 Meldon, J., *Structural Funds and the Environment: Problems and Prospects* (1992, An Taisce), p. 57.
57 Case C-396/92 *Bund Naturshutz in Bayern and Others v Freistaat Bayern* [1994] ECR I-3717, para. 71.
58 [1994] 4 All ER 352.
59 *Twyford Down Parish Council v Secretary of State for the Environment* [1990] 1 Environmental Law Reports 37. The European Court has not ruled on the accuracy of the assumption that projects in respect of which an application for development consent had been submitted prior to the deadline for implementing the directive are not subject to EIA. This was the approach adopted by the Advocate-General in supra, n. 55. In Case C-431/92 *Commission v Germany* [1995] ECR I-2189 the Court found that a project could not benefit from the pipeline defence where there had been merely informal contact between the developer and state authority prior to the deadline.

The amended directive does not seek to redefine or clarify the concept of a project. It does, however, provide in Annex III that the characteristics of a project must be considered having regard (*inter alia*) to 'the cumulation with other projects'. Projects are to be viewed 'in context': two projects, identical in and of themselves, may be distinguished in terms of characteristics according to their juxtaposition vis-à-vis other projects. While the directive provides merely that this information is to be taken into account, and hence in UK administrative law would represent a mandatory relevant consideration, this change does militate in the direction of Advocate-General Gulman's determination to read the directive in such a way as to preclude evasion through cumulative effects which might reasonably have been anticipated to be known at the time of the application for development consent.

More broadly, questions surrounding the concept of a 'project' within the framework of the EIA directive, highlight an issue of fundamental importance. Since 1990 there has been under discussion the idea of introducing some form of strategic EIA. The Commission published its latest draft for such a directive in 1996. In order to be enacted the proposal must be accepted unanimously in Council. The previous UK government was vehemently opposed to the introduction of such legislation. The stance to be adopted by the present incumbents is as yet uncertain. This proposal seeks to move beyond the sphere of individual project appraisal, to the environmental evaluation of national strategy at the level of plans and programmes; these being defined as 'town and country planning plans and programmes', including those in the areas of transport, energy, waste and water management, industry, telecommunications and tourism.[60] As will be seen in the next chapter, a limited form of programmatic or 'strategic' EIA has been introduced in the context of the Community's regional development policy and Member State implementation thereof.

The second aspect to the case currently pending against Ireland which is, to an extent, addressed by the recent amendments to the EIA directive concerns the location of the proposed project. The Commission contends that the Irish system of thresholds under Article 4(2) and Annex II does not adequately reflect the importance of location and, in particular, it does not distinguish between projects in areas which have recognized importance and value

---

60 Supra, n. 5, Article 2.

for nature conservation and those which do not; notwithstanding that Article 2(1) of the 1985 directive explicitly refers to location as a factor to be considered in assessing whether the project is likely to have significant effects on the environment. Having regard to earlier discussions about SPAs and SAsC, it it is striking that projects falling within the scope of Annex II need not necessarily undergo an EIA, where these fall beneath the thresholds established by the Member States. A proposal to introduce mandatory assessment in such areas was rejected by the Member States. Instead, the amended directive will simply regard this (and other location factors) as a relevant consideration to be taken into account. Much depends over the coming years upon the intensity of review which national and European courts apply in assessing whether the Annex III considerations have in fact been taken into account. Review will be considerably facilitated by virtue of the introduction of an obligation on Member States to make available to the public, the main reasons and considerations on which any decision to grant or refuse development consent has been taken.[61]

In the case of review by national courts, the issue of direct effect is pertinent. Until now the UK courts have refused to countenance the possibility that Article 4(2), relating to Annex II projects, be capable of adjudication before them; this even in circumstances where whole classes of project have been *a priori* exempted from assessment.[62] Whereas prior to the amendments, Member State discretion under Article 4(2) was virtually unconstrained, this is no longer the case in that they are obliged to reach their decision on the basis of certain objective criteria. It might be anticipated that the new Article 4(2) (when it takes effect) is such that direct effect will be conceded in so far as national courts are asked to examine whether all relevant considerations were indeed taken into account. The question of direct effect is, of course, a question of interpretation to be determined by the European Court. Thus far, it has had little, if indeed anything, to say on this subject. In *Commission* v *Germany*[63] the Court considered whether Article 2 (among others) was sufficiently clear, precise and unequivocal for

---

61 Supra, n. 4, Article 9.
62 For an overview of the case law see Ward, A., 'The Right to an Effective Remedy in European Community Law and Environmental Protection: A Case Study of United Kingdom Judicial Decisions Concerning the Environmental Impact Assessment Directive' (1993) 5 JEL 221. On the latter point remember supra, n. 51.
63 Supra, n. 59, paras. 39–40.

its application by national authorities to be mandatory. It concluded that it was. The test applied closely resembles that for direct effect. Moreover, a national court is a national authority, subject also to Article 5 EC. However, it may well be the case that to say that a directive imposes an absolute obligation on competent authorities within Member States is not at all to say that the directive is to be regarded as justiciable before national courts. It is also relevant to note that, in the light of the facts of this case, the Court was considering the application of Article 2 to an Article 4(1) Annex I project, in respect of which assessment is mandatory.

More recently, the European Court considered the role of national courts in ensuring that Member States do not exceed the limits to their discretion under Article 4(2).[64] These limits are to be found in Article 2(1), which requires assessment in the case of projects having significant effects on the environment. The question of whether these limits have been exceeded, through the establishment of thresholds and/or criteria, is to be determined not on a project by project basis, but in the light of an overall assessment of the characteristics of the category of project concerned. The European Court concluded that '[t]he fact that in this case the Member States have a discretion under Articles 2(1) and 4(2) of the directive does not preclude judicial review of the question whether the national authorities exceeded their discretion'.[65] Equally, where national courts must or may raise, of their own motion, pleas based on binding national rules, they are also obliged to take into account the relevant provisions of a directive, in an action for judicial review. It is interesting to observe that Judge Edward (writing extra-judicially) stresses that the Court in this case did not follow the advice of Advocate-General Elmer, who argued in favour of direct effect. What the Court decided, he suggests, 'is not "direct effect" in the traditional sense and it would perhaps be as well to find another formula in order to avoid confusion'.[66] Perhaps the crucial point here is that Judge Edward is emphasizing that the relevant parts of the EIA directive do not necessarily confer rights upon individuals which the national courts are obliged to pro-

[64] Case C-72/95 *Kraaijeveld BV* v *Gedeputeerde Staten van Zuid-Holland* [1996] ECR I-5403.
[65] Ibid., para. 59.
[66] 'Foreword' in Holder, J., *The Impact of EC Environmental Law in the United Kingdom* (Wiley, 1997), p. xiv.

tect.[67] This would remain true even in an action brought against a developer who happens to be an emanation of the state. It is simply that the national courts, in the performance of their *public* law functions, are obliged to police the boundaries of Member State discretion as constituted by the directive. The directive is justiciable before national courts in public law actions. This distinction is important in the wake of *Francovich*.[68] If to say that a directive is directly effective is to imply that it confers rights on individuals, that is also to say that it satisfies the first of the conditions governing state liability in damages for a breach of Community law. This is precisely what the Court, it seems, was careful to avoid concluding.

What does EIA involve?

In essence, EIA involves the drawing up of an environmental impact statement. The information to be included, in as much as Member States consider this relevant and that a developer reasonably be required to supply this information, is specified in Annex III of the original directive, and Annex IV, as amended. As a minimum, the EIS is to include the information specified in Article 5(2) (Article 5(3) as amended). This includes a description of the project and of the measures envisaged to avoid, reduce or, if possible remedy, significant adverse effects, such data as is required to identify and assess the main effects, together with a non-technical summary. Further to the recent amendments, developers will also be required to supply an outline of the main alternatives to the proposed project which were studied by the developer, and the main reasons for the final choice, taking into account the environmental effects.

The amendments also introduce the possibility of what has come to be known as 'scoping'. Member States may require that the competent authorities issue an opinion on the scope of the information to be supplied. Such an opinion is without prejudice to any later decision to request additional information. Before issuing an opinion, the relevant authority is obliged to consult both with

---

67 See Edward and Lane, *EC law: an Introduction* (Butterworths/Law Society of Scotland, 1995), para. 133, where the authors define direct effect in terms of individual rights.
68 Cases C-6 & 9/90 *Francovich and Bonifaci v Italian State* [1991] ECR I-5357. See Ch. 8.

the developer and with other bodies with specific responsibilities for the environment, as designated by the Member States pursuant to Article 6(1). Member States may, alternatively, merely provide for such scoping at the specific request of the developer. This is designed to 'permit interested parties, the local planning authority and statutory consultees to ascertain the scope and intensity of the investigation'.[69]

The information gathered is to be communicated to those bodies referred to in Article 6(1), which shall have an opportunity to express an opinion on the request for development consent and (further to the amendments) on the information supplied. One of the major concerns over recent years has been the wide variation in the quality of EISs. By providing an opportunity for bodies with detailed and specialist environmental knowledge to comment on the information supplied, deficiencies may be revealed and corrected by way of a request for further information. There is also a duty to consult with the public, originally before the initiation of the relevant project and, further to the amendments, before the granting of development consent.[70] This clarifies a certain ambiguity. Article 8 has always demanded that information gathered, including that which accrues through public consultation, is to be taken into consideration in the development consent procedure. Were the public consulted after the granting of development consent, even though before the project commenced, it is apparent that Member States would be vulnerable to the allegation of a breach of Article 8. As was noted above, with the entry into force of the recent amendments, Member States will be obliged to inform the public, not only of the decision taken and any conditions attaching thereto, but also of the reasons for the decision, and of the considerations upon which it is based. This will facilitate effective enforcement, but the language of 'be taken into consideration' exemplifies starkly the purely procedural nature of EIA obligations. If the recent reforms of the EIA directive have sought to constrain Member State 'exit' as regards the kind of projects requiring assessment, Member State 'voice', in adjudging whether development consent ought to be granted, remains clearly audible.

[69] Supra, n. 50, p. 399.
[70] Supra, n. 4, Article 6(2). Note also the existence of Article 7 (and its recent amendment) regarding consultation between Member States where a project in one Member State is likely to have a significant impact upon the environment in another Member State. On this, see supra, n. 51.

It is clear from the above discussion that, over recent years, the Commission has been proactive in striving to promote the proper application of the EIA directive. This has proved necessary largely due to the ambiguity which surrounds many of the concepts deployed in the directive, and hence the impossibility (according to Member State courts) of direct effect. Language such as 'where Member States consider' or 'significant effects' is such as to preserve Member State autonomy and to render judicial review problematic. It is striking that, at a time when the European Court has demonstrated a willingness to curtail the procedural autonomy of Member States courts in a bid to ensure that vindication of Community law rights is not made 'excessively difficult',[71] the latest Commission proposals pertaining to Strategic Environmental Assessment, provide:

> No provision of this Directive shall give rise to a right to seek judicial review in respect of a legislative act by which a plan or programme has been adopted.[72]

This seems to be a watered-down version of the legislative exemption in Article 1(5) of the EIA directive. This provides that the directive does not apply to projects adopted by a specific act of national legislation. While the Commission has sought to maintain that this exemption applies only where a comparable EIA is made in the process of adopting the new legislation, there is really nothing in the wording of this provision to guarantee this outcome.[73] This provides for the exemption 'since', rather than 'if', the objectives of the directive are achieved through the legislative process. This SEA 'ouster clause', were it to be enacted, would be conceptually significant. We already saw, in Chapter 5, the inclusion in the preamble to a Council Decision of a statement seeking to exclude the possibility of judicial application. As the European Court strives to further the *effet utile* of Community law, there is evidence that the Community legislator is beginning to fight back. Ouster clauses of this kind have not been willingly upheld by the English courts.[74] It is not, in this writer's view, inconceivable that the European Court would strike down such a provision, on the

---

71 See Ch. 8.

72 Supra, n. 5, Article 10(3).

73 Letter from the Commission to the RSPB, cited by Geddes, A., 'Environmental Impact Assessments' (1991) 88 Law Society Gazette 24, p. 24.

74 See Craig, P., *Administrative Law* (OUP, 1994), Chapter 16.

basis that it is contrary to Article 5 of the Treaty. Only time will tell.

Conclusion

Few areas of Community environmental law are as deeply controversial as those which affect land use and development activities. It is apparent from the above that Member States are reluctant to cede control over such areas of economic life. The shortcomings which inhere in the three directives under discussion bear considerably on the topic to be examined in the next chapter. The Community today represents an important source of development funding. Such funding is to accrue in a manner which is compatible with Community environmental law and policy. In so far as Community environmental law is characterized by an increasing reluctance to silence Member State 'voice', at the interface between environment and development, and in so far as Community environmental policy is hard to enforce, the principle of environmental compatibility as it pertains to Community funding cannot be expected to realize the Community's commitment to sustainable development.

CHAPTER SEVEN

Regional policy and environment

A decade on from the World Wide Fund for Nature's 'European Campaign against the Structural Funds', controversy over the environmental dimension of the Community's development activities continues unabated. Legislative changes notwithstanding, the tension between ecology and economy remains palpable.[1] Following repeated critical intervention on the part of the Court of Auditors,[2] the European Parliament has threatened to block funding should the situation not improve. The Commission itself acknowledges that 'it has for several years been receiving complaints concerning infringements of environmental legislation in the implementation of projects assisted by Community funds'.[3] Somewhat cynically, it indicates that 'it views this situation seriously in that it damages public perception of Community Activity'.[4]

The Community – post-Maastricht – was committed to a strategy of 'sustainable growth ... respecting the environment'.[5] This, the Commission insists, is no oxymoron, '... there is no linear relationship between economic growth and its impact on the environment'.[6] On the contrary, environment and development are presented as of 'complementary character'.[7] With Amsterdam, the new Treaty leitmotiv would take the form of 'sustainable development'. Nonetheless, within the context of the geographic dimen-

---

1 The Community's 1988 regulations governing the operation of the structural funds were amended wholesale in 1993. See, in particular, Council Regulation 2081/93 OJ 1993 L193/5 (the 'framework' regulation) and Council Regulation 2082/93 OJ 1993 L193/21 (the 'coordination' regulation).
2 OJ 1992 C245/7.
3 COM(95) 509 final, *Commission Communication: Cohesion Policy and the Environment*, p. 1.
4 Ibid.
5 Article 2 EC.
6 COM(97) 27 final, *1997 Annual Economic Report*, p. 61.
7 Supra, n. 3, p. 2.

sion of the Community's social and economic cohesion objective, development is taken to imply the pursuit of accelerated economic growth in the Community's poorer regions and Member States.[8] The Community's very poorest regions ('objective 1' regions, so-called) are identified on the basis of their exceptionally low per capita GDP, relative (less than 75% than) to the overall Community average. Principal among the Community instruments supporting this objective are the three structural funds (the European Regional Development Fund, the European Social Fund and the Guidance Section of the European Agricultural Guidance and Guarantee Fund) and the more recently established Cohesion fund.[9] Together, these absorb almost one-third of the Community's entire budget.

Article 130r(2) provides that '[e]nvironmental protection requirements must be integrated into the definition and implementation of other Community policies' (see also Article 6 to be introduced by The Treaty of Amsterdam.). Today, the structural funds, in so far as they pursue regional policy objectives,[10] dedicate 7% of total funding to environmental projects. During the first two years of the Cohesion fund's operation, the balance between environmental and transport infrastructure projects was struck at 45% and 55% respectively. Moreover, in keeping with this integration obligation, the regulations governing the structural and cohesion funds establish the principle of what may be called environmental compatibility. This stipulates that measures financed by these funds are to be in conformity with the (EC) Treaty, with instruments adopted pursuant thereto and with Community policies, including that in the area of environmental protection.[11] Fine words indeed! But how, the ever sceptical lawyer asks, is compliance to be secured? The Acheloos dam, the Tagus bridge and the Fuerteventura windmill park have sown seeds of doubt in the minds of all but the most complacent.[12] This chapter will examine

[8] See Articles 130a–130e EC and COM(96) 542 final, *First Cohesion Report*.

[9] On the latter see Council Regulation 1164/94 OJ 1994 L130/1.

[10] Article 1 of the framework regulation (supra, n. 1) provides that the funds are to contribute to six objectives, four of which are regionally defined. Around 70% of total funding accrues to 'objective 1' regions with a view to promoting the development and structural adjustment of regions whose development is lagging behind. Typically, such regions have a GDP per capita average of less than 75% of the Community average.

[11] Article 7(1) of the framework regulation, supra, n. 1 and supra, n. 10, art. 8(1).

[12] For examples of projects highlighting the tension between the Community's environment and development objectives see op. cit., n. 2, Scott, J., *Development Dilemmas in the European Community* (Open UP, 1995) and the references cited therein.

this issue principally in the context of Community structural funding. It will begin by considering the role of the courts, European and national, in ensuring respect for this principle, and hence in policing the sensitive interface between environment and development. The first section will be dedicated to the apparently esoteric, but profoundly important, issues arising out of the recent judgments of the European Courts in *An Taisce and WWF(UK)* v *Commission*.[13] This will focus upon the difficulties associated with establishing the existence, in the context of the implementation of Community structural funding, of a reviewable Community level 'act' within the meaning of Article 173 EC.

Environmental compatibility before the European courts

On 21 December 1989 the Commission approved, by decision, an 'operational programme' for tourism submitted by the Irish government. This programme '... which did not address specific projects but merely analysed in general terms a number of sub-programmes on infrastructure, plant, training and marketing ...', was to be part-financed by Community structural funding. On 22 April 1991 the Irish Minister of State at the Department of Finance, announced plans for the construction of a visitors' centre (and interpretative centre) in a disused quarry at the foot of the Mullaghmore mountain in County Clare. This project, which following machinations in the Irish courts is still awaiting planning permission,[14] would also involve the construction of an access road, car park and waste water treatment plant. It would attract an estimated 60,000 visitors each year. The initiative was hallmarked to receive Community assistance to the tune of 2.7 million Irish pounds. Mullaghmore is situated in the Burren in an area of

---

13 Case T-461/93 (CFI) [1994] ECR ll-733 and Case C-325/94P (ECJ) [1996] ECR 1-3727.
14 See *Howard* v *Commissioners for Public Works* [1994] IR 101 (High Court), 123 (Supreme Court) and 395 (No. 3, Supreme Court) and *The Irish Times*, 17 March 1997 for a discussion of allegations that the Minister for Arts, Culture and the Gaeltacht is holding north County Clare 'to ransom' over his revised plans for the visitors' centre. The suggestion is the Minister is making public funding of three existing centres conditional upon a grant of planning permission in respect of the Mullaghmore project. As things stand, the centre is only half built.

'outstanding national beauty and of considerable geological, botanical and archaeological interest'.[15]

On 19 June 1992, the Director-General for environment (DG XI) informed the Irish permanent representative in Brussels of his intention to recommend the commencement of Article 169 proceedings against Ireland, a request to which the College of Commissioners ultimately did not accede. The Commission expressed, in a press release, confidence that the Burren project was in conformity with Community environmental law and, specifically, with the Environmental Impact Assessment (EIA) and Groundwater directives.[16] This though the latter had not yet been correctly implemented in Irish law.

Others were less sanguine. An Taisce and the WWF, having earlier lodged a complaint about the project with the Commission, initiated an action for judicial review pursuant to Article 173 EC. This was heard, at the outset, by the Court of First Instance (CFI) and subsequently, on appeal, by the European Court. Neither court deemed it necessary to address the substance of their complaint, which centred upon the application of the concept of environmental compatibility. Each dismissed the action for annulment as inadmissible. Their decision to do so was predicated not upon the familiar issue of *locus standi* (an issue which will be considered below), but upon the rather more arcane question of whether the defendant (the Commission) had adopted a decision sanctioning Community financing of the project, and hence whether there was in existence a legal act which could form the subject matter of the action. They concluded that it had not.

At first glance such a conclusion appears to fly in the face of common sense and clearly raises issues of accountability in respect of so-called *Community* structural funding. There was no doubt that the project was to receive assistance from the structural funds, but merely uncertainty as to where responsibility for determining that fact lay. An appreciation of the difficulties faced by the applicants in this case demands some understanding of the development planning process.

Since 1988, Community structural assistance has been largely programme, as opposed to project, based. Financial support accrues to a limited number of 'operational programmes' which take

15 Ibid., *Howard.*, p. 109.
16 Council Directives. 85/337 OJ 1985 L175/40 and Council Directive 80/68 OJ 1980 L20/43.

the form of multi-annual packages of consistent development measures.[17] Operational programmes are often thematically defined, hence the Irish operational programme on tourism. Programme applications need contain only the basic information necessary to identify objectives set and the broad measures chosen to meet them. They need not contain the details of specific, individual, projects to be financed. As noted above, such programmes are approved by way of a formal Commission decision,[18] a decision which, incontrovertibly, constitutes a reviewable act. Yet, by the time that plans for the Burren initiative were announced, the deadline (two months) for challenging this decision had long since passed. At any rate, this decision was impervious to challenge on its merits. It explicitly endorsed the principle of environmental compatibility, providing that operations funded thereunder be in conformity with Community environmental law and policy. The applicants were not objecting to this decision as such, but rather to an alleged failure to abide by its terms (and the terms of the framework regulation) further down the road of the development planning process. As we proceed down this road, to the point of (operational) programme implementation, Community legislation governing structural funding emerges as increasingly opaque with regard to governance structures. And so the Commission is able to assert, with some credibility, that programme implementation is 'under the competence of the Member States'.[19] Responsibility for project selection, within the framework of an operational programme, is said to accrue exclusively at a national, rather than a Community, level. Such devolution, pursued initially in a bid to achieve managerial efficiency, is today celebrated in the name of subsidiarity.

The applicants, by two separate but identical letters, wrote to the Commission Director-Generals for environmental and regional policy, requesting access to Commission documents relating to the examination of the Burren project and specifically to the question of the availability of structural funding. Access was refused on the basis of a need to protect the Commission's interest in the confidentiality of its proceedings. This led to a further action before

---

17 Supra, n. 1, Article 5(5) of the framework regulation.
18 These decisions are published in the Official Journal but not the text of the operational programmes themselves. These are available (only in the language(s) of the Member State concerned) from the relevant national authorities or from DGXV1 (regional development).
19 Supra, n. 3, p. 10.

the CFI, concerned with the issue of access to information. The CFI annulled the Commission's decision to deny access, on the basis of Community rules governing openness and transparency. It did so, however, on narrow grounds in that the Commission had failed to adequately reason its decision or to explain why the documents fell within the scope of the exceptions relied upon.[20]

In view of the Commission's reticence over its internal deliberations, it is not surprising to find that the applicants arguments in *An Taisce* were somewhat speculative in nature. They took, as their starting point, the Commission's decision not to commence (Article 169) infringement proceedings against Ireland, a decision which in itself is not reviewable.[21] They argued that this implied the adoption of a second decision not to suspend, reduce, or cancel assistance, pursuant to Article 24(2) of the co-ordination regulation. Neither the CFI, nor the European Court, was convinced:

> A decision adopted under Article 24 of Regulation No 4253/88 is therefore distinct from [the] institution of Article 169 proceedings or from a decision not to pursue such proceedings. These two procedures are independent of each other, serve different aims and are subject to different rules. . . . [T]he Commission's decision not to institute proceedings under Article 169 of the Treaty cannot implicitly entail the taking of a separate decision based on Article 24 . . .[22]

While the European Court, in its order, confirms that a positive decision to suspend or reduce funding would, in principle, be actionable, it does not address the question of the status of a decision not to do so. It merely denies, in this case, that such a decision had in fact been taken. Leaving aside the evidential difficulties in establishing the existence of a negative decision of this kind,[23] it is by no

---

[20] See Case T-105/95 *WWF UK* v *Commission*, judgment of 5 March 1997, nyr.

[21] For recent confirmation of this see, C-107/95P *Bundesverband der Bilanzbuchhalter* v *Commission* [1997] ECR I-947.

[22] Case C-325/94P, supra, n. 13, paras 25–6.

[23] The Commission is obliged, prior to exercising its powers to reduce or suspend assistance, to conduct an examination and to give the Member State concerned the opportunity to submit comments. It need not inform the Member State of the action that it proposes in view of the results of the examination and the comments received. Given the Commission's approach to the disclosure of documents pertaining to internal deliberations, it would seem to be extraordinarily difficult in practice to adduce evidence of the existence of a decision not to reduce or suspend funding.

means clear that such a decision exhibits the characteristics associated with an 'act' within the meaning of Article 173. The CFI emphasizes, correctly, in *An Taisce,* that the Commission may take such a decision 'at any time, including after the completion of the work . . .'.[24] A negative decision of this kind is neither strictly binding, nor definite and unequivocal. The Commission may change its mind. According to this analysis, it does not appear to be an act possessing the necessary legal effects to be reviewable.[25]

In view of the above, the applicants in the more recent *Greenpeace* case[26] sought to navigate a very different, and altogether more plausible, tack in the search for the missing act. Their oral arguments on appeal, before a full Court, were heard on 17 June 1997. The outcome is pending. The application concerns the implementation of a Commission decision ((91) 440) approving Community financing for two fossil fuel power stations in Spain. It is alleged that development consent was granted for this project, and construction commenced, prior to an appropriate environmental impact assessment. As to the identity of the putative Community act, the arguments presented were complex but broadly took the following form: a sum representing around one-quarter of total Community funding for this initiative was paid to Spain at the time of the adoption of the Commission decision.[27] This decision, in keeping with the co-ordination regulation,[28] provided that subsequent disbursements were to be effected on an annual basis. Whereas the first payment flowed automatically as a consequence of the Commission decision, and hence did not enjoy a distinct legal identity, it is alleged that subsequent payments were disbursed by way of separate Commission decisions taking the form of reviewable acts. By October 1993 the Commission conceded that it had released 40 million ECU to the Spanish government in respect of this project; some 12 million ECU more than the sum devolved upon project approval. The applicants are seeking annul-

---

24 Case T-461/93, supra, n. 13, para. 36.
25 For a fuller discussion of this issue and of the case law of the courts, see Hartley, T., *The Foundations of European Community Law* (OUP, 1994), pp. 347–50, 395–7.
26 Case T-585/93 *Stichtung Greenpeace Council and Others* v *Commission* [1995] ECR ll-2205.
27 As in *An Taisce*, this decision appeared to endorse the principle of environmental compatibility and was impervious to challenge.
28 Supra, n. 1, Articles 25–6.

ment of this alleged decision to release a second tranche of Community finance.

The arguments presented by the applicants are cogent. They draw not only upon the financial plan annexed to Commission Decision 91(440) but also upon the Community's financial regulation.[29] Financial assistance from the structural funds is subject to the relevant rules of this.[30] In terms of financial management, the financial regulation requires compliance with a four-stage procedure, allegedly on each occasion that funding is released; commitment, validation, authorization and payment of expenditure. Validation is defined as 'the act whereby the authorizing officer shall . . . verify the existence of the creditor's claim . . . determine or verify the existence and the amount of the sum due . . . [and] *verify the conditions under which payment falls due*'. Validation, the applicants argue, requires verification of environmental compatibility in accordance with the framework regulation and Decision 91(440).[31] Thus, 'the disbursement of individual payments (after the initial payment) . . . is not simply a question of "administrative implementation" as is suggested by the Commission . . . [e]ach disbursement of funds . . . was required to be authorized by an act which is in substance a decision and [is] therefore open to challenge under Article 173 EC Treaty'.[32]

Regardless of the final outcome of this particular case, it must be observed that the circumstances giving rise to it are not altogether typical. Annex 1 of Commission Decision 91(440) specifies that funding is to be dedicated to the construction of energy infrastructure, consisting of two thermal groups of 80 MW, in Granadila de Abona (Tenerife) and San Bartolome de Tirajana (Gran Canaria). It, unlike the decision approving the Irish operational programme, does contain information relating to specific projects to be financed.[33] Within the framework of operational

[29] Financial Regulation OJ 1977 L356/1.

[30] Article 19(1), co-ordination regulation, supra, n. 1.

[31] The preamble to this decision provides that '[w]hereas given the characteristics of this investment, and its environmental impacts, it is compulsory to comply with Community law in this matter, and above all with . . . [the EIA Directive]'.

[32] *Observations submitted by the applicants in respect to the objection as to Admissibility (Reg. 29964) submitted by the defendant in Case T-585/93*, supra, n. 26, p. 9.

[33] This situation is more akin to that arising in the context of the cohesion fund which is project as opposed to programme based.

programmes, financial commitments and payment relate to 'measures'. An operational programme on tourism may, by way of example, comprise distinct measures relating to the provision or upgrading of tourist accommodation, training to improve tourism skills, and the development of tourist attractions and facilities. Such measures are not project specific.

The Commission on this basis may argue that validation operates at a high level of generality and that payment merely implies the transfer (albeit in tranches) of sums pertaining to measures, not individual projects. Such transfers may be thought, as the Commission argued in *An Taisce*, merely to afford Member States the opportunity to build certain projects of their choice. Formally, for operational programmes, this does indeed appear to be the case. Equally, were it to be accepted that responsibility for project selection rests exclusively with the Member States – an issue to which we will return – then the Commission may legitimately contend that it is not until final payment falls due (which may be as little as 20% of the relevant commitment) that it can be expected to possess detailed information on specific projects. Disbursement of final payments (in respect of each annual commitment) is conditional upon the submission, by Member States, of the reports referred to in Article 25(4) of the co-ordination regulation. Reporting procedures laid down by the Commission establish that such reports (annual and final reports) are to include a list of projects approved by measures, details of the amount of grant awarded, together with summary information given by the monitoring system.[34] Unless the Commission insists on receiving this information, it is difficult to see how it intends 'to play a more active role in the *prevention of infringements of environmental rules* within Structural Funds' . . . operations . . . [and to] make use of strict sanctions as envisaged in the provisions in force, including the reimbursement of Community Funds'.[35] At this stage it might consequently be argued that validation operates at a project specific level, and hence that disbursement of final payment constitutes an act capable of forming the subject matter of an action.

---

[34] See, for example, in relation to the Highlands and Islands Single Programming Document, *Annual Progress and Final Reports on Structural Fund Operations: Reference Format and Suggested Tables* (July 1995). Such documents may be presumed to constitute the 'jointly agreed reporting procedures' pursuant to Article 25(1) of the co-ordination regulation, supra, n. 1.

[35] Supra, n. 3, p. 11.

What, though, of the Commission's claim that responsibility for programme implementation lies with the Member State concerned? This is true, but Member States are, in this context, to act within the framework of 'partnership'.[36] This necessitates close consultations between the Commission, the Member States, regional and local government and a range of intermediate associations, acting in pursuit of a common goal. Hence, responsibility for programme implementation is shared. The clearest institutional expression of partnership takes the form of the establishment of monitoring committees.[37] Again, though, the governing regulations are obscure on this point, the Commission insists that 'project selection and implementation, are the remit of the monitoring committees'.[38] In practice, at least in many regions, this does appear to be the case.[39] The Commission is entitled to representation on such committees (DG XI and DG XVI). Moreover, crucially it (in the form of DG XVI) asserts, in this context, a 'non-negotiable right of veto', with a view to ensuring, *inter alia*, the conformity of operations financed with Community environmental law and policy.[40] Approval of a given project application by a monitoring committee might thus imply a decision by the Commission not to exercise this right of veto. Might this constitute a decision susceptible to review? If so, as will be seen below, this may have significant connotations in relation to *locus standi*. The answer to this question is, however, by no means clear. Formally, the role of monitoring committees in determining the fate of project applications is ambiguous, as is the legal status (effects) of their decisions and of the Commission's internal guide. The difficulty here is the elliptical nature of the governing legislation. Procedures for programme implementation have evolved in something approaching a legal vacuum. Equally, it is by no means certain to what extent an alleged decision adopted, but not in writing, by a Commission official within the framework of a monitoring committee, constitutes an act of the Commission producing legal effects, which would be susceptible to review.

Against such a backdrop the Commission seeks *de facto* to ass-

---

[36] Article 4(1), framework regulation, supra, n. 1.
[37] Article 25, co-ordination regulation, supra, n. 1.
[38] Supra, n. 13, p. 8.
[39] See, by way of example, Scott, J., 'From Rio to Inverness: Environment and Development in the Highlands and Islands "Objective 1" Enterprise Area' in Holder, J. (ed.), *The Impact of EC Environmental Law in the UK* (Wiley, 1997).
[40] DG XVI internal document, *Guide a l'usage des rapporteurs*.

ert some authority, but to deny all responsibility. Normatively, the applicants in *An Taisce* must be right: '. . . the Community cannot disclaim all responsibility for the possible environmental effects of projects which it finances, especially since most projects financed by Community structural funds would not be carried out by the Member State without such financing'.[41] The Commission's contentions in *Greenpeace* that the applicants are seeking to 'create a sort of "fiction" as regards the contested measure' is not only formalistic, but opportunistic. The CFI, however, elected not to address these arguments, declaring the application to be inadmissible on other grounds. Neither Greenpeace nor the 'others' were deemed to be 'individually concerned' by the putative act and, hence, given that the contested decision was not addressed to them, their standing to sue was denied. It is to this issue of *locus standi*, in the context of Community structural funding, that this chapter will now (briefly) turn.

Locus standi, Community structural funding and environmental compatibility

Much has been written criticizing the European Courts' restrictive approach to the question of standing, not least from the perspective of protecting the public interest in a clean and healthy environment.[42] The order of the CFI in *Greenpeace* merely adds grist to this particular mill. The applicants in this case were a mixed bag. Three environmental associations were joined by sixteen local residents. Each of the sixteen individuals asserted a credible interest in the contested act, be it economic, environmental, or quality of life-based.[43] But none was affected 'by reason of certain attributes . . . peculiar to them or by reason of circumstances in which they are differentiated from all other persons . . .'.[44] On the contrary, they were affected 'in the same manner as any other local resident, fisherman, farmer or tourist who is, or might be in the future, in the same situation'.[45] As such, they were not individually

---

41 Case T-461/93, supra, n. 13, para. 23.
42 See, generally, Reich and Micklitz (eds), *Public Interest Litigation Before the European Courts* (Nomos, Verlag, 1996).
43 They included, *inter alia*, a fisherman, ornithologist, doctor, taxi driver and windsurfer.
44 Case 25/62 *Plaumann & Co v Commission* [1963] ECR 95, p. 107.
45 Supra, n. 6, para. 55.

concerned. Likewise, the environmental associations, claiming to represent the general interest in environmental protection, did not succeed in demonstrating individual concern on the part of one or more of their members. On this basis, in the absence of 'special circumstances', their standing was denied.[46] Gérard, rightly, condemns this approach in the following terms:

> ... the Court seems to endorse the paradoxical situation by which the more people ... are adversely affected by Community decisions ... the less chance they have of being heard. ... The underlying problem is that concepts of individual interest are fundamentally antithetical to the environment. Environmental interests, by nature, are collective, concerning the many rather than the few. The Court here says, in essence, that environmental interests of a natural or legal person cannot ever usefully be invoked against a Community decision because they will not meet the test for admissibility. Held up against this, the Commission's own emphasis on access to justice for environmental associations [and individuals] in the Fifth Action Programme ... seems naive or even [dis]ingenuous [*sic*.].[47]

It should, however, be emphasized that there is a chink of light in the reasoning of the CFI, such as might give some hope to future applicants litigating in the name of environmental compatibility. Two of the individual applicants, and one of the applicant associations, sought to adduce 'special circumstances' in a bid to establish their individual concern. Whereas the former had submitted official complaints to the Commission over the construction of the power stations, the latter (Greenpeace) had both met, and exchanged correspondence with, the Commission. The CFI dismissed these factors as irrelevant, emphasizing that, nonetheless:

> No specific procedures are provided for whereby individuals may be associated with the adoption, implementation and monitoring of decisions taken in the field of financial assistance granted by the ERDF ... [and further that] the Commission did not, prior to the adoption of the contested decision, initiate any procedure in which

[46] Ibid., para. 59.
[47] Gérard, N., 'Access to Justice on Environmental Matters – a Case of Double Standards?' (1996) 8 JEL 149, pp. 152–3. The Fifth Action Programme insists that '[i]ndividuals and public interest groups should have practicable access to the court to ensure that their legitimate interests are protected and that prescribed environmental measures are effectively enforced and illegal practices stopped'.

Greenpeace participated; nor was Greenpeace in any way the interlocutor of the Commission with regard to the adoption of the basis Decision C91(440) and/or of the contested decision.

The implications appear to be that, in principle, participation in procedures associated with, or leading to the adoption of, a decision may be such to confer a special interest, justifying *locus standi*. This is entirely consistent with established jurisprudence. Individuals and associations playing a part in state aid proceedings under Article 93(2) (including complainants) have been granted standing;[48] their membership merely of an open category of persons affected by the decision, notwithstanding.[49] Comparable conclusions have been reached in respect of competition and anti-dumping proceedings.[50] Similarly, in the area of structural policy, the CFI has cited 'repeated participation in the meetings organized by the Commission, and the MAF, and thus in the procedure in conclusion of which the contested decision was adopted' as one factor attesting to the individual concern of an applicant seeking to challenge a Commission decision.[51]

It has nonetheless been argued that 'mere participation is, as a rule, insufficient to establish standing', evidence of 'specific injury' also being required.[52] In practice, such injury has typically taken the form of market prejudice, giving rise to a substantive economic interest, albeit an economic interest which does not distinguish the applicant individually.[53] In *Greenpeace*, however, the CFI chooses not to distinguish between economic and environmental interests in defining the parameters of individual concern. The same rules remain '. . . applicable whatever the nature, economic or other-

---

48 The status of complainants to challenge a negative Commission decision not to initiate proceedings varies according to the substantive issue at hand. For example, this is possible in the case of anti-dumping proceedings but not in competition cases.

49 See, for example, Case 169/84 *Cofaz v Commission* [1986] ECR 391 and Cases 67–8 and 70/85 *Van der Kooy v Commission* [1988] ECR 219 and, in respect of complainants, Case 198/91 *Cook v Commission* [1993] ECR I-2487.

50 See, generally, supra, n. 25, pp. 378–83.

51 Case T-465/93 *Consorzio Gruppo di Azione Locale Murgia Messapica* v *Commission* [1994] ECR II-361, para. 26.

52 Bernard, N., 'Citizenship in a Polycentric Polity' (unpublished manuscript).

53 See Case T-37/92 *BEUC and NCC v Commission* [1994] ECR II-285, where consumer associations representing the economic interests of consumers generally were able to challenge a Commission decision by virtue of their status as a complainant pursuant to Article 85.

wise, of those of the applicants' interests which are affected'.[54] There is nothing here to suggest that participation in the procedures associated with the adoption of a reviewable act, backed up by evidence of a collective environmental interest, would not be such as to confer standing.

What, then, is the relevance of this for structural funding? It is to be found in the operation of the concept of partnership, outlined above. Were it to be accepted that the Commission 'acts' within the framework of a monitoring committee, by deciding whether or not to exercise the non-negotiable right of veto to which it lays claim, then a broad range of actors may be thought to be closely associated with the adoption of this decision; certainly those organizations represented on this committee, and arguably even those comprising technical sub-committees established to advise the monitoring committee. The identity of such persons will vary according to the composition of the partnership established. It is then apparent that issues of standing are inextricably tied to the vexed question of the identity of the contested act. Conclusions in respect of the latter may have important implications for the former.

Advocate General Cosmas recently issued his opinion in the *Greenpeace* appeal. In this he argues that it may be possible to identify a closed class of persons who are affected in a different and more intense manner, by virtue of proximity to the environmental intervention or the extent (gravity) of the consequences suffered. This concession does not, however, lead him to uphold the appeal, having regard to the specific facts of this case.

Environmental compatibility before the national courts

The European Court's approach to issues of standing is eclectic. It has been argued that a number of policy considerations influence its conclusions in this respect.[55] One factor 'which *has* been alluded to in some judgments . . . is whether there is any alternative remedy open to the applicant . . . . Such a remedy would normally be in the national courts . . .'.[56] In the absence of such a remedy,

[54] Supra, n. 26, para. 50.
[55] Supra, n. 25, pp. 376–7.
[56] Ibid., p. 377.

standing has tended to be more readily conceded. In view of the difficulties outlined above in establishing the existence of a Community level act, and Member States' putative responsibility for programme implementation, it may be thought that national courts represent the appropriate forum for the enforcement of environmental compatibility:

> It is, after all, a matter of national jurisdiction to ensure legal protection for private parties in order to safeguard the rights that individuals derive from the direct effect of provisions of Community law. If the project was not in accordance with Community environmental law or policy, a national court would have had to defer the implementation measures or declare them void . . .[57]

Two principal difficulties inhere in this approach, each militating in favour of European court involvement in policing the application of environmental compatibility. First, by no means all Community environmental law is susceptible to effective enforcement in national courts, by way of the established principles of direct and 'indirect' effect. One need merely recall here discussion in the previous chapter concerning the EIA directive; a measure of primary importance for structural funding.

Second, the principle of environmental compatibility is commendably broad. It is predicated upon a tripartite distinction between the Treaty, instruments adopted thereunder, and environmental policy. The effect of this trichotomy is to make clear that conformity requires compatibility not only with binding Community instruments, but also with Community policy more broadly defined. This was particularly salient prior to the entry into force of the Maastricht Treaty, at which time Community environmental action programmes (policy) were not formally adopted under the Treaty. Post-Maastricht, the Treaty provides that the act-ivities of the Community shall include a policy in the sphere of the environment.[58] This policy encompasses all manner of legal acts under Article 189, together with international agreements to which the Community is party, and environmental action programmes. Community environmental policy, as such, today com-

---

57 Comijs, D., 'Individual Legal Protection under the Structural Funds' (1995) 2 MJ 187.
58 Article 3(k).

prises both binding and non-binding enactments.[59] 'Policy', in Scots 'the pleasure-grounds surrounding a mansion', extends also, in Community environmental discourse, to the mansion itself.

In principle, the effect of Article 7(1) of the framework regulation is to compel compliance, on the part both of the Community and of its Member States, with instruments and concepts which, in other circumstances, would not be regarded as binding at all (action programmes), or binding merely upon the Community legislature (Article 130r principles). The objectives which inhere in such measures tend to be broadly defined and to necessitate the exercise of broad discretion. To this extent, they are inherently unsuited to adjudication before national courts. Though even the European courts may be anticipated to favour a 'light touch' approach to judicial review on the basis of instruments merely comprising broad policy orientations, experience in other spheres suggests that they would, at least, intervene to correct a patent or manifest error, or to prevent a misuse of power.[60]

The development planning process and environmental compatibility

Litigating in the name of environmental compatibility should be viewed as a last resort; not least, but not only, in view of the difficulties outlined above. It is necessary to add to these: the cost of litigation; the time factor; the principle that preventive action should be taken; and the breakdown in communication and trust between actors (repeat players in an on-going relationship) which it implies. Nonetheless, the threat of successful litigation represents a powerful incentive for actors, at all levels, to ensure that the development planning process proceeds in a manner which is environmentally sagacious. This is of particular importance as the legislation governing structural funding is laconic as regards the place of environmental considerations in development planning.

Though Member States are required to submit to the Commission information pertaining to the environmental dimension of

---

[59] A pedant might suggest at this point that the time has come to delete, as devoid of any independent meaning, the reference to instruments adopted under the Treaty.

[60] On this issue of 'intensity of review' see Craig and de Burca, *EC Law*, pp. 501–5.

development plans, programmes and projects, the parameters of the data to be provided is defined only in the most general terms. Consequently, the quality of environmental assessment undertaken, in practice, (at both a strategic and project specific level) varies considerably across the Community's regions.[61] Development plans submitted by Member States are to include an appraisal of the environmental situation in the area concerned, and an evaluation of the environmental impact of the proposed development strategy and operations. The latter is to be provided 'in terms of sustainable development in agreement with the provisions of Community law in force'.[62] Also to be included are details of arrangements made to associate environmental authorities in the preparation and implementation of the plan and to ensure compliance with Community environmental rules.[63] Member State applications for assistance, including that devolving to operational programmes, shall include such information as is necessary to permit verification of environmental compatibility.[64]

At the level of programme implementation, it is for Member States to determine the composition and operating procedures of the monitoring committees, and the role of environmental bodies therein. Formulation of project selection criteria is the responsibility of the Member State concerned. Additional information is to be submitted pursuant to the jointly agreed reporting procedures. Again, this is defined in the broadest terms; for example, description of programme delivery and management structures, methodology and criteria for project selection, composition and operation of the monitoring committees, information relating to the observance of Community policies at the level of each measure and steps undertaken to ensure observance of these policies.

The Commission conceives its role in terms of the 'encouragement, screening and coordination of national practices which will be managed in a climate of partnership rather than obligation'.[65] There is much to be said in favour of such an approach. It implies a genuine sharing of responsibility, which is essential given the

---

61 For an assessment of the manner in which environmental considerations have penetrated the development planning process in the Highlands and Islands objective 1 region see supra, n. 39.

62 See, for example, in relation to objective 1 regions, Article 9(8), framework regulation, supra, n. 1.

63 Ibid.

64 Article 14(2), co-ordination regulation, supra, n. 1.

65 Supra, n. 3, p. 9.

Commission's limited resources. It is predicated upon an acceptance of diversity and devolution in governance, such as is in keeping with the concept of (substantive) subsidiarity. The notion of partnership is conceptually exciting, offering immense possibilities in thinking about the realization of meaningful (participatory) democracy in the European Union, within the framework of a polity which is simultaneously big and small. But, as the Commission itself notes, there is a pressing need to develop a clearer role for environmental authorities in programme implementation, to further develop appropriate project selection (as well as *ex post* impact) criteria, and to promote dialogue with representative environmental NGOs, operating within the framework of the partnership.[66] In addition, the quality of strategic environmental assessment (at the level of plans and programmes) needs to be assured, not only through constructive dialogue, but also by the promulgation of a clearer legal framework[67] outlining minimum obligations and conditions for the granting of Community assistance. Mutual trust may be enhanced, rather than undermined, by a clearer articulation of the respective obligations of actors participating in development planning.

It is not being suggested that the Commission can realistically scrutinize the details of every project to receive structural funding. However, it is realistic to ask that the Commission more thoroughly supervise the management systems which are put in place in order to ensure respect for the principle of environmental compatibility. A recent Commission regulation establishes detailed arrangements for the financial control by Member States of operations co-financed by the Structural Funds.[68] This requires Member States to notify the Commission of the description of their management and control systems, and to up-date this information on a regular basis. It further requires Member States to organize internal controls and on-the-spot checks in order to verify the effectiveness of national systems. This includes an obligation to verify compliance with the principle of environmental compatibility.[69] This initiative is to be welcomed, although in practice its effectiveness depends upon the quality of information which the

---

[66] Ibid.
[67] See Ch. 6.
[68] Pursuant to Article 23(1) of the co-ordination regulation, supra, n. 1. Commission Regulation 2064/97 OJ 1997 L290/1.
[69] Ibid., Article 4 (final paragraph).

Commission insists upon receiving. The prospect of a successful action against the Commission before the European Courts, under Article 173, may provide just the incentive required to ensure proper scrutiny.

Conclusion

It is undeniable that, over recent years, the environment has been accorded a high profile in the operation of the Community's regional policy. There remain, however, significant problems associated with the enforcement of the principle of environmental compatibility. These are complicated by virtue of the uncertainty which arises, against a backdrop of what are quite dramatically new forms of shared (or multi-level) governance, as to the identity of the authorities with responsibility for ensuring compliance with this principle. The concept of partnership, a concrete expression of the Community's commitment to 'shared responsibility' in the environmental sphere, carries with it the danger, alluded to in Steinbeck's *The Grapes of Wrath*, that we don't (figuratively) know 'who to shoot'. Devolution in decision-making, pursued in the name of both efficiency and democracy, must imply, or so the Commission contends, a transfer not only of power but of responsibility. But where the transfer is not absolute, lines of accountability become confused.

'Partnership' has been defined, by the former Commissioner responsible for regional development, as implying the 'close involvement of regional and local bodies with the Commission and national authorities in planning and implementing development measures'.[70] It requires that Community operations be established through close consultations between the Commission, the Member State concerned and the competent authorities and bodies including, within the framework of national rules and practices, the so-called social and economic partners designated by the Member State at national, regional, local or other level. With its emphasis upon shared governance and participation by intermediate associations (both governmental and non-governmental), together with the apparently non-hierarchical, conversational, nature of deci-

---

70 Millan, B., 'Introduction' to the *Community Support Frameworks* for the Programming Period 1989–1993 (Commission of the European Communities).

sion-making structures which it implies, it appears to represent a genuine experiment in responsive law-making and democratic (civic) participation. It should, however, be observed that 'partnership' in practice, takes a myriad of forms, reflecting national constitutional traditions.

It is, of course, no coincidence that it is in the area of development policy that such experiments in democracy and devolution have been piloted in the Community. The certainty which appears once to have surrounded the idea of development as an unqualified human value, universal in its connotations and progressive in its orientation, is today frequently greeted with incredulity. Development has become 'development' – inverted commas representing a slim defence against allegations of imperialist posturing and cultural (economic) hegemony. Even in a world characterized by inequality and disabling poverty, 'development' is perceived as threat as well as opportunity. Attempts to transcend the narrow and unidimensional logic of economic development (as per capita GDP or GNP) and to rescue development's human face (through, for example, the language of 'basic needs') have been perceived as yet more threatening to life quality and culture, not least by virtue of their insidious appeal.[71] It is against such a backdrop that notions of participation in development should be understood – as an attempt to recover the legitimacy of development discourse. 'Partnership' represents a Community version of a global phenomenon.

In that this chapter (and indeed the previous one) has been concerned, in part, with issues of enforcement in Community law, it leads on to the concluding chapter to this volume. The topic of enforcement is vast and multi-faceted. The final chapter will consider briefly the adequacy of existing enforcement mechanisms, but also examine a number of new approaches to the challenge of enforcement, including recourse to environmental agreements.

[71] Illich, I., 'Needs' in Sachs, W., *The Development Dictionary* (1992, Pluto).

CHAPTER EIGHT

Enforcing EC environmental law

In the first chapter of this book we looked at the rationale for EC environmental law. This was considered against a backdrop of environmental externalities and the danger of 'free-riding', where enjoyment of the benefits associated with environmental amelioration cannot be confined to those contributing to the improvement. It was recognized that, though the collectivity may benefit from a change in behaviour, such a change was unlikely to be achieved in the absence of intervention. Law may be viewed as a means of generating trust between actors, and of creating a level of predictability (in terms of behaviour) such as may counter the phenomenon of free-riding. However, for it to serve such a function, the law which seeks to manage environmental change, must be (and be perceived to be) enforceable and enforced. It is with this issue of enforcement that this chapter is concerned. The term 'enforcement' is used as a convenient shorthand to cover a multitude of forms of compliance or non-compliance with Community law, including formal implementation and practical application.

Needless to say, enforcement represents only one aspect of law's claims to legitimacy. Roger Cotterrell expresses this well in the language of *voluntas* and *ratio* in law.[1] Whereas the former speaks to law's 'capacity to decree', the latter is concerned with its 'capacity to persuade':

> Law's authority as *voluntas* can promote peace, order, and security, but usually only when it is constrained and channelled by doctrinal principles that make it sufficiently predictable and rational in operation. Conversely, the elaboration of *ratio* in legal doctrine can provide intelligible principles of justice in social relationships, yet these have only limited practical significance unless

1 *Law's Community* (OUP, 1995), pp. 317–20.

they can be imposed by authority on those for whom the general reasonableness of moral persuasiveness of principle is an insufficient motive for compliance in the face of conflicting specific interests.[2]

Though, as will be seen in this chapter, there are substantial problems inherent in existing mechanisms for the enforcement of Community law, relatively, as a species of non-state law, European Community law is remarkably strong on *voluntas*. It may, however, be thought to be rather weaker in terms of *ratio*. As Cotterrell tells us, the two are, ultimately, interdependent. Concerns surrounding deficiencies of enforcement in Community law should not be allowed to conceal the very fundamental questions surrounding the legitimacy of EC law.

This chapter will begin by examining the role of the Commission as 'watchdog' of Community law, and the role of courts, European and national, in securing compliance with Community environmental law. It will, in this context, return to the crucial question of interim protection alluded to in Chapter 6. It will turn finally to consider briefly the Commission's recent communication on environmental agreements, and the role of such agreements in securing effective enforcement. Wherever possible, examples will be drawn from the area of water quality; a substantive topic of enormous significance which has not been examined in its own right in this book (see generally COM(96)59 final).

The Commission as 'watchdog'

The EC Treaty places the Commission at the heart of the system for the enforcement of Community law. A brief survey of the table of cases to this book serves to exemplify the significance of the Commission as an agent of enforcement. Article 169 provides that:

> If the Commission considers that a Member State has failed to fulfil an obligation under this Treaty, it shall deliver a reasoned opinion on the matter after giving the State concerned the opportunity to submit its observations.
>
> If the State concerned does not comply with the opinion within the period laid down by the Commission, the latter may bring the matter before the Court of Justice.

Article 169 enforcement actions thus comprise both an administra-

2 Ibid., p. 319.

tive and a judicial phase. The vast majority of proceedings commenced never reach the European Court. In its twelfth report on monitoring the application of Community law,[3] the Commission notes that in 1994, as regards Member State failure to notify measures implementing environmental directives, it issued 42 Article 169 letters, 46 reasoned opinions and only three referrals to the European Court.[4] The secrecy which surrounds Commission/ Member State negotiations during the administrative stage is such that it is difficult to assess with any accuracy whether this low referral rate constitutes a vindication of the effectiveness of the administrative phase, or an indictment of Commission diffidence.

For a long time, criticism of this enforcement mechanism focused upon the declaratory nature of the European Court's judgment, finding a Member State to be in breach of its EC law obligations. Today, pursuant to the entry into force of the Maastricht Treaty, the Commission may institute a new action against any Member State failing to comply with a judgment of the Court. The European Court may, in such circumstances, impose a lump sum or penalty payment upon the offending Member State.[5] The current Commissioner with responsibility for environment (Ritt Bjerregaard) has instituted a number of follow-up actions under Article 171. The scale of the potential fines involved (for example, up to quarter of a million ECU per day in respect of a German failure to respect Community law regulating the environmental quality of groundwater), and the widespread publicity which has surrounded Bjerregaard's tough stance, has had the desired effect of 'persuading' recalcitrant states to step into line. Recent successes, however, should not be allowed to obscure the very real problems associated with the Commission's role as watchdog of Community environmental law.

Rhiannon Williams was formerly a lawyer working for DG XI (environment). She offers a vivid portrait of the Commission at work in the performance of its role as watchdog.[6] Of the many trenchant criticisms which she makes, none is more telling than

---

3   COM(95) 500 final.

4   See Macrory and Purdy, 'The Enforcement of EC Environmental Laws Against Member States' in Holder, J., *The Impact of EC Environmental Law in the United Kingdom* (Wiley, 1997) for an analysis of this report. They suggest that the figures should have read as follows: 62 letters, 53 reasoned opinions and three referrals.

5   Article 171 EC.

6   'The European Commission and the Enforcement of Environment law; an Invidious Position' (1994) YEL 351.

that pertaining to the politicization of the Commission's enforcement function. There is, she argues, a suspicion that 'good infringement cases . . . may be sacrificed to political causes'. She adds (provocatively) that 'good men' may be similarly sacrificed. She refers here to the fate of Ludwig Kramer, who was transferred from his position as Head of the DG XI Legal Affairs Unit (to Waste), allegedly due to his reluctance to 'compromise on issues of legal principle in enforcement investigations and infringement proceedings'.[7] She argues that 'political factors' may 'influence the case at a variety of stages'; when the Head of the DG XI Legal Affairs Unit considers whether to recommend the commencement of infringement proceedings, when the DG XI Technical or Policy Units comment on the proposal, when the Commission legal service comments upon it, and finally when the proposal is considered by the Heads of Cabinet (Chefs de Cabinet) and the Commissioners.[8] As was emphasized in the previous chapter, the Commission has total discretion when it comes to the question of whether to institute proceedings. Notwithstanding recent pressure from the Ombudsman, Jacob Sodermann, the Commission 'has stopped short of promising to explain why it has decided not to proceed with particular infringement cases'.[9]

Williams offers two specific illustrations in support of her thesis. One of these relates to the delay which surrounded the oral hearing before the European Court, in a case against the United Kingdom for failure to comply with the bathing waters directive.[10] The hearing was originally scheduled for March 1992. It was deferred on two occasions, once until after the United Kingdom general election, and for the second time upon United Kingdom assumption of the Council Presidency. Ultimately, following oral argument on 27 October 1992, the Court issued judgment on 14 July 1993, more than three years after the Commission's Article

7 Ibid., p. 358.
8 Ibid., p. 364. A formal decision of the College of Commissioners is required to open infringement proceedings, except where these relate to a failure to notify the Commission of implementing measures in relation to a directive.
9 Linton, L., 'Infringement procedure to be made more open' *European Voice* http://www.european-voice.com
10 Council Directive 76/160 OJ 1976 L31/1. The other relates to the Twyford Down 'pipe-line' project mentioned in Ch. 6. Since his resignation, Ripa de Meana, formerly Commissioner with responsibility for the enviroment, has spoken out about the political pressure exerted to dissuade the Commission from taking an action against the United Kingdom, just at the time that Maastricht negotiations were at a crucial stage.

169 application.[11] In its judgment the Court held that the quality
of bathing waters of Blackpool and of those adjacent to Southport
failed to conform with the target standards laid down in the directive. The United Kingdom's defence that it had taken all practicable steps to meet these standards (although it had not established
the physical impossibility of so doing) was rejected by the Court.
In another water case, concerning the drinking water directive,[12]
the Court insisted that neither practical or administrative difficulties, nor financial difficulties, could excuse Member States from a
failure to fulfil their obligations.[13]

Allegations of the sort put forward by Williams are impossible
to substantiate. What is, however, clear is that there is a *perception* that political factors such as, for example, the need to garner
Member State support for a particular legislative proposal or
Treaty amendment, influence the Commission in the performance
of its enforcement functions. A survey, cited by Williams, of environmental NGOs confirms this. This is, in itself, important, and leads
on to a second fundamental criticism of the Commission's capacity
to act as guardian of the Treaty.

The Commission's capacity to perform its enforcement function
is contingent upon the quality of information which it receives. In
the absence of a Commission environmental inspectorate, complaints by private parties and NGOs are crucial in alerting the
Commission to possible infringements. Were would-be complainants to be deterred by a perception that the Commission is unlikely
to fully or adequately investigate or follow through complaints,
this would have the effect of exacerbating the 'information gap'
with which the Commission must contend.[14] The Commission itself concedes that it:

> ... has only limited powers to monitor the correct application of
> Community environmental law. It is almost entirely dependent on
> information supplied to it on an ad hoc basis by complaints, by
> petitions to and written and oral questions from the European
> Parliament, by non-governmental organisations, by the media and
> by the Member States themselves.[15]

11 Case C-56/90 *Commission* v *United Kingdom* [1993] ECR I-4109.
12 Council Directive 80/778 OJ 1980 L229/11.
13 Case C-42/89 *Commission* v *Belgium* [1990] ECR I-2821.
14 Macrory, R., 'The Enforcement of Community Environmental Law: Some
    Critical Remarks' (1992) 29 CMLRev. 347, p. 362.
15 COM(96)500 *Communication on Implementing Community Environmental
    Law*, p. 5.

This information deficit is particularly acute in relation to 'implementation in practice' as opposed to 'black letter implementation'.[16] As to the latter, Member States are obliged to communicate to the Commission the texts of the main provisions of national law adopted to implement a directive. As to the former, Member States are obliged, according to the terms of many environmental directives, to submit periodic reports to the Commission on the implementation of Community law measures. All the evidence suggests that Member State compliance with these reporting requirements is poor.[17] Ludwig Kramer suggests that no more than 10% of reports are received by the Commission.[18] In 1991 a directive was adopted standardizing and rationalizing environmental implementation reports, this in a bid to ensure the reliability and comparability of data received.[19] Within nine months of receiving the relevant reports, the Commission is to publish a Community-wide report. The first sectoral report, which concerns the water sector, was due to be published in 1997. The Commission has stressed the need to more closely involve the Environment Agency in the assessment and follow up of these reports.[20] More generally, it recognizes the significance, in terms of implementation, of this agency in that it is intended to provide the Community, and the Member States, with objective, reliable and comparable information on the state of the environment.[21]

It is significant, however, that the Commission stops short of proposing any formal inspectorate or enforcement function for the Agency. On the contrary, the proposals which the Commission puts forward militate strongly in the direction of the devolution of responsibility for enforcement. This is consistent with the approach which was considered in the previous chapter in respect of environmental compatibility and Community structural funding.

---

16 Ibid.
17 See Wilkinson, D., *The State of Reporting by the EC Commission in Fulfilment of Obligations Contained in EC Environmental Legislation* (Institute of European Environmental Law, 1994), and House of Lords Select Committee on the European Communities, *Report on the Implementation and Enforcement of Environmental Legislation* 1991–2, 9th Report, HL Paper 53-I, pp. 17–18.
18 Cited in Davies, P. G. G., 'The European Environment Agency' (1994) YEL 313, p. 334.
19 Council Directive 91/692 OJ 1991 L377/48.
20 Supra, n. 15, para. 59. See Council Regulation 1210/90 on the Establishment of the European Environment Agency and the European Environment Information and Observation Network, OJ 1990 L120/1.
21 Ibid.

The Commission presents, in its communication on implementation, three main 'new areas for action'.[22] The first to be 'considered' relates to the drawing up of guidelines establishing minimum criteria for Member State inspections in relation, for example, to the monitoring of industrial emissions and environmental quality standards (target standards). It is proposed that it may be necessary to combine this with the establishment of a 'limited Community body' with responsibility for auditing Member State fulfilment of their inspection duties.[23]

The second would take us yet further down this road of decentralized enforcement. The Commission proposes to consider adopting guidelines governing non-judicial complaint investigation procedures in Member States. Citizen complaints would, in the first instance, be directed to, and investigated by, appropriate bodies within the Member States. The Commission observes that such procedures already exist in a number of Member States and that they take, generally, one of two forms; an independent ombudsman or a system of administrative review.

Finally, the Commission returns to a theme which has long been familiar: access to justice. The Commission emphasizes that, at present, responsibility for enforcement of environmental law 'mainly rests with public authorities, and is dependent on their powers, resources and goodwill', and that there is a need to provide 'supplementary avenues for improving enforcement'.[24] Steps need to be taken to promote access, by citizens and NGOs seeking to promote the protection of ecological interests, to Member State courts. In particular, environmental associations recognized by Member States should be accorded *locus standi* to bring actions before these courts. The Commission proposes to examine the need for guidelines on access to national courts by representative associations. It acknowledges frankly that 'there is no possibility that the resources in time and personnel which are available to the Commission and to the Court of Justice in Luxembourg will ever be sufficient for, not even a majority, of environmental cases arising in all Member States to be dealt with through direct actions brought by the Commission in the Court of Justice'.[25]

These Commission proposals have much merit, this notwith-

22 Supra, n. 15, pp. 8–13.
23 Ibid., p. 9.
24 Ibid., p. 11.
25 Ibid., p. 12.

standing a certain irony surrounding its observations on access to justice in view of the Community's own rules on standing. As is so often the case in the Community, proposals born of pragmatism may be defended in the language of subsidiarity. It is to the role of Member State courts in enforcing EC environmental law that this chapter will now turn.

Community environmental law before Member State courts

In February 1996 the English High Court quashed two decisions of the Secretary of State for the Environment adopted pursuant to the Urban Waste Water Treatment (England and Wales) Regulations 1994.[26] By these decisions the Secretary of State had designated the outer estuarine limits of the Humber and Severn estuaries, for the purpose of the application of the Community's urban waste water directive.[27] The significance of the Minister's decisions lay in the type of treatment required to be applied to waste water discharged. Waste discharged from agglomerations of more than 150,000 people was in general to be subject to both primary (physical and/or chemical) and more expensive secondary (biological) treatment. Only in exceptional circumstances, where it could be demonstrated that the latter would not produce any environmental benefit, and where the discharge was to 'less sensitive areas' of *coastal* waters, was primary treatment to suffice.[28] Hence, by designating stretches of what we think of as the Humber and Severn rivers as coastal waters, substantial cost savings were to accrue (to the quite recently privatized water companies).

The directive itself was unhelpful on the question of designation; an estuary being defined as a transitional area at the mouth of a river between fresh-water and coastal waters, and coastal waters as the waters outside the low-water line or the outer limit of an estuary.[29] The definitions laid down were thus circular in na-

---

26 *R* v *Secretary of State for the Environment*, ex p *Kingston-upon-Hull City Council* and *R* v *Secretary of State for the Environment*, ex p *Bristol City Council and Woodspring District Council* [1996] 8 JEL 336, including a commentary by Caroline Blatch.

27 Council Directive 91/271 OJ 1991 L135/40.

28 Ibid., Articles 8(5) and 6(2). Annex II B lays down the criteria for the identification of less sensitive areas.

29 Ibid., Article 1.

ture. As the directive does not establish criteria for designation, the Court held that Member States enjoy considerable discretion. It would not be right to confine them, in exercising this discretion, to considerations of salinity (as the applicants had argued) or topography (as the respondent argued, having used the Humber and Severn bridges as marking the outermost limit of coastal waters). The most that could be required was that 'there must be a genuine and rational assessment in each case of what actually constitutes the estuary having regard to all the relevant circumstances relating to the characteristics of the area of water in question and having regard to the purpose of the Directive'.[30] The purpose of the directive to prevent adverse environmental effects may be taken into account. However, cost considerations may not. These constitute irrelevant considerations. 'An area of water either is or is not an estuary regardless of what it will cost to treat waste water discharged into it.'[31] This conclusion was confirmed through recourse to the directive, Article 3(1) of which provides that water collecting systems need not be provided where this would involve 'excessive cost'. There is no similar cost/benefit facility under Article 8(5). Harrison J, being satisfied that cost considerations had 'played a major role' in designating the outer limits of the estuaries, and having heard no other credible explanation, granted orders of *certiorari* to quash both the Hull and the Severn decisions.

It would be easy to gain the impression, 'as we await the first successful case on direct effect of an environmental directive',[32] that national courts have no role to play in the enforcement of EC environmental law. This recent case reminds us that this is not so. The applicants in this case were not seeking to vindicate rights arising from the directive and hence the question of direct effect did not arise. Direct effect is not invariably a prerequisite for a national court to be seized with an issue of Community law. There appear to be three situations in which national courts will be required to adjudicate upon Community law questions, even where the relevant Community law is not capable of direct effect.

The first arises out of a concept sometimes known (confusingly) as 'indirect effect'. This is a mechanism developed by the European Court which serves, partially, to fill the enforcement gap generated by the distinction between 'vertical' and 'horizontal' direct effect

30 Ibid., p. 343.
31 Ibid.
32 Holder, J., 'Introduction' in supra, n. 4, p. 7.

of directives; directives being, in principle, capable of the former but not the latter.[33] According to this, national courts are obliged to construe national law, as far as is possible, in the light of the wording and purpose of a directive in order to achieve the result pursued by that directive.[34] There are limits to this obligation ('as far as possible') which the European Court has expressed through recourse to the Community law general principles of legal certainty and non-retroactivity. All that we know with any certainty is that a directive cannot, independent of implementing legislation, have the effect of determining or aggravating the criminal liability of persons who act in contravention of it.[35]

The second situation in which non-directly effective Community law may be justiciable before national courts is exemplified by the estuary case under discussion. This takes us back also to Chapter 6 and to the recent judgment of the European Court in *Kraaijeveld*.[36] We saw there that Community law may enjoy 'public law effect', whereby national courts will be obliged to have regard to the relevant Community law in assessing whether public law powers have been exercised in a manner which is lawful. Crucially, to conclude that a Community measure is not capable of direct effect, is not to conclude that it is not susceptible to application before national courts, even directly in an action for judicial review. In this sense the Commission is correct to be stressing the importance of national level *locus standi* rules. It is, however, apparent that there are limits to the effectiveness of judicial review as a mechanism for the enforcement of Community environmental law. As Rehbinder puts it:

> ... the effectiveness of judicial review of administrative action ... depends on the availability of, and access to, administrative review, the remedies of the parties and the powers of the court, including the availability of interim relief, the kind of decisions that are subject to judicial review, the scope of judicial review as to procedure and the merits, and the distribution of the costs of

---

[33] Case C-91/92 *Faccini Dori* v *Recreb* [1994] ECR I-3325. But see Case 129/94 Criminal Proceedings against Rafael Ruiz Berualdez [1996] ECR I-1829.

[34] See Case 14/83 *Von Colson & Kamann* v *Land Nordrhein-Westfalen* [1984] ECR 1891 and Case C-106/89 *Marleasing* v *La Comercial Internacionale de Alimentacion SA* [1990] ECR I-4135.

[35] Case 80/86 *Criminal Proceedings against Kolpinghuis Nijmegen BV* [1987] ECR 3969, para. 14.

[36] Case C-72/95, [1996] ECR I-5403. See also Case 168/95 *Criminal Proceedings Against Arcaro* [1996] ECR I-4705, at para. 41 for a stricter statement of the limits to 'indirect' effect.

litigation. There are great differences between the Member States in this respect.[37]

That said, the European Court has been prepared to deprive Member State courts of a degree of autonomy (procedural and substantive) with a view to securing the effective protection of directly effective Community law rights. National rules which make it excessively difficult to vindicate such rights are to be set aside.[38] We will see an example of this, in the context of interim protection, below. To what extent the European Court might be prepared to limit national judicial autonomy where the relevant provisions of Community law are not directly effective, and where they do not confer rights on individuals – enjoying merely 'public law effect' – remains to be seen.

The third scenario in which non-directly effective Community law may generate a right of action before national courts arises as a result of the European Court's judgment in *Francovich*.[39] Here the Court established the principle of state liability in damages for breach of Community law. The availability of this remedy is not contingent upon the relevant provision of Community law being (or not being) directly effective. It depends rather upon the rule in question being such as to confer rights on individuals (the content of which is identifiable), the seriousness of the Member State breach, and the existence of a causal link between the breach and the damage sustained. So far the case law of the Court has focused upon the requirement that the breach of Community law be 'sufficiently serious'. Certain breaches are to be regarded as automatically so, such as where there is settled case law of the Court on the matter. Otherwise, by way of analogy with Article 215, it must be demonstrated that the Member State has gravely and manifestly disregarded the limits on its discretion. The Court has identified a number of factors which may be taken into consideration by the national court in assessing the seriousness of the breach. These include the clarity and precision of the rule breached, the measure of discretion which the rule accorded to the Member State, the ques-

---

37 Rehbinder, E., '*Locus Standi*, Community Law and the Case for Harmonization' in Somsen, H., *Protecting the European Environment* (Blackstone, 1996), pp. 163–4.
38 For an excellent overview of the law in this area see Flynn, L., 'Taking Remedies Too Seriously? National Procedural Autonomy in the European Court of Justice' (1996) 31 Irish Jurist 110.
39 Cases C-6 & 9/90 *Francovich and Bonifaci* v *Italian State* [1991] ECR I-5357.

tion of whether the breach was intentional or involuntary, or ex-
cusable or inexcusable, and consideration of whether the position
taken by a Community institution may have contributed to the
breach.[40]

It is apparent that the threat of liability in damages represents a
powerful incentive for Member State to strive to comply with their
Community law obligations. Yet the utility of this remedy in the
area of environmental law is by no means certain. Particularly
problematic is the first of the three conditions cited, namely the requirement that the Community measure confer rights upon individuals.[41] A small number of Community environmental directives
self-evidently confer rights upon individuals. This is readily apparent, for example, in relation to the access to environmental information directive.[42] This provides that Member States shall ensure
that public authorities, and bodies with public responsibilities for
the environment and under the control of public authorities, are
required to make available information relating to the environment to any natural or legal person, without that person having to
prove an interest.[43] Subject to a number of public interest exceptions,[44] this establishes a right of access to certain environmental
information. Any person who considers that his or her request for
information has been unreasonably refused or ignored, or inadequ-
ately answered, may seek judicial or administrative review of this
decision.[45] Similarly, the EIA directive, discussed in Chapter 6,
confers certain information and consultation (participation) rights
on individuals.

Most Community environmental measures, however, do not ex-

---

40   See, especially, Cases C-46 & 48/93 *Brasserie Du Pecheur SA* v *Germany* and *R*
     v *Secretary of State for Transport* ex p *Factortame Ltd and Others* [1996] ECR
     I-1029; Case C-392/93 *R* v *H.M. Treasury,* ex p *British Telecommunications*
     [1996] ECR I-1631; Case C-5/94 *R* v *Ministry of Agriculture, Fisheries & Food,*
     ex p *Hedley Lomas (Ireland) Ltd* [1996] ECR I-2553.
41   See, generally, Hilson, C., 'Community Rights in Environmental Law: Rhetoric
     or Reality?' in Holder, supra, n. 4.
42   Council Directive 90/313 OJ 1990 L158/56. See House of Lords Select
     Committee on the European Communities, *Freedom of Access to Information
     on the Environment* Session 1989–90, First Report.
43   Ibid., Articles 3(1) and 6.
44   Ibid., Article 3(2). These include, for example, confidentiality of proceedings of
     public authorities, international relations, or national defence; public security;
     commercial and industrial confidentiality; and where disclosure would make it
     more likely that the environment to which the material is related would be
     damaged.
45   Ibid., Article 4.

plicitly confer rights on individuals, but simply create obligations which are binding on Member States as regards environmental quality. The European Court has, nonetheless, been prepared to concede on a number of occasions that directives regulating water quality (through the introduction of target and performance standards) are intended to confer rights on individuals. Thus, in *Commission* v *Germany*, the Court concluded that 'whenever non-compliance with the measures required by the [drinking water] directives in question might endanger the health of persons, those concerned should be able to rely on mandatory rules in order to enforce their rights'.[46] Similarly, in another action against Germany, concerning the groundwater directive, the Court accepts that the purpose of the directive is to 'create rights and obligations for individuals'.[47] A comparable approach has been adopted as regards air quality legislation.[48]

Though, in the case of the groundwater directive, the link between the measure and the protection of human health was not explicit, each of the directives under consideration in these cases was intended to protect the public interest in a healthy environment. Individuals have a direct, personal, interest in the quality of the water which they drink or in which they bathe, and in the quality of the air which they breath. Their physical health depends upon it. It has been argued that in this the Court does not go far enough. 'Concentrating on the protection of human health is anthropocentric. . . . True environmental rights will only arise if rights are also granted to citizens in respect of EC directives which have nothing to do with the protection of human health, such as nature conservation directives'.[49]

There are those who consider that state liability in damages is a remedy which will be available in the event of an appropriate breach of an environmental provision. Advocate-General Lenz, in *Commission* v *United Kingdom and Ireland*, found the action to be admissible even though, between the commencement of infringement proceedings and the date of the oral hearing, steps had been taken to implement the directive regulating water quality in-

---

46 Case C-58/89 [1991] ECR I-4983, para. 14. Council Directive 75/440 OJ 1975 L194/26.
47 Case C-131/88 *Commission* v *Germany* [1991] ECR I-825, para. 7. Council Directive 80/68 OJ 1980 L20//43.
48 Case C-361/88 *Commission* v *Germany* [1991] ECR I-2567, para. 16.
49 Supra, n. 41, pp. 57–8.

tended for human consumption. In his view there was a legal interest in the continuation of the proceedings, which consisted 'in providing a basis for the liability of a Member State for its Treaty infringement with respect to another Member State, the Community or individuals'.[50] Though a prior finding of the Court is not necessary to establish liability, where there has been such a finding any breach will, automatically, be sufficiently serious.[51] Others, however, are more sceptical. Hilson, quite rightly, stresses the difficulties associated with seeking to prove causation between the breach and the damage suffered.[52] In keeping with the principle of national procedural autonomy, it will be for Member States to determine the nature of the burden of proof applying, and evidential rules regarding the admission of expert (medical and other) evidence; subject as ever to the principle of non-discrimination and to the requirement that national rules must not make it excessively difficult to obtain reparation. Whatever the standard, proving a link between a medical condition (Hilson cites examples such as asthma or gastric cancer) and a specific Member State's failure to comply with Community environmental standards (on air or water quality) will pose, in many (if not most) cases, insurmountable problems. Talk of gastric cancer leads on nicely to the next issue to be addressed. The availability of pecuniary compensation as one lies on a hospice bed dying of cancer, or even visits the car park where once the Lappel Bank curlew and redshank waded, is of little consolation. As Bjerregaard noted, launching the latest round of Article 171 Commission actions, 'We do not want to see the money. We want to see the problem solved'; one might add, 'before it is too late'. Given the lengthy delays associated with litigation as a mechanism for the enforcement of Community law, whether before European or national courts, the issue of interim protection is profoundly significant.

Environmental protection and interim relief

Under Article 186 EC, the Court is empowered, in cases before it, to prescribe any necessary interim measures. Even out of term, the

---

[50] Case C-337/89 [1992] ECR I-6103, para. 41.
[51] Supra, n. 40, *Brasserie*, para. 57.
[52] Supra, n. 41, pp. 65–7.

President of the Court (or another judge, usually from Luxembourg or Belgium) will be 'on call' to hear applications for interim relief. It is not unknown for these to be heard within a matter of days. The Court's Rules of Procedure establish that an application for interim measures shall state the subject matter of the proceedings, the circumstances giving rise to urgency and the pleas of fact and law establishing a *prima facie* case for the interim measures applied for.[53] The Commission may apply for such relief in the context of Article 169 infringement proceedings. It did so in the *Leybucht dyke* case, discussed in Chapter 6.[54] The application was lodged on 14 July 1989. Oral argument was heard on 9 August 1989, and the Order of the President issued one week later. On this occasion the application was rejected on the basis that the Commission had failed to establish the urgency of the need to interrupt work on the site, which not only had already started, but was almost complete. Evidence presented to the Court did not lead it to the conclusion that the remaining construction work, in comparison with that already completed, would have a significant effect on the conservation of wild birds protected under Annex 1 of the wild birds directive.[55]

This decision offers an insight into the conditions governing the availability of interim relief. The Commission, in its application, must demonstrate a *prima facie* case against the Member State concerned. It must demonstrate the urgency of the measure, in that it must be shown to be necessary to prevent (and capable of preventing) serious and irreparable harm. '[P]urely financial damage cannot, as the Court has held on numerous occasions, be regarded in principle as irreparable'.[56] It is also notable that each of the parties to the hearing put forth arguments outlining the alleged consequences of any interim order suspending work. While the Commission contends that such an order would have no appreciable financial consequences, resulting merely in a delay of around 18 months, the German government points both to the financial consequences of cessation of work, and also to the dangers to human life inherent in delaying completion of coastal defence structures. This reflects the practice of the Court in having regard

---

53 OJ 1991 L176/23, Article 83(2).
54 Case C-59/89R *Commission v Germany* [1989] ECR I-2607.
55 Ibid., paras. 16–22.
56 Cases C-143/88 & C-92/89 *Zukerfabrik Süderdithmarschen AG v Hauptzollamt Itzehow & Paderborn* [1991] ECR I-415, para. 29.

to the 'balance of interests' in considering whether to grant interim relief.[57]

When it comes to the availability of interim relief before national courts, the situation is less clear cut. Particularly important is the question of the availability of interim relief at national level pending a preliminary ruling from the European Court. In the early *Simmenthal*[58] the European Court insisted that a national court must do 'everything necessary . . . to set aside national legislative provisions which might prevent Community rules from having their full force and effect'. In *Factortame*[59] the Court went further, observing that:

> . . . the full effectiveness of Community law would be just as much impaired if a rule of national law could prevent a court seized of a dispute governed by Community law from granting interim relief in order to ensure that the full effectiveness of the judgment to be given on the existence of the rights claimed under Community law. It follows that a court, which in those circumstances would grant interim relief if it were not for a rule of national law, is obliged to set aside that rule.

If then, in principle, interim relief is to be available, even in an action against the Crown, this judgment leaves two questions unanswered. First, to what extent is interim relief to be available in cases involving the application of Community law which is not directly effective, and which does not confer rights upon individuals, enjoying merely what we have called 'public law effect'? In such circumstances national courts are similarly charged with ensuring the effectiveness of Community law, in that they are responsible for policing the outer limits of the discretion conferred by Community law. There is, therefore, no reason to expect that the European Court would not equally, in this situation, insist upon the availability, of interim protection in appropriate circumstances.

Second, in what circumstances, and according to what criteria, is interim relief actually to be granted? The European Court in *Factortame* did not specify the conditions to be applied, apparently leaving this to national law, subject only to the principles of non-

---

[57] See, for example, Case 246/89R *Commission* v *United Kingdom* [1989] ECR 3125.

[58] Case 106/77 *Ammistrazione delle Finanze dello Stato* v *Simmenthal SpA* [1978] ECR 629, para. 22.

[59] Case C-213/89 *R* v *Secretary of State for Transport*, ex p *Factortame Ltd (No. 2)* [1990] ECR I-2433, para. 21.

discrimination and effectiveness. In England this procedural autonomy has created certain problems from the perspective of environmental protection. Though the English courts have stressed that, in
relation to interim relief, 'there are no absolutes, only variables',[60]
there is, in the case of an application for an interim injunction, a
clear expectation that a cross-undertaking in damages be given as
a condition of the relief. In the *Lappel Bank* case, discussed in
Chapter 6, the Royal Society for the Protection of Birds (RSPB),
was not prepared (or could not afford) to give such an undertaking, because the commercial losses which would be incurred were
the project to be delayed pending judgment of the European Court
would be very large. By applying for an interim declaration, rather
than an interim injunction, the RSPB hoped to avoid the necessity
of giving such an undertaking. The House of Lords, however, took
the view that they were 'seeking to achieve the same result [as with
an interim injunction] without the risk of incurring very substantial expenditure and thereby asking ... [the] House to adopt a
most unusual course'.[61] It concluded that a declaration that the
Secretary of State acts unlawfully if he fails to act in a particular
way is, in effect, a mandatory order which would usually be
granted in the form of an injunction. Hence, in the absence of a
cross-undertaking, relief was denied, although it was 'fairly clear'
from existing case law that their application (following the preliminary ruling of the European Court) was likely to succeed.[62]

It seems, therefore, that irreparable damage is to be prevented
only where nature has a spokesperson willing and able to offer security for financial risk accruing. There is nothing in the case law
of the European Court to suggest that such a rule, relating to
cross-undertakings in damages, needs be set aside on the basis that
it undermines the effective application of Community law. Indeed,
even if, as some have argued, the proper criteria to be applied in
considering an application for interim relief are those which the
Court has developed in the context of a challenge to the validity of
a *Community* regulation, the European Court has accepted there
that '[i]f the grant of interim relief represents a financial risk for

---

60 *R v HM Treasury*, ex p *British Telecommunications* [1994] 1 CMLR 621,
   p. 647.
61 *R v Secretary of State for the Environment*, ex p *RSPB* (1995) 7 JEL 262, p. 266.
62 Prospects for success counts among Sir Thomas Bingham's 'variables' in supra,
   n. 60. He points also to the nature of the legislation to be disapplied. Interim
   relief is less likely to be granted where primary legislation is involved, as opposed
   to secondary legislation affecting few people.

the Community, the national court must also be in a position to require the applicant to provide adequate guarantees, such as the deposit of money or other security'.[63] There is a problem here. The very area of Community law most likely to give rise to serious and irreparable damage, in the event that it is not correctly applied, is also the area in which big business has no economic stake in securing its application. Those who speak for the environment, before courts of law, may speak in the name of the public interest, but are they are sustained more by principle and passion, than by cash.

Environmental agreements

Towards the end of 1996 the Commission issued a Communication on Environmental Agreements.[64] This was followed by a Commission Recommendation concerning Environmental Agreements implementing Community directives.[65] Self-consciously presented as marking progress in broadening the range of environmental policy instruments deployed, the Communication identified a number of roles for such agreements. They might be used as a supplement to binding legislation, promoting a 'let's work together' as opposed to a 'thou shalt not' approach.[66] They may serve as 'a transitory complement to an environmental tax', conclusion of an environmental agreement being made a prerequisite for total or partial exemption from the tax.[67] Most significantly, the Commission suggests that '[t]hey can also be a means for implementing – in a cost-effective manner – regulatory objectives established by Community Directives'.[68]

Though the Commission's endorsement of environmental agreements as an implementation tool has been criticized by a number of environmental NGOs,[69] its proposals are in fact relatively modest. For one thing, it recommends that they be deployed against a

---

[63] Supra, n. 56, para. 32 and Cases C-465-6/93 *Atlanta Fruchhandelsgesellschaft mbH* v *Bundesamt für Ernahrung und Forstwirtschaft* [1995] ECR I-3761, para. 45. See Steiner, J., *Enforcing EC Law* (Blackstone, 1995), p. 49.

[64] COM(96) 561 final.

[65] OJ 1995 L333/59.

[66] Supra, n. 64, para. 1.

[67] Ibid., para. 14.

[68] Ibid., para. 3.

[69] See European Environmental Bureau Comments concerning the Commission Proposal on Environmental Agreements – on line at http://www.envirocom.com/eeb/

backdrop of what the Commission (not very elegantly) calls 'legis-latory fall-back'.[70] That is to say, implementing legislation will be required in order to bind those not party to an agreement, or those who fail to comply with the terms of a relevant agreement. In ad-dition, such agreements between public authorities and industry are to be contractual in form, and hence binding and enforceable before national courts.[71] The objectives to be achieved pursuant to a particular agreement are, in addition, to be quantified, hence fa-cilitating verification of compliance.[72]

Moreover, the Commission acknowledges that recourse to envi-ronmental agreements will not be appropriate in the case of all types of environmental directives. They are presented as repre-senting an appropriate and adequate implementation tool in rela-tion to those directives which provide 'for the setting up of general programmes or for the achievement of general targets'.[73] For example, the Commission points to a Community directive on containers of liquids for human consumption, and requires Mem-ber States to draw up programmes for reducing the tonnage and the volume of such containers.[74] This was implemented in France by way of industry agreements, and the Court accepted that such agreements could, in principle, were they to include quantified ob-jectives and a timetable for completion, constitute programmes within the meaning of the directive.[75] It is, however, significant that the Commission considers that where directives are intended to create rights and obligations for individuals, implementing legis-lation is required to ensure that individuals are in a position to as-certain the full extent of their rights. The use of the conjunction 'and' suggests that, simply because a directive confers rights on in-dividuals, is not in itself a reason to preclude recourse to such agreements. The implication seems to be that this new instrument of environment policy is suitable in cases where directives are 'once removed' in nature, imposing obligations on Member States, but leaving it to them to determine the distribution of the pollution abatement burden. This would be true of directives imposing envi-

---

70 Supra, n. 64, para. 34.
71 Ibid., para. 19.
72 Ibid., para. 20.
73 Ibid., para. 32.
74 Council Directive 85/339 OJ 1985 L176/18 (subsequently repealed by the packaging directive: European Parliament and Council Directive 94/62 OJ 1994 L265/10).
75 Case C-225/93 *Commission* v *France* [1994] ECR I-4949.

ronmental quality standards, or those imposing non-firm specific performance standards.

The Commission thus adopts a cautious approach to the topic of environmental agreements, especially in so far as these are conceived as an instrument for implementing Community environmental law. In a bid to enhance the effectiveness and credibility of this instrument, the Commission's model is a prescriptive one which barely moves beyond 'command and control'. It is premised upon a 'let's work together' or else 'thou shalt do' approach. For François Ost, 'the fundamental question raised by environmental contracts' is precisely whether they are intended 'to replace the normative [regulatory] framework':

> does government ultimately need to divest itself of its regulatory power and seek to secure through negotiation some of the objectives it no longer thinks it can attain by traditional policy actions? Or is the point more to anticipate future regulation by experimenting, in collaboration with firms, with the feasibility of objectives considered . . .? Or, is the point to secure the execution of the existing regulations by associating the addressees with their implementation.[76]

In the Commission's view, they are clearly not intended to do so. Ost points out that, were environmental contracts or agreements to replace more traditional forms of regulation, this would carry with it a number of dangers. He points to three in particular; 'the risk of breakdown of equality between firms', 'the risk of the authorities being "captured" by the firms they are supposed to control . . .', and 'the risk of reducing the democratic nature of public action by "privatization" '.[77] These may outweigh the advantages of 'rapidity, flexibility and responsibilization'.[78]

It is the latter concept of 'responsibilization' which holds the key to an understanding of much current theoretical debate on the future of environmental law. This would have us believe that a quest for ever more *voluntas* is not only unrealistic, but also counterproductive. It takes as its starting point the undeniable reality of corporate 'resistance' to external regulation, but conceives this resistance neither in terms of economic power, nor in terms of

---

[76] 'A Game Without rules?: The Ecological Self-Organization of Firms' in Teubner, Farmer and Murphy (eds), *Environmental Law and Ecological Reponsibility* (Wiley, 1995), p. 347.

[77] Ibid., pp. 347–8.

[78] Ibid., p. 349.

the practical deficiencies associated with existing mechanisms of enforcement.[79] It conceives it rather in the language of 'auto-poiesis', or in the self-referentiality or closure of 'systems', including law, such as cautions '[d]o not try to teach from the outside'.[80] This has created a momentum in the direction of 'maximum feasible self-regulation'.[81] For self-regulation to be feasible, the object of regulation (for example, the firm) must be endowed with an internal morality such as promotes socially (ecologically) responsible behaviour. One function of law, according to this thesis, is to make 'institutions ... sensitive to the social effects which their strategies for the maximization of their specific [for example, profit focused] rationality trigger'.[82] This has been expressed equally in the language of the need for law to ' "irritate" economic and technological practices and induce them to produce new ecological knowledge'.[83] By way of concrete example, one could point to Community initiatives promoting voluntary 'eco-management and auditing'[84] and 'eco-labelling'.[85] The former at least is predicated upon an expectation that clearer corporate understanding of patterns of environmental behaviour may induce a change in behaviour, stimulating corporate self-responsibility.

It may be frustrating to end a book just at the point at which a whole new paradigm of thinking about environmental law has been alluded to. It is, however, in a sense, appropriate for a book of this sort. It serves to remind both the author and the reader of the intellectual richness of the discipline under consideration. It is hoped that this book will serve as a starting point for those who wish (returning to the notion of the starry plough) to gaze at the stars while not losing sight of the need to furrow the land (though not, of course, the meadows).

---

79 Farmer and Tuebner, 'Ecological Self-Organization' in supra, n. 76, p. 5.
80 Ibid.,
81 Selznick, P., 'Self-Regulation and the Theory of Institutions' in Teubner, Farmer and Murphy, supra, n. 76, p. 395. See also Selznick, P., *The Moral Commonwealth* (University of California Press, 1992).
82 Teubner, G. (ed.), *Juridification of Social Spheres: a Comparative Analysis in the Areas of Labour, Corporate, Antitrust and Social Welfare Law* (de Gruyter, 1987), p. 38.
83 Supra, n. 76, p. 8.
84 Council Regulation 1836/93 OJ 1993 L168/1.
85 Council Regulation 880/92 OJ 1992 L99/1.

Further Reading

Many suggestions for additional reading appear in the footnotes to the text. The following books offer a good starting point, in addition to journal articles. The main environmental journals covering EC developments are the *Journal of Environmental Law*, *Ecology Law Quarterly*, and the *European Environmental Law Review* and *Water Law*. Other excellent journals include *Environmental Politics* and *Environmental Values*. General EC law journals also frequently carry articles on this subject. The *Yearbook of European Law* has been particularly good over recent years. The monthly *ENDS Reports* (Environmental Data Services) are invaluable in terms of keeping up to date with recent developments.

Holder, J. (ed.), *The Impact of EC Environmental Law in the United Kingdom* (Wiley, Chichester, 1997)

Jacobs, M., *The Green Economy* (Pluto Press, London, 1991)

Jans, J., *European Environmental Law* (Kluwer, London, 1995)

Johnson and Corcelle, *The Environmental Policy of the European Communities* (Kluwer, London, 2nd edn, 1995)

Kramer, L., *The EC Treaty and Environmental Law* (Sweet & Maxwell, London, 2nd edn, 1995)

Sagoff, M., *The Economy of the Earth: Philosophy, Law and the Environment* (CUP, Cambridge, 1990)

Somsen, H. (ed.), *Protecting the European Environment: Enforcing EC Environmental Law* (Blackstone, London, 1996)

Teubner, Farmer and Murphy (eds), *Environmental Law and Ecological Responsibility* (Dartmouth, Aldershot, 1994)

Turner, Pearce and Bateman (eds), *Environmental Economics: An Elementary Introduction* (Harvester Wheatsheaf, London, 1994)

Winter, G., *European Environmental Law: a Comparative Perspective* (Dartmouth, Aldershot, 1996)

The internet today provides an invaluable resource. The author finds the following sites particularly useful in EC environmental law. Many provide additional useful links to other sites:

http://europa.eu.int/ (European Community)

http://europea.eu.int/dj/index.htm (Court of Justice)

http://www.unimass.nl~egmilieu// (European Environmental Law Homepage of the University of Maastricht)

http://www.envirocom.com/eeb/ (European Environmental Bureau)

http://www.european-voice.com/ (European Voice)

Readers are advised to ask their local law librarian about access to CELEX, a database of European Community Law. For access a username and password is needed as this service is not free. Most law schools in the United Kingdom will enjoy access through their libraries.

Appendix – Treaty of Amsterdam

The treaty of Amsterdam was concluded by the governments of the Member States on 2 October 1997. It is unlikely to be ratified by all Member States until 1999 at the earliest. It will not enter into force until this time. The Treaty would introduce important substantive changes to both the Treaty on European Union, and the EC Treaty. In addition it would result in a renumbering of the Treaties. While the most important implications of Amsterdam for environmental policy have been highlighted in this book, this appendix sets out the text of relevant extracts from the post-Amsterdam consolidated EC Treaty, and indicates the new article numbers in areas referred to in this book.

Article 2 (formerly Article 2)

The Community shall have as its task, by establishing a common market and an economic and monetary union and by implementing common policies or activities referred to in Articles 3 and 4, to promote throughout the Community a harmonious, balanced and sustainable development of economic activities, a high level of employment and of social protection, equality between men and women, sustainable and non-inflationary growth, a high degree of competitiveness and convergence of economic performance, a high level of protection and improvement of the quality of the environment, the raising of the standard of living and quality of life, and economic and social cohesion and solidarity among Member States.

Article 6 (new)

Environmental protection requirements must be integrated into the definition and implementation of the Community policies and activities referred to in Article 3, in particular with a view to promoting sustainable development.

Article 28 (formerly Article 30)

(unchanged)

Article 30 (formerly Article 36)

(unchanged)

Article 95 (formerly Article 100a)

1. By way of derogation from Article 94 [formerly Article 100] and save where otherwise provided in this Treaty, the following provisions shall apply for the achievement of the objectives set out in Article 14 [formerly Article 7a]. The Council shall, acting in accordance with the procedure referred to in Article 251 [co-decision, formerly Article 189b[1]] and after consulting the Economic and Social Committee, adopt the measures for the approximation of the provisions laid down by law, regulation or administrative action in Member States which have as their object the establishment and functioning of the internal market.

2. Paragraph 1 shall not apply to fiscal provisions, to those relating to the free movement of persons nor to those relating to the rights and interests of employed persons.

---

[1] It should be noted that the nature of the co-decision procedure would change pursuant to the entry into force of this Treaty. In particular, where the Conciliation Committee does not approve a joint text, the proposed act shall be deemed not to have been adopted. Previously, were the Council to confirm the common position agreed prior to conciliation, the measure could be adopted in the absence of an agreed text, unless the European Parliament voted, by absolute majority, to reject this text. Relatively, the powers of the Parliament have been further enhanced under this new procedure.

3. The Commission, in its proposals envisaged in paragraph 1 concerning health, safety, environmental protection and consumer protection, will take as a base a high level of protection, taking account in particular of any new development based on scientific facts. Within their respective powers, the European Parliament and the Council will also seek to achieve this objective.

4. If, after the adoption by the Council or by the Commission of a harmonisation measure, a Member State deems it necessary to maintain national provisions on grounds of major needs referred to in Article 30 [formerly Article 36], or relating to the protection of the environment or the working environment, it shall notify the Commission of these provisions as well as the grounds for maintaining them.

5. Moreover, without prejudice to paragraph 4, if, after the adoption by the Council or by the Commission of a harmonisation measure, a Member State deems it necessary to introduce national provisions based on new scientific evidence relating to the protection of the environment or the working environment on grounds of a problem specific to that Member State arising after the adoption of the harmonisation measure, it shall notify the Commission of the envisaged provisions as well as the grounds for introducing them.

6. The Commission shall, within six months of the notifications as referred to in paragraphs 4 and 5, approve or reject the national provisions involved after having verified whether or not they are a means of arbitrary discimination or a disguised restriction on trade between Member States and whether or not they shall constitute an obstacle to the functioning of the internal market.

In the absence of a decision by the Commission within this period the national provisions referred to in paragraphs 4 and 5 shall be deemed to have been approved.

When justified by the complexity of the matter and in the absence of danger for human health, the Commission may notify the Member State concerned that the period referred to in this paragraph may be extended for a further period of up to six months.

7. When, pursuant to paragraph 6, a Member State is authorised to maintain or introduce national provisions derogating from a harmonisation measure, the Commission shall immediately examine whether to propose an adaption to that measure.

8. When a Member State raises a specific problem on public health in a field which has been the subject of prior harmonisation measures, it shall bring it to the attention of the Commission which shall immediately examine whether to propose appropriate measures to the Council.

9. By way of derogation from the procedure laid down in Articles 226 and 227 [formerly Articles 169 and 170], the Commission and any Member State may bring the matter directly before the Court of Justice if it considers that another Member State is making improper use of the powers provided for in this Article.

10. The harmonisation measures referred to above shall, in appropriate cases, include a safeguard clause authorising the Member States to take, for one or more of the non-economic reasons referred to in Article 30 [formerly Article 36], provisional measures subject to a Community control procedure.

Article 133 (formerly Article 113)

(largely unchanged though the decision-making procedures to apply are now set out in Article 300 (formerly Article 228). In addition a new paragraph 5 provides:)

5. The Council, acting unanimously on a proposal from the Commission and after consulting the European Parliament, may extend to application of paragraphs 1 to 4 to international negotiations and agreements on services and intellectual property insofar as they are not covered by these paragraphs.

Articles 158–162 (formerly Articles 130a–130e)

(These articles, relating to economic and social cohesion, remain largely unchanged. However, new Article 162 provides that henceforth implementing decisions under the ERDF are to be taken according to the co-decision rather than co-operation procedure.[2])

2   ibid

Article 174 [formerly Article 130r]

(This is largely unchanged though the obligation to integrate environmental protection requirements into the definition and implementation of other Community policies has been deleted due to the introduction of the new Article 6 referred to above.)

Article 175 (formerly Article 130s)

1. The Council, acting in accordance with the procedure referred to in Article 251 [formerly Article 189b[3]] and after consulting the Economic and Social Committee and the Committee of the Regions, shall decide what action is to be taken by the Community in order to achieve the objectives referred to in Article 174 [formerly Article 130r].

(This brings about a move from co-operation to co-decision in environmental decision-making, other than in those areas specified in paragraph 2, and provides for the compulsory consultation of the Committee of the Regions. The rest of the article remains largely unchanged though paragraphs 2 and 3 also now provide for the consultation of the Committee of the Regions.)

Article 176 (formerly Article 130t)

(unchanged)

Article 226 (formerly Article 169)

(unchanged)

Article 227 (formerly Article 170)

(unchanged)

---

[3] supra n. 1

Article 228 (formerly Article 171)

(unchanged except for reference to newly numbered Article 227, formerly Article 170)

Article 230 (formerly Article 173)

(unchanged)

Article 234 (formerly Article 177)

(unchanged)

Bibliography

Ackermann and Stewart, 'Reforming Environmental Law' (1985) 37 Stanford LR 1333

Adams, J.G.U., '. . . and how much for your grandmother?' (1974) Environment and Planning A/6

Adams, J.G.U., 'The Emperor's Old Clothes: The Curious Comeback of Cost-benefit Analysis' (1993) 2 Environmental Values 247

Albritton, E., 'The Endangered Species Act: the Foundation Darter Teaches what the Snail Darter Failed to Teach' (1994) 21 ELQ 1007

Anderson, B., *Imagined Communities* (Verso, London, 1983)

Bernard, N., 'Discrimination and Free Movement in EC Law' (1996) 45 ICLQ 82

Bernard, N., 'The Future of European Economic Law in the light of the Principle of Subsidiarity' (1996) 33 CMLRev. 633

Bernard, N., 'Citizenship in a Polycentric Polity' (unpublished, 1996)

Boehmer-Christiansen, S., 'Environmental Quality Objectives versus Uniform Emission Standards' in Freestone and Ijlstra (eds.), (1990)

Boucquey, N., 'Hot Spots in the Bubble: Ecological Liability in Markets for Pollution Rights' in Teubner, Farmer and Murphy (eds.), (1994)

Brinkhorst, L., 'The Road to Maastricht' (1993) 20 ELQ 7

de Burca, G., 'The Quest for Legitimacy in the European Union' (1996) 59 MLR 349

Casey, S., *Drums Under the Windows* (Macmillan, Basingstoke, 1946)

Chalmers, D., 'Environmental Protection and the Single Market:

An Unusual Development. Does the EC Treaty Need a Title on the Environment?' (1995) LIEI 65

Comijs, D., 'Individual Legal Protection under the Structural Funds' (1995) 2 MJ 187

Cotterrell, R., *Laws Community* (OUP, Oxford, 1995)

Craig and de Burca, *EC Law: Text, Cases and Materials* (OUP, Oxford, 1995)

Craig, P., *Administrative Law* (OUP, Oxford, 1994)

Crosby, S., 'The Single Market and the Rule of Law' (1991) 16 ELR 451

Davies, P.G.G., 'The European Environment Agency' (1994) YEL 313

Demaret, P., 'Environmental Policy and Commercial Policy: the Emergence of Trade-Related Environmental Measures (TREMs) in the External Relations of the European Community' in Maresceau, M. (ed.), (1993)

Demaret and Stewardson, 'Border Tax Adjustments under GATT and EC Law and General Implications for Environmental Taxes' (1994) 28 JWT 5

Dine and Watts (eds), *Discrimination Law* (Wiley, Chichester, 1996)

Düerkop, M., 'Trade and Environment: International Trade Law Aspects of the Proposed EC Directive Introducing a Tax on Carbon Dioxide Emissions and Energy' (1994) 31 CMLRev. 807

Dwyer, J.P., 'The Use of Market Incentives in Controlling Air Pollution: California's Marketable Permits Programme' (1993) 20 ELQ 103

Eeckhout, P., *The European Internal Market and International Trade: a Legal Analysis* (OUP, Oxford, 1994)

Eeckhout, P., 'The Domestic Status of the WTO Agreement: Interconnecting Legal Systems' (1997) 34 CMLRev. 11

Ehlermann, C.-D., 'Application of GATT Rules in the EC' in Hilf, Jacobs and Petersmann (eds.), (1986)

Elworthy, S., 'Legal Obstacles to Integrating Environmental Concerns into the CAP' in Van Dael (ed.), *Recente Ontwikke-Lingen in het Europees Milieurect* (Kluwer, London, 1997)

Elworthy and Holder, *Environmental Protection: Text and Materials* (Butterworths, London, 1997)

Emiliou and O'Keefe (eds), *The European Union and World Trade Law* (Wiley, Chichester, 1996)

Faure and Lefevere, 'The Draft Directive on Integrated Pollution Prevention and Control: an Economic Perspective' (1996) EELR 112

Flynn, L., 'Taking Remedies Too Seriously? National Procedural Autonomy in the European Court of Justice' (1996) 31 Irish Jurist 110

Freestone and Ijlstra (eds.), *The North Sea: Perspectives on Regional Environmental Co-operation* (Graham & Trotman/Martinus Nijhoff, London/Dordrecht, 1990)

Geddes, A., 'Environmental Impact Assessments' (1991) 88 Law Society Gazette 24

Gérard, N., 'Access to Justice on Environmental Matters – a Case of Double Standards?' (1996) 8 JEL 149

Gilsdorf, P., 'Portée et délimitation des compétences communautaires en matiére de politique commerciale' (1989) RMC 195

Gormley, L., 'Reasoning Renounced? The Remarkable Judgment in *Keck & Mithouard* (1994) European Business LR 63

Hahn and Stavins, 'Incentive-Based Environmental Regulation: A New Era from an Old Idea?' (1991) 18 ELQ 1

Haigh, N., *EEC Environmental Policy and Britain* (Longman, London, 1990)

Harden, I. (ed.), *State Aid: Community Law and Policy* (Trier Academy of European Law/Bundesanzeiger, Koln, 1993)

Hardin, G., 'The Tragedy of the Commons' (1968) 162 Science 1243

Hartley, T., *Foundations of European Community Law* (OUP, Oxford, 1994)

Held, D., *Political Theory and the Modern State* (Polity, Cambridge, 1989)

Hession and Macrory, 'Balancing Trade Freedom with the Requirements of Sustainable Development' in Emiliou and O'Keefe (eds), (1996)

Hilf, Jacobs and Petersmann (eds.), *The European Community and the GATT* (Kluwer, Deventer, 1986)

Hilson, C., 'Community Rights in Environmental Law: Rhetoric or Reality?' in Holder, J. (ed.) (1997)

Hinsley, F.H., *Sovereignty* (CUP, Cambridge, 1986)

Holder, J. (ed.), *The Impact of EC Environmental Law in the United Kingdom* (Wiley, Chichester, 1997)

Illich, I., 'Needs' in Sachs, W. (ed.), (1992)

Jacobs, M., *The Green Economy* (Pluto, London, 1991)

Jans, J., *European Environmental Law* (Kluwer, London, 1995)

Johnson and Corcelle, *The Environmental Policy of the European Communities* (Kluwer, London, 1995)

Kelman, S., 'Cost-Benefit Analysis: an Ethical Critique' (1981) 5 Regulation 33

Kramer, L., *European Environmental Law: Casebook* (Sweet & Maxwell, London, 1993)

Kramer, L., *The EC Treaty and Environmental Law* (Sweet & Maxwell, London, 2nd edn, 1995)

Lowenfeld, A., 'Remedies Along with Rights: Institutional Reform in the New GATT' (1994) 88 AJIL 477

Macrory, R., 'The Enforcement of Community Environmental Law: Some Critical Remarks' (1992) 29 CMLRev. 347

Macrory and Purdy, 'The Enforcement of EC Environmental Law Against Member States' in Holder, J. (ed.), (1997)

Marenco, G., 'Pour une interprétation traditionnelle de la notion de mesure deffet équivalent' (1984) Cahiers de Droit Européen 291

Maresceau, M. (ed.), *The European Community's Commercial Policy after 1992: the Legal Dimension* (Martinus Nijhoff, Dordrecht, 1993)

Meldon, J., *Structural Funds and the Environment: Problems and Prospects* (An Taisce, Dublin, 1992)

Menell and Stewart, *Environmental law and Policy* (Little, Brown & Co., Boulder, 1994)

Mishan, E.J., *Cost-Benefit Analysis* (Allen & Unwin, London, 1988)

Montana I Mora, M., 'A GATT with Teeth? Law Wins Over Politics in the Resolution of International Trade Disputes' (1993) 31 CJIL 103

Ogus, A., *Regulation: Legal Form and Economic Theory* (OUP, Oxford, 1994)

O'Keefe and Twomey (eds), *Legal Issues of the Maastricht Treaty* (Wiley/Chancery, Chichester, 1994)

Oliver, P., *Free Movement of Goods* (Sweet & Maxwell, London, 1995)

Ost, F., 'A Game Without Rules? The Ecological Self-Organization of Firms' in Teubner, Farmer and Murphy (eds), (1994)

Pedler and Schaefer (eds), *Shaping European Law and Policy: the Role of Committees and Comitology in the Policy Process* (European Institute for Public Administration, Maastricht, 1996)

Pescatore, P., 'Some Critical Remarks on the Single European Act' (1987) 24 CMLRev. 9

Petersmann, E.-U., 'Application of the GATT by the Court of Justice of the European Communities' (1993) 20 CMLRev. 1147

Porras, I.M., 'The Rio Declaration: a New Basis for International Cooperation' in Sands, P., (1993)

Rehbinder and Stewart, *Environmental Protection Policy* (Walter de Gruyter, Berlin, 1985)

Rehbinder, E., '*Locus Standi, Community Law and the Case for Harmonization* in Somsen, H. (ed.) (1995)

Reich & Micklitz (eds), *Public Interest Litigation Before the European Courts* (Nomos Verlag, Baden-Baden, 1996)

Rose-Ackermann, S., *Controlling Environmental Policy: the Limits of Public Law in Germany and the United States* (Yale UP, New Haven,1995)

Rubenstein, M., *Equal Pay for Work of Equal Value* (Macmillan, Basingstoke, 1984)

Sachs, W. (ed.), *The Development Dictionary* (Pluto, London, 1992)

Sagoff, M., *The Economy of the Earth: Philosophy, Law and the Environment* (CUP, Cambridge, 1990)

Sands, P., Greening International Law (Earthscan, London, 1993)

Sands, P., *Principles of International Environmental Law* (MUP, Manchester, 1995)

Schoenbaum, T.J., 'International Trade and Protection of the Environment: The Continuing Search for Reconciliation' (1997) 91 AJIL 268

Scott, J., *Development Dilemmas in the European Community: Rethinking Regional Development Policy* (Open UP, Milton Keynes, 1995)

Scott, J., 'The GATT and Community Law: Rethinking the "Regulatory Gap" ' in Shaw and More (eds.), (1995)

Scott, J., 'From Rio to Inverness: Environment and Development in the Highlands and Islands Objective 1 Enterprise Area' in Holder, J. (ed.), (1997)

Selznick, P., *The Moral Commonwealth* (University of California Press, Berkeley, 1992)

Selznick, P., 'Self-Regulation and the Theory of Institutions' in Teubner, Farmer and Murphy (eds), (1994)

Shaw, J., *EC Law* (Macmillan, Basingstoke, 1995)

Shaw and More (eds), *New Legal Dynamics of European Union* (OUP, Oxford, 1995)

Somsen, H. (ed.), *Protecting the European Environment: Enforcing EC Environmental Law* (Blackstone, London, 1996)

Stewart, R., 'Environmental Regulation and International Competitiveness' (1993) 102 Yale LJ 2039

Steiner, J., 'Subsidiarity under the Maastricht Treaty' in O'Keefe and Twomey (eds), (1994)

Steiner, J., *Enforcing EC Law* (Blackstone, London, 1995)

Teubner, G. (ed.), *Juridification of Social Spheres: a Comparative Analysis in the Areas of Labour, Corporate, Antitrust and Social Welfare Law* (de Gruyter, Berlin, 1987)

Teubner, Farmer and Murphy, *Environmental Law and Ecological Responsibility* (Wiley, Chichester, 1994)

Toth, A., 'A Legal Analysis of Subsidiarity' in O'Keefe and Twomey (eds), (1994)

Turner, Pearce and Bateman, *Environmental Economics: an Elementary Introduction* (Harvester Wheatsheaf, London, 1994)

Ward, A., 'The Right to an Effective Remedy in European Community Law and Environmental Protection: a Case Study of United Kingdom Judicial Decisions Concerning the Environmental Impact Assessment Directive' (1993) 5 JEL 221

Weatherill, S., 'Beyond Preemption? Shared Competence and Constitutional Change in the European Community' in O'Keefe and Twomey (eds), (1994)

Weatherill and Beaumont, *EC Law* (Penguin, Harmondsworth, 2nd edn, 1995)

Weatherill, S., *Law and Integration in the European Union* (OUP, Oxford, 1995)

Weiler, J. H. H., 'The Transformation of Europe' (1991) 100 Yale LJ 2403

Weiler, J. H. H., 'Does Europe Need a Constitution? Reflections on Demos, Telos and the German Maastricht Decision' (1995) 1 ELJ 219

White, E., 'In Search of the Limits to Article 30 of the EEC Treaty' (1989) 26 CMLRev. 235

Wilkinson, D., *The State of Reporting by the EC Commission in fulfilment of Obligations Contained in EC Environmental Legislation* (Institute of European Environmental Policy, London, 1994)

Wils, W.P.J., 'The Birds Directive 15 Years Later: a Survey of the Case Law and a Comparison of the Habitats Directive' (1994) 6 JEL 218

Wils, W.P.J., 'Subsidiarity and EC Environmental Policy: Taking People's Concerns Seriously' (1994) 6 JEL 85

Winter, G. (ed.), *European Community Law: a Comparative Perspective* (Dartmouth, Aldershot, 1996)

Wyatt and Dashwood, *European Community Law* (Sweet & Maxwell, London, 1993)

Index

Access to Environmental Information: 159
Access to Justice:
  locus standi (ECJ), 131, 139–41, 155
  locus standi (national courts), 154–5, 157–8
Acid Rain: 34
Agenda 2000: 54
Agri-Environmental Measures: 54
Agriculture Agreement (WTO): 54
Air Quality: 24–39
Amsterdam Treaty: 10, 14–2, 90, 128, Appendix
  Protocol on Subsidiarity and Proportionality, 10, 11, 15, 18
An Taisce: 130–4
Article 100a(4): 40–3
Assimilative Capacity: 33–4
Autonomy (of nations): 13, 85
Auto-Oil Programme: 27, 29
Autopoiesis: 168

Bathing Waters: 151–2
BAT: 28, 32, 36
BATNEEC: 28, 36

BSE: 72–3
Burren: 130–34

Chemicals (trade in): 86
CITES: 87, 88
Citizenship: 22
Climate Change: 46
Cohesion Fund: 129, 135
Cohesion Report: 129
Comitology: 21
Command and Control Regulation: 24–37, 44, 167 (*see also* standards)
Commission Communications
  Cohesion and the Environment, 128
  Implementation, 152–3
Common Agricultural Policy: 53–5
Common Commercial Policy: 88–91
  common rules for imports, 91
  specific authorization, 88, 92
Common Concern of Mankind: 16
Common Heritage of Mankind: 16, 83
Competence (Community): 3–10, 86, 88–91

Jurisdictional 'Mutation', 4, 6
(*see also* legal basis)
Cost-Benefit Analysis: 17, 18–23, 37, 59, 70, 109, 156
Cost-Effectiveness: 29–30, 33, 36–7, 58, 60
Court of Auditors: 128

Danish Bottles: 66–8, 69–70, 80
Dead Red Grouse: 80–3
Democracy: 8–9, 21–2, 144, 147, 167
Direct Effect: 94–5, 111, 122–3, 126

Eco-labelling: 104, 168
Eco-management and audit: 168
Economic Instruments: 44–63
    environmental taxes, 45–50, 51, 52
    financial instruments, 53
    internal market, 62
    state aids, 50–3
    tradeable emissions permits, 50–60
Economic and Social Cohesion: 40, 129
Efficiency: 17–19, 22
Emission standards; (*see* standards; performance)
Enforcement: 35, 37, 148–68
    Commission communication on implementation, 152–3
    Commission's role, 93, 122–3, 126, 133, 149–53, 161
    direct effect, 94–5, 111, 122–3, 126, 156–7

environmental agreements, 165–7
indirect effect, 141, 156–7
interim protection, 112, 161–5
Member State reports, 153
public law effect, 123–4, 126, 157
state liability in damages, 124, 158–61
(*see also* environmental compatibility)
Enumerated Powers: 4
Environment Agency: 153
Environmental Action Programmes: 6
    Fifth Action Programme, 24, 31, 55, 139
Environmental Agreements: 165–7
Environmental Compatibility (structural funds): 129–45
Environmental Impact Assessment Directive: 107, 117–26, 131
    Annex 1, 118–19, 123
    Annex 2, 118–19, 121–2
    amendments, 119, 120, 124–5
    direct effect, 122–3, 126
    public consultation, 125
    public law effect, 123–4, 126, 157–8
    salami effect: 119–21
    scoping, 124–5
    screening, 119
    (*see also* strategic EIA)
Environmental Quality Objectives: (*see* standards; target)
Environmental Rights: 123–4, 159–60

Environmental Taxes: 45–50
   Carbon/Energy Tax: 45–50, 51, 52
   Road Taxes, 45–6
Exhaustive Harmonization: 65, 78, 81
   Externalities: 11–13
   (*see also* spillovers)

Flora and Fauna: 86, 87, 90
Francovich 124, 158–61
Free Movement of Goods 62–85
   Article 30, 65–6, 76–7
   Article 34, 66
   Article 36, 65, 68–9, 71, 73, 91, 92
   (*see also* mandatory requirements and trade)
Free-riding: 12, 34, 37, 39, 148

GATT: 92–102
   direct effect, 94–5
   dispute settlement, 94–5, 98–100, 103, 105
   exceptions, 98–101
   justiciability before ECJ, 94
   Most favoured nation, 95
   national treatment, 95, 97
   quantitative restriction, 95, 97
German Beer: 71
German Crayfish: 69
Gourmetterie: 80–3
Greenpeace:
   Structural Funds, 134–41
THORP: 120
Groundwater: 160
Habitats Directive: 17, 106–8, 112–15
   protection of species, 116–17

(*see also* SAsC)
Harmonization: 5, 78, 81
   external, 91
(*see also* minimum harmonization)
Hormones: 103

Independent Agencies: 18
'Indirect' Effect: 141
Industrial Plants: 26–7, 32–3, 38–9
Integration Obligations: 79, 129 (*see also* evironmental compatibility)
Interdependence: 13, 65, 79
Interim Relief: 112, 158, 161–5
IPPC: 28, 30, 31–3

Judicial Review (Article 173): 8, 90, 130–41
   locus standi, 131, 139–41, 155
   reviewable act, 130–8
Judicial Review (national courts): 111, 123–4, 126, 154–8, 161–5
   (*see also* interim relief)

Keck: 75–7

Lappel Bank (RSPB): 110, 111, 161, 164
Legal Basis: 7, 16, 86
   Article 100, 4–7
   Article 100a, 7–10, 16, 40, 90
   Article 113, 88–93, 97
   Article 130s, 7–9, 40, 88–9, 90, 92, 97
   Article 235, 5–7, 108
   choice of, 8–10, 88–93

Leghold Traps: 86, 90, 96, 101–2
Legislative Procedures: 6–10, 26, 28, 39, 108
Leybucht dykes (wild birds): 109, 110, 162
LIFE: 53
Locus Standi (*see* access to justice)

Maastricht Treaty (*see* Treaty on European Union)
Mad Cows: (*see* BSE)
Mandatory Requirements: 67, 68, 73, 77, 83, 91, 92
    distinctly and indistinctly applicable measures, 73–9
    least restrictive means, 69, 70
    necessity, 69, 70, 84
    proportionality, 69, 70, 84
Marleasing doctrine: 157
Minimum Harmonization: 40, 43, 64, 81, 89
    Article 130t, 40–2
Molitor Report: 23, 31
Motor Vehicles: 27, 29
Mutual Recognition: 65, 104

Natura 2000: 107, 108, 112, 113
Nature Conservation: 106–16
Non-Governmental Organizations: 22, 128, 139, 145, 152, 154
Notification (of Commission): 41–2 (*See also* Article 100a(4))
Notification Directive: 42, 50

Ozone depleting substances: 86, 87, 90

Paris Summit: 5
Partnership: 137, 141, 144, 146
Peene Valley, 112, 113
Polluter Pays Principle: 34
Precautionary Principle: 71, 103, 117
Pre-emption: 64
Preventive Action: 143
Product Regulation: 5, 26, 27–8, 83
Production Process Regulation: 5, 26, 27–8, 104, 83
Proportionality:
    general principle in relation to goods, 69–70, 84
    legislative 11, 31
Public Goods: 12, 60
Public Law Effect: 123–4, 126, 157–8

Quantitative Restrictions: 66, 76, 95, 97

Regulatory Competition: 8, 14–16, 43, 85, 104
Risk: 70–2, 103–4
RSPB (Lappel Bank): 110, 111, 164

Sanitary and Phytosanitary Measures Agreement: 93, 102–4
Santona Marshes (wild birds): 109–10
Scientific Reason: 35–6, 70, 72–3, 103–4, 105
Seal pups: 86, 87
Shared but Differentiated Responsibility: 39
Shared Responsibility: 31, 64, 144

Single European Act: 4, 7, 40
Social Cost: 11–12, 60, 61
Sovereignty: 13, 33, 65, 85,
    105, 115
Special Areas of Conserva-
    tion (SAsC): 108, 112–
    15, 122
  derogation on economic
    grounds, 112–13
  designation, 112, 113–15
Special Protection Areas (SPA):
    108–12, 115, 122
  derogation on economic
    grounds, 109–10
  designation, 108–12
Spillovers: 13–18
  Economic, 14–16, 18, 33
  Physical, 13, 17, 83
  Psychic, 16–17, 19–20, 23
Standards:
  differentiation, 37–43
  Performance: 26–8, 30–2,
    35, 37, 55, 56–7
  Specification, 28–9, 30–2, 37
  Target, 25–6, 30–5, 37
State Aids: 50–3
State Liability in Damages:
    124, 158–61
Stockholm Conference: 6
Strategic EIA: 121, 126,
    143–5
Structural Funds: 126, 129,
    131, 143–5, 153
  development planning and
    environment, 143–5
  financial control, 145
  monitoring committees,
    137, 141
  objective 1, 129
  partnership, 137, 141, 144,
    146

Programme approach, 130–2
    (see also environmental com-
    patibility)
Subsidiarity: 3, 10, 11, 13–18,
    43, 132, 144
Sustainable Development:
    128
Sustainable Growth: 128

Technical Barriers to Trade
    Agreement: 93, 102–4
Technocracy: 18, 21
Titanium Dioxide: 8–9, 90
Tradeable Emissions Permits:
    55–60
  banking, 55, 56
  bubbles, 55, 56
  grandfathering, 57
  hoarding, 57
  hot-spots, 61
  netting, 55, 56
  offsets, 55, 56
Trade and Environment: 64–
    105
  external relations perspec-
    tive, 85–105
  extra-territoriality, 80–4,
    87–8, 100–2
  internal market perspective,
    64–85
Tragedy of the Commons: 12
Transparency: 133, 138–41
Treaty on European Union: 9,
    128, 142, 150
Tuna/Dolphin Panel: 96, 98,
    100, 102
Twyford Down: 120, 151

Urban Waste Water: 155–6
Uruguay Round: 54, 93

Wallonian Waste: 77–9
Waste: 77–9, 86
   radioactive, 86, 87, 90
Wild Birds: 6, 17, 80–3, 106–
   12, 115
   direct effect, 111

species, 116–17
(see also SPA)
World Trade Organization
   Agreement: 86, 88, 92–5,
   101, 105
WTO Opinion: 93